Strategic Management Accounting
text and cases

Strategic Management Accounting
text and cases

Malcolm Smith BA (Econ), MBA, PhD, ACA, FCPA, FCMA
Professor of Management Accounting, Sheffield Hallam University

Butterworth-Heinemann
Linacre House, Jordan Hill, Oxford OX2 8DP
A division of Reed Educational and Professional Publishing Ltd

   A member of the Reed Elsevier plc group

OXFORD   BOSTON   JOHANNESBURG
MELBOURNE   NEW DELHI   SINGAPORE

First published by Reed International Books Pty Limited
trading as Butterworths 1995
First published in Great Britain 1997

British Library Cataloguing in Publication Data
Smith, Malcolm
    Strategic management accounting: text and cases
    1. Managerial accounting
    I. Title
    658.1'511

ISBN 0 7506 3097 3

Library of Congress Cataloguing in Publication Data
Smith, Malcolm.
    Strategic management accounting:text and cases/Malcolm Smith.
    p.   cm.
    Includes bibliographical references and index.
    ISBN 0 7506 3097 3 (pbk.)
    1   managerial accounting.   2   Strategic planning – Accounting.
    I. Title.
    HF5657.4.S56   96–36315
    658.15'11 – dc20   CIP

Composition by Scribe Design, Gillingham, Kent
Printed and bound in Great Britain

Contents

Preface   *ix*
Acknowledgements   *xi*
List of Figures   *xiii*

Introduction   **1**

Chapter 1

Case Study Method   **3**

1.1 Introduction   3
1.2 Case Analysis   4
1.3 Oral Report   6
1.4 Written Report   9
1.5 Example Case   10
     Case 1: Cambridge Business Conferences   11

Chapter 2

Accounting Ethics   **21**

2.1 Introduction   21
     Case 2: Kambalda Manufacturing   32
     Case 3: SLI Holdings   34

Chapter 3

Management Accounting Information Systems (MAIS)   39

3.1 Introduction   39
3.2 Internal Control   42
3.3 Performance Evaluation   46
3.4 Non-financial Indicators   47
     Case 4: Inner City Cycles   52
     Case 5: Pinewall Furnishings   61

Chapter 4

Strategic Management Accounting (SMA)   **67**

4.1 Introduction   67
4.2 Corporate Objectives   67
4.3 Current Situation Analysis   68
4.4 The Product Life Cycle (PLC)   72
4.5 Boston Consulting Group (BCG) Portfolio Matrix   74

Contents

4.6 Environmental Analysis   78
4.7 Performance Benchmarking   82
4.8 Strategy Alternatives   83
4.9 Evaluation of Achievements   84
     CASE 6: VERTEX PRINTING GROUP   87
     CASE 7: GEELONG TEXTILES   92
     CASE 8: HARSTON EXPLORATION   97
     CASE 9: EASTON PRINTING SERVICES   105

Chapter 5

Product and Customer Profitability   **107**

5.1 Introduction   107
5.2 Product Mix   107
5.3 Activity Based Costing   108
5.4 Implementing ABC   111
5.5 Activity Based Management   113
5.6 Customer Profitability Analysis   122
     CASE 10: WILLINGHAM FURNITURE LTD   126
     CASE 11: ESAU CREEK WINERY   130
     CASE 12: SUBIACO TECHNOLOGY   131
     CASE 13: FIBRO LTD   133
     CASE 14: DERRICK'S CONFECTIONERY   136
     CASE 15: PITCAIRN ELECTRONICS   138

Chapter 6

Project Appraisal   **140**

6.1 Introduction   140
6.2 Returns   140
6.3 Risk   142
6.4 Quality   145
6.5 Time   146
     CASE 16: THE SANDY BAY DEVELOPMENT   151
     CASE 17: JARRAHDALE MINESITE   153
     CASE 18: ALUMINA REFINERIES   159
     CASE 19: BOUTIQUE FASHIONS   164

Chapter 7

Total Quality Management   **166**

7.1 Introduction   166
7.2 Implementing TQM   168
     CASE 20: BLACKBURN CHEMICALS   173
     CASE 21: SPICK'N'SPAN DRY CLEANERS   178

Contents

Chapter 8

Management Science   179

8.1 Introduction   179
8.2 Decision-making Models   180
8.3 Time Series Analysis   185
8.4 Regression Analysis   194
8.5 Discriminant Analysis   206
     CASE 22: THE REDFERN MUTUAL ASSURANCE COMPANY   218
     CASE 23: CHARITY SHOPS   222
     CASE 24: COUNTRYWIDE STORES   225
     CASE 25: WHITTLESFORD HARDWARE GROUP   229
     CASE 26: BRITISH MOTORS   234
     CASE 27: BALMAIN BREWERIES   250

Index   253

Preface

Many accounting undergraduates begin their studies with quite serious misconceptions about management accounting. Far too many of them still imagine the management accountant as an inarticulate male chained to a desk at head office, calculator in one hand and spreadsheet in the other. In an effort to change these perceptions I arrive for my first year class in fancy dress—the hard hat, safety goggles and steel toe-capped boots that I wore for my most recent management accounting assignment!

Most students have little experience of a manufacturing environment or of the pivotal role the management accountant can play in planning and control. Often such work is conducted in noisy, dirty, hazardous locations immediately adjacent to the manufacturing process—not in clean, safe offices far removed from the action—and a growing number of management accountants are female.

This book is intended to give students a flavour of such an environment, by reflecting my own workplace experiences over an extended period. It cannot pretend to be a substitute for first-hand personal observation but aims to provide a readily available, if sanitised, alternative. It also highlights the importance of other related disciplines, particularly management, marketing and organisational psychology.

Management accounting courses are increasingly being assessed through case study scenarios. The cases supplied here are designed to be useful both for class teaching and for preparing students for professional accounting examinations, in particular those of the Chartered Institute of Management Accountants.

The book is intended to fill a significant gap in the market by providing practical cases with a true *strategic* dimension. The cases are all class-tested and student-friendly; they provide guidance while still allowing flexibility of response. Theory and mathematical exposition are limited to the minimum needed for competent completion of the case requirements. The supporting material is designed to help both students and instructors make the best possible use of the case material, and a great deal of time has been spent producing a comprehensive instructor's manual. Too many case books skimp on detail and don't give sufficient guidance to teachers; I hope such a criticism cannot be leveled at this text.

My gratitude is due to my wife, Beth, who has seen many hours that she quite reasonably deemed to be hers taken up by the production of two volumes and supporting materials on disk. The constructive feedback of fellow accounting educators will make the project worthwhile!

MALCOLM SMITH

Acknowledgements

The thoughts and suggestions of many colleagues have been invaluable in the development of the cases and supporting text in this volume.

Special thanks should go to Shane Dikolli and Mardi Gooding of Curtin University; Keith Houghton, Melbourne University; Richard Taffler, Al Russel, Ann Brown and Ronnie Lessem, City University, London; Ped Ristic, Ralph Sunley, John de Reuck and Colette Raby, Murdoch University; John Cullen and Alan Coad, Sheffield Hallam University; Michael Brett, Peter Philips, Colin Drury and Roy Liversage.

Figures

Chapter 1

Figure 1   Analytical Tools in Management Accounting   5
Figure C1.1   Break-even Output   14
Figure C1.2   Conference Costs for CBC   14

Chapter 2

Figure 2   22
Figure C2.1   Kambalda Manufacturing Divisional Structure   32

Chapter 3

Figure 3   Measuring Process Performance   41
Figure 4   Matrix of Non-Financial Performance Indicators   48
Figure C4.1   Organisational Structure Chart   53
Figure C4.2   Financial Structure of ICC   54
Figure C4.3   Estimated Current Financial Position   55
Figure C4.4   Bikes On Order and In Hand   57
Figure C4.5   Till Point Sales Record   58
Figure C4.6   Projected Financial Position on Expansion   59
Figure C4.7   Competitors for Inner City Cycles   60
Figure C5.1   Theoretical Organisation Chart   62
Figure C5.2   Current Factory Layout   65
Figure C5.3   Job Flows and Responsibilities   66

Chapter 4

Figure 5   The Strategic Management Accounting Approach   68
Figure 6   SWOT Analysis   69
Figure 7   Alternative Market Diversifications   72
Figure 8   The Product Life Cycle   73
Figure 9   BCG Portfolio Matrix   75
Figure 10   Strategy Outcomes in BCG Portfolio   77
Figure 11   Solving the Throughput Problem   84
Figure C6.1   Divisional Structure   88
Figure C6.2   Royal Printing — Distribution of Outlets   88

Figures

Figure C6.3   Royal Printing Pricing Policy   88
Figure C6.4   Equipment Requirements and Costings for Nuneaton Upgrade   90
Figure C6.5   Nuneaton Division — Cost Rate Calculation   91
Figure C7.1   Geelong Textiles — Organisation Chart 1992   93
Figure C7.2   Production Flows at Geelong Textiles   94
Figure C7.3   Revenue and Earnings Trends   95
Figure C7.4   Cost Structure   96
Figure C8.1   Numerical Responses for Five Companies   99
Figure C8.2   Harston Exploration — Benchmarking Outcomes   100
Figure C8.3   Holcroft Diamonds — Benchmarking Outcomes   101
Figure C8.4   Sheepcote Mining — Benchmarking Outcomes   102
Figure C8.5   Bolton Extractive — Benchmarking Outcomes   103
Figure C8.6   Burwell Minerals — Benchmarking Outcomes   104

Chapter 5
Figure 12   Four Activities and Five Products   109
Figure 13   Activity Based Costing of Products   110
Figure 14   The Drivers of Activity Based Management   114
Figure 15   Aspects of Value Added Management (VAM)   114
Figure 16   Alternative Product Scheduling Systems   120
Figure 17   Customer Portfolio Matrix   124
Figure C10.1   Sales and Production Flow at Willingham   127
Figure C10.2   Quarterly Profit and Loss Statement (Year Ending 30/6/93)   129
Figure C10.3   Ratio Analysis for Willingham Furniture   129
Figure C12.1   Range of Products   131
Figure C12.2   Matrix of Hourly Usage within each Department
per Item of Product   132
Figure C12.3   Daily Sales and Sales Projections   132
Figure C13.1   Fibro Production Process   134
Figure C13.2   Material Usage by Product (per day)   135
Figure C14.1   Sales Distribution by Customer   136
Figure C14.2   Profiles for Derrick's Customer Base   137
Figure C15.1   Product Cost Information   139
Figure C15.2   Product Pricing   139

Chapter 6
Figure 18   Probability Distribution of Projected Returns   142
Figure 19   Decision Trees for Cable Technology   144

Figures

Figure 20	Gantt Chart	148
Figure 21	FCFS Matrix for Job Schedule	149
Figure C16.1	Network of Activities in Sandy Bay Development	152
Figure C16.2	Target Costs and Completion	152
Figure C17.1	Alternative Scenarios for Caterpillar Front End Loaders	153
Figure C17.2	FEL Operating Hours	156
Figure C17.3	Percentage Availability/Utilisation of FELs	156
Figure C17.5	Maintenance Costs for FEL Fleet	157
Figure C17.4	Projected FEL Management	158
Figure C18.1	Maintenance Costs ($£$)	160
Figure C18.2	Cost Savings and Increased Profits ($£$)	161
Figure C18.3	10 Year Appraisal for Mobile Crane and Aerial Work Platform	162

Chapter 7

Figure 22	The PRAISE System of Quality Improvement	169
Figure 23	Process for Reviewing the Management Accounting Function	171

Chapter 8

Figure 24	Normal Distribution Simulation	184
Figure 25	Classical Time Series Decomposition	185
Figure 26	Time Series Analysis for Exploration Holdings	188
Figure 27	Cyclical Component (Additive Model)	190
Figure 28	Cyclical Component (Multiplicative Model)	190
Figure 29	Ordinary Least Squares (OLS) Regression Fit	195
Figure 30	Evidence of Mis-specification	198
Figure 31	Dataset for Gresham State Bank	208
Figure 32	Financial Ratios for Gresham Z-model	209
Figure C22.1	Dataset for Redfern Assurance Company	219
Figure C23.1	Charity Shops Data	223
Figure C24.1	Store Data for Countrywide	226
Figure C24.1a	Store Data for Countrywide (cont)	227
Figure C25.1	Group Structure (1985–89)	229
Figure C25.2	Summary Financial Data (1983–92)	230
Figure C25.3	Four Year Performance of Subsidiaries	231
Figure C25.4	Industry Average Performance Measures	232
Figure C25.5	Framework for Recovery Analysis	233
Figure C26.1	Distribution of British Motors Dealerships	234

List of Figures

Figure C26.2   Failed Dealerships (1987–1992)   236
Figure C26.3   Live Dealerships (1992)   237
Figure C26.4   Live Dealerships (1993)   243
Figure C27.1   Weekly Depot Data of Balmain Cartons   251

Introduction

This book improves on the management accounting offerings currently available by: providing practical cases based on actual situations, and which concern the latest issues of strategic management accounting.

The cases are almost exclusively based on the author's employment and consulting experiences. They provide the opportunity for applying the 'new tools' of management accounting in realistic situations.

Each chapter provides an overview of the area, or identification of the key issues and references for further reading. Each major case provides a practical scenario covering diverse aspects of each of the topic areas; in addition numerous Minicases, together with worked solutions, are included. The cases are written for an intended audience comprising MBA and second and third year undergraduate students in management accounting, but will be useful in a variety of other professional courses.

Some of the cases include large amounts of data and require the use of statistical packages. A datadisk is supplied to facilitate the use of available computer software.

The 27 major cases are distributed by topic area, within issues, as follows:

		Page
1.	**CASE STUDY METHOD**	
	CASE 1: Cost-volume-profit analysis	11
2.	**ACCOUNTING ETHICS**	
	CASE 2: Self-interested management manipulation	32
	CASE 3: Executive level fraud	34
3.	**MAIS**	
	CASE 4: Management and inventory control	52
	CASE 5: Management accounting systems	61
4.	**SMA**	
	CASE 6: Action for loss-making subsidiaries	87
	CASE 7: Activity management	92
	CASE 8: Benchmaking	97
	CASE 9: Diversification strategies	105
5.	**PRODUCT AND CUSTOMER PROFITABILITY**	
	CASE 10: Marketing Strategies	126
	CASE 11: Product-mix analysis	130
	CASE 12: Product pricing and elimination	131
	CASE 13: Product costing and non-financial indicators	133

CASE 14:	Customer profitability analysis	136
CASE 15:	Activity based costing	138

6. PROJECT APPRAISAL
CASE 16:	Network analysis	151
CASE 17:	Investment appraisal	153
CASE 18:	Post-audit of capital expenditures	159
CASE 19:	Probabilistic evaluation of risk and returns	164

7. TQM
CASE 20:	Process of implementation	173
CASE 21:	Corporate goals and improvement opportunities	178

8. MANAGEMENT SCIENCE
CASE 22:	Price setting (regression analysis)	218
CASE 23:	Sales forecasting (regression analysis)	222
CASE 24:	Sales forecasting (regression analysis)	225
CASE 25:	Turnaround strategies (ratio analysis)	229
CASE 26:	Failure prediction (discriminant analysis)	234
CASE 27:	Inventory control (time-series analysis)	250

The varying complexity of these cases allows them to be categorised into three equal sized groups of nine cases each. The recommended use of cases based on the author's class experience is:

In-class discussion: Cases 1,2,3,9,11,14,16,20,21

Individual/small group exercises: Cases 6,7,8,12,13,15,18,19,25
(1–3 persons)

Large group projects: Cases 4,5,10,17,22,23,24,26,27
(2–5 persons)

The Tutor Manual (accompanying this volume) gives an indication of the type of answer that might be anticipated from good students.

Worked solutions are provided for *Case 1: Cambridge Business Conferences*, to illustrate the case study method, and for the following Minicases:

Minicase A:	Ashley-Yeats Retailing	(Accounting Ethics)	27
Minicase B:	Bakewise Holdings	(Throughput)	118
Minicase C:	Cable Technology	(Decision Tree Analysis)	143
Minicase D:	Donovan Furnishings	(Job Scheduling)	147
Minicase E:	Exploration Holdings	(Time Series Analysis)	187
Minicase F:	Ferrous Castings	(Regression Analysis)	200
Minicase G:	Gresham State Bank	(Discriminant Analysis)	207

The datadisk contains spreadsheet datafiles for each of the following cases, held under their respective casename:

Cases: 10, 13, 15, 18, 22, 23, 24, 25, 26, 27
Minicases: E, F, G

Chapter 1

Case Study Method

1.1 INTRODUCTION

In the absence of a period of relevant work experience, the case study provides a next-best alternative for exposure to decision-making in an organisational context. Ideally, cases will be realistic, preferably abstractions of situations that have actually occurred. The great majority of the cases in this book have the advantage of being based on real situations in which the author was directly involved: we are, there-fore, able to gain an insight into the complexities of the situation and the decisions that were actually made (these are revealed in the companion Tutor Manual).

The practicalities of the case study environment, with students as active rather than passive participants, mean that the scenarios will necessarily be incomplete. Pressures of time and information overload make this situation inevitable. Inconsistencies, uncertainties and shortage of information are par for the course — often introduced deliberately by the author in order to gauge the reaction of students. As long as realistic assumptions are made and a sensitivity analysis conducted to test the impact of alternative assumptions on outcomes, such deficien-cies are easily overcome. The existence of alternative sets of assumptions, all equally acceptable, means that there is frequently no unique solution. This absence of a 'right' answer often causes problems to students, especially in accounting, and leads to suspicion of the case study method until they become more familiar with it. Such ambiguity and uncertainty are good practice for a career in management! It soon becomes apparent that a decision, articulately argued from among the alternatives and substantiated by the appropriate numerical information, is more important than an interminable search for an outcome which is indisputably 'correct'.

To paraphrase W Edwards Deming: 'In God we Trust, All others bring Data' and 'Someone with an Opinion and No Data is just another person with an opinion'. Support of arguments with relevant financial and non-financial informa-tion is essential; this means the use of appropriate mathematical and statistical methods to facilitate information processing.

The cases in this volume require the use of a number of different techniques: decision trees, network analysis, break-even analysis, discounted cash flows, linear programming, regression analysis, discriminant analysis and time series analysis. Such tools are an essential part of the management accountant's survival kit, and are now facilitated by ease of access to suitable computer software in the form of spreadsheets and statistical packages.

Students should be aware of a number of important guidelines for case analysis and the presentation of their oral and written findings. These are explored in the following sections with the intention of eliminating the most glaring errors and improving the overall standard (of content *and* presentation) of case study reports.

1.2 CASE ANALYSIS

The case study is usually designed to represent a scenario close to that which would be found in a working environment. There is often no unique solution and analysis frequently requires the adoption of a multi-disciplinary approach.

A systematic approach is necessary for efficient case evaluation. Many are available, but all have the same objective — to prevent the case participants from jumping to quick-fix solutions by ignoring essential steps in the analytical process. The following process — designated by the **RAPIDE** acronym — provides a six stage guide for case analysis:

- **Read the Case.** How this is accomplished is largely dependent on individual taste, but may combine three elements:
    - (i)   an initial skim of the case to become aware of its scope;
    - (ii)   a detailed reading to digest all key aspects;
    - (iii) a third reading when notes are made, key points highlighted and relationships between points established through sketch diagrams.

- **Analyse the Case.** Identify the key facts, issues and potential problems. A SWOT analysis (Strengths, Weaknesses, Opportunities, Threats) is often a useful technique at this stage of the analysis in order to begin categorising the key internal and external issues. It may, however, be incomplete, requiring analysis in greater depth to finalise some areas.

- **Problem Identification.** Arrange the issues of the case in order of priority to allow the statement of major and minor problems that can be corrected. These will become the key focus of the analysis. Take care not to confuse 'symptoms' with real problems at this stage, nor to focus unnecessarily on peripheral or irrelevant issues.

- **Investigation of Problems.** Examine in full all prioritised problems, utilising all of the material available in the case and any relevant additional sources available locally (e.g. current and trend, industry data). This stage will include quantitative analysis and the use of appropriate mathematical and statistical tools. These are examined in depth, with reference to specific cases, in subsequent chapters. Detail of their range of application is supplied by Figure 1.

- **Development of Alternative Solutions.** Suggest alternative solutions to each of the problems, identifying financial and non-financial costs and benefits. Do not overlook the non-financial factors, even though these may be played down in the case — they are often the most important aspects of any decision, especially if they have strategic implications. Identify difficulties of implementation and potential consequences of different actions, quantifying their likelihood if feasible.

- **Evaluation of Alternatives.** Judge the alternative solutions and select the best course of action based on the available data. Some compromise will be inevitable, because it will be impossible to quantify all of the potential impacts. Integrating complex and sometimes conflicting outcomes is difficult — it may seem like trying to add 'apples and oranges' at times, but must be attempted. It may help to establish decision criteria:

(i)   What characteristics *must* be satisfied?
(ii) Which characteristics are desirable but not essential?
(iii) Which outcomes are consistent with short and long-term organisational goals?
(iv) Which outcomes are congruent with the strategic direction of the enterprise?
(v)   Which alternative is *financially* the most desirable?
(vi) Which non-financial measures, if any, outweigh the financials for relative importance?

	APPLICATIONS	**TECHNIQUES**
PLANNING	Plant location Job scheduling Throughput	Transportation methods Network analysis Queuing theory Product life cycle (PLC) analysis BCG portfolio matrix analysis
CONTROL	Product mix Inventory modelling	Linear programming Economic order quantity (EOQ) Simulation methods
FORECASTING	Cost behaviour Sales planning Failure prediction	Regression analysis Time series analysis Financial ratio analysis Discriminant analysis Logit/probit models
DECISION MAKING	Lease <u>or</u> buy Make <u>or</u> buy Capital expenditure Risk management	Break-even analysis Discounted cash flow (DCF) Probability/decision trees

Figure 1: Analytical Tools in Management Accounting

Where the case study includes questions at the end, do *not* allow your analysis to focus unnecessarily on an attempt to answer these. Treat them as additional information, issues which are regarded by one person (the author) as important and thus worthy of consideration, but not necessarily deserving priority treatment.

Throughout this process, be aware of interesting and creative alternatives for both analysis and presentation. Remember, you will have to present your findings (both oral and written) and may have to 'sell' your recommendations to reluctant colleagues. The next two sections focus on these issues.

1.3 ORAL REPORT

In addition to the judgment necessary to conduct a case study analysis, students need to develop presentation skills in order to communicate their findings. Whether this communication is in an oral or written format, students will need to organise their material by graphing and tabulating results prior to presenting them to the target audience.

Both oral and written reports are concerned with content and presentation and comprise basic components which can be simplified as three commandments:

- tell them what you are going to tell them (i.e. an overview);

- tell them (i.e. main body of the report);

- tell them what you have just told them! (i.e. summary and conclusions).

The differences between target audiences provide the fundamental differences in the requirements for oral and written reports, since they will govern both the material to be presented and the manner of its presentation.

The oral report demands close attention to a number of key features. In terms of the acronym below, successful oral reports are **STRIPED**:

- **Simplicity.** Do not attempt to communicate too much. This is easily the most common mistake in case presentations. Complex arguments and a multiplicity of intricate relationships are likely to lose a majority of the audience. Be aware of their needs and capabilities, so that the content and tone of the presentation can be tailored appropriately. The resulting 'bespoke' presentation may comprise only two or three essential issues emphasised and reiterated within a simple framework. A SWOT analysis is often a suitable means of accomplishing this focus within a simple structure, since it allows a narrowing down of attention to the key issues while recognising that other peripheral issues do exist.

  The question of simplicity applies equally to the content of the slides used in the presentation, whether these are overhead projector transparencies or computer generated screens from Harvard Graphics or Powerpoint, for example. They should be brief and uncomplicated — a small number of bullet pointed items, say, in an 18 point font or bigger, for ease of reading. Graphs and tables should be similarly uncluttered:

- do *not* copy pages of an A4 report directly onto slides;

- do *not* transfer spreadsheet output directly;

- do *not* try to represent more than three variables simultaneously on the same graph;

- but *do* use slides as a focus for attention to indicate direction and to highlight key points and statistics.

- **Timing.** You should know how much time is allowed or expected for the presentation, and make the best use of it. On no account overrun — better to finish two minutes early, but better still to finish right on time. This requires practice. Once the intended material has been organised a dry run is essential, even if it is only you talking to the wall! Make allowances for nerves, which may cause your delivery to be quicker in the *actual* presentation, but ensure that you are not attempting to deliver too much material in the allowable time.

- **Rules of the Game.** Establish the parameters of your presentation at the outset. If you are prepared to field questions during your presentation then make this clear at the beginning, but beware because they can:

  - upset your timing;

  - disrupt your flow by causing you to deal with issues earlier than your intended sequence;

  - get you bogged down in unnecessary detail (especially numerical) that you might have hoped to avoid.

It is simpler to field detailed questions at the end of the presentation and only allow interjections that are necessary to clarify points. If this is your chosen course, make it clear in your opening remarks that this is how you intend to proceed.

Leaving questions to the end has other advantages. During the planning process it should be apparent which areas will present the most difficulty and which are likely to prompt questions. Indeed, it will be possible to anticipate some of the questions, giving you an opportunity to prepare answers in advance, and to prepare overhead transparencies to support the explanations. The more devious of students may even have 'planted' questions in the audience to ensure that they have the opportunity to demonstrate their competence in a particular area! Where there are multiple presenters questions can be funneled through a single recipient to the presenter with the greatest expertise, to ensure efficient conduct of the question session.

- **Interest.** Your introduction should grab the audience and demonstrate that you will be interesting and that your report will be worth listening to. An initial burst of humour or the use of relevant props often serve as ice-breakers which allow the audience to settle down and get accustomed to the speaker. These may need to be repeated at intervals in order to maintain a hold over the audience.

Maintaining interest can be more of a problem when multiple speakers are being employed. The use of two or three speakers in a single case presentation can have significant benefits when handled properly — if not, it can be disastrous! Detailed organisation and efficient time management are necessary to achieve:

- distinct and separate roles for each of the speakers;
- effective and timely change-over between speakers;
- absence of overlap and redundancy of content.

A change in style and pace for different components of the presentation can be most refreshing, but makes prior communication between the speakers absolutely essential. The worst case scenario is when large teams insist that everybody speaks (at least once), but no clear roles have been enunciated. The result is a repetitive procession where the same ground is explored and re-explored and even the overheads are re-used.

- **Practicality.** Do not blind the audience with theory. They will not want to hear it in a case environment. A theoretical background may be essential, but take care to blend it in with the requirements of the case. The worst presentations have several seemingly unrelated components and presenters who make no attempt to integrate them: this is particularly apparent when theory and practice are two of the separate components. Link the issues together carefully as part of the overall thrust and use the case to illustrate any theoretical concepts that are introduced.

- **Eye Contact.** Maintain eye contact with the audience at all times to gauge reaction. Glazed eyes, nodding heads and fluttering eyelids are all good indicators that the speaker must act, to increase the level of activity, change the tone of voice and/or adjust the level of complexity of the content. Perhaps the worst evils of presentation are attempting to read notes or talking to the whiteboard or screen. The audience does not need to see the top or back of the presenter's head.

It is not generally a good idea to distribute handouts before or during the presentation since this provides an opportunity for distraction:

- the audience will read the handout rather than listening to the explanations;
- the action of mid-presentation distribution will inevitably generate avoidable paper-shuffling and talking among members of the audience.

The only instance when prior distribution is recommended is when the handout is to be used as part of the presentation (e.g. to talk the audience through a series of graphs/tables which are too complex to present in the form of an overhead slide). Otherwise, leave the distribution of handouts (e.g. executive summary or hard-copy of slides) until the end of the presentation and inform the audience at the outset that they will not need to make onerous notes because copies will be available at the end.

- **Direction.** The introduction to the presentation should include a road map specifying exactly where the presentation is going — what content will be examined, in what order and why. Materials should be organised accordingly and the route followed, with references back to the original map where necessary to ensure that the audience is not lost and is still on track towards the conclusions and recommendations. The thrust and direction of the report should, therefore, always be apparent, as will be the planning that has been undertaken to reach the intended goal. Part of this will be a strong ending emphasising the key issues and the major recommendations. Do not meander to an end dealing with minor or peripheral issues; do not finish abruptly because of shortage of time with key issues remaining unaddressed; both are symptomatic of poor planning and an absence of directional focus.

1.4 WRITTEN REPORT

Although the key issues and the overall thrust will be the same as in the oral report, the written version provides an opportunity to develop much more detailed arguments and to substantiate arguments with supporting evidence. Just as in the oral report, both presentation and content must be addressed but the requirements are different.

The final document should be professionally presented. It must be word-processed, without grammatical or spelling errors, and assembled in the manner of a management report. There are a number of texts available which provide guidance on business communication and effective writing and plenty of on-line computer-based help in the form of Spellcheck (to avoid spelling errors) and Grammatik V (to avoid grammatical errors). The latter will also measure the readability of the text to give an indication of available compositional improvement.

The content of the report should conform to a standard structure so that it can be used effectively by a reader whose needs may be driven by time constraints. The reader is, therefore, allowed to access information of increasing levels of detail. The following is a typical structure:

1. Cover page — including case study title and authors' names;

2. Table of contents — detailing by page number the location of the components of the report;

3. Recommendations — one-page brief for the executive who has little time to devote to the report, detailing recommended strategies for adoption;

4. Executive summary — a case brief, including the background scenario, key issues, alternatives considered, analysis conducted and results.

These first four stages should occupy only a few pages and should be easy to read in five minutes or less. They give a clear indication of the scope of the problem and the recommended course(s) of action.

5. Background — relevant facts relating to the key issues which provide essential material for decision making (peripheral material, if included at all, should be consigned to an appendix).

6. Problem statement — clear specification of the key issues and problems requiring solution. The SWOT analysis outcomes might be employed at this stage to provide a focus for direction.

7. Analysis — the guts of the report, normally comprising the identification and evaluation of a number of alternative strategies which are consistent with the perceived objectives of the organisation. This section would normally include clearly labelled graphs and tables to support the arguments.

8. Recommendations and conclusions — detailed recommendations including action plans and implementation strategies as well as a recognition of limitations and potential drawbacks. No new material should be introduced at the conclusion stage. The material up to here in the report should stand alone but be capable of even further embellishment by reference to detailed tables, graphs, proofs, etc.

9. Appendixes — material which is too technically complex or which is so detailed that it disrupts the flow of argument in the analytical sections should be assigned to an appendix and referenced in the main text. References to relevant literature which might be viewed to provide even more detailed explanations could be cited here.

The overall report should be as brief as possible, consistent with it including all essential material. The top copy should be bound securely and neatly, and at least one other copy made for reference. All materials should be maintained on computer disk because the opportunity may arise to modify the written report in the light of comments made on the oral presentation.

1.5 EXAMPLE CASE

The next step is to test how well the RAPIDE procedure outlined above works in practice. To accomplish this, *Case 1: Cambridge Business Conferences* is used as an example to illustrate potential analysis and reporting problems.

CASE 1: CAMBRIDGE BUSINESS CONFERENCES

This case focuses on the use of relevants costs in a practical decision making frame-work. It requires a distinction between fixed, variable, sunk and discretionary costs and a facility with break-even analysis.

Cambridge Business Conferences (CBC) is a company skilled in the organisation and running of conferences and seminars. It normally runs six or seven events per year and is currently planning a two day conference to take place at the University Arms Hotel, Cambridge, in August 1996. The conference will be titled 'Information Technology in the 21st Century' and will present 12 speakers of international repute, five from the UK, three from western Europe and two each from Australia and the US. The booking of the venue has incurred the payment of a non-refundable deposit of £2000.

The conference organiser, Linda Winzar, estimates the following costs and revenues to be applicable.

Costs

(a) A daily delegate rate of £30 per head on each day of the conference, to cover tea/coffee and use of all hotel facilities.

(b) Meals charged at a standard rate — breakfast £12, lunch £18, dinner £28.

(c) Overnight rate for double room of £49.50.

(d) Stationery and conference papers costing £10 per delegate pack.

(e) Conference speakers are to be paid a combination of fee + expenses, and will be offered meals and overnight accommodation at the company's expense.

The following fees have been agreed (and must be paid even in the event of the prior cancellation of the conference):

3 @ £500; 2 @ £600; 2 @ £100; 1 @ AUD$800; 1 @ US$2800

The remaining speakers have either offered their services free or are prevented from charging a fee (i.e. government departments and foreign embassies). Expenses (estimated at £100 out-of-pocket expenses + travelling expenses per person) are only payable after they have been incurred.

(f) An advertising budget of £1500 has been agreed for the period March to June.

(g) The major marketing thrust will be via mail shot. An initial print run of 5000 brochures has been agreed for distribution by post. Envelopes and covering letters can be reckoned to make the total cost of the mailout 55p per addressee.

11

Printing costs can be calculated at £500 set-up + 15p per brochure. Confirmation letters will be sent to those delegates making firm bookings by post at a further cost of 50p per addressee.

(h) Administration costs and the costs of word-processing mailing lists are estimated to amount to £7000.

Revenues

Pilot testing reveals that delegates will be prepared to pay a conference fee of around £700, the rate to include overnight accommodation between the days of the conference and inclusive of all meals between lunch on Day One and lunch on Day Two. Any delegates requiring overnight accommodation prior to Day One will be billed separately. The venue can accommodate a maximum of 150 delegates in theatre style or 90 delegates seminar style, over each of the two days of the conference. Linda is actively seeking other means of raising additional conference related revenue.

You are required to evaluate the viability of this conference and recommend alternative courses of action, consistent with the short and long-term goals of CBC. Your analysis should embrace break-even and sensitivity analyses associated with the proposed event together with an exploration of the cancellation option.

CASE ANALYSIS: CAMBRIDGE BUSINESS CONFERENCES

READ THE CASE

An initial reading reveals that the case is short, but with an abundance of cost information. Data allowing the conduct of a break-even analysis is apparently readily available.

More detailed attention to the first paragraph reveals more than just numbers. The conference under consideration is apparently not a one-off event; Cambridge Business Conferences (CBC) is apparently in this business in the long-run so this single event cannot be considered in isolation. More detailed attention to the numerical content reveals a plethora of assumptions, so that unique outcomes will not be feasible, and sensitivity in a number of areas, notably with regard to exchange rates.

A third reading raises issues relating to the short and long-term goals of the company and the potential impact of decision making on alternative strategies. Sketching out the relationships reveals that a fixed/variable cost division does not work particularly well and neither does a sunk/discretionary cost division. The focus is clearly on relevant costs, and the conference activity and its timing reveal a possible avenue of analysis.

ANALYSE THE CASE

The key issues of the case appear to be:

Case Study Method

- a company with goals of survival and long-term profitability;
- a single event, 'Information Technology in the 21st Century', which may or may not contribute to company profitability;
- the strategic importance of this event to the long-term viability of the company;
- the financial impact of the success/failure of this event.

Clearly the company would like this event to make a contribution to profitability and will take pains to ensure that it does so. But its long-term reputation may be more important, so that strategic decisions may be necessary to cope with loss-making contingencies.

A SWOT analysis is probably not appropriate to this case because very little information is provided on the group, its staffing or its alternative 'products'. The calculations are the simplest starting point because they will provide some of our unknowns regarding this particular event. However, we must remain fully aware that the financials, whatever message they give, may be peripheral to the strategic actions eventually undertaken.

A simple break-even analysis requires that we establish relationships for costs and revenues. Our first assumptions require the formulation of linear relationships:

$$C = a + bq$$

and

$$R = pq$$

where
C = Total Costs; R = Total Revenues

a = fixed costs (particularly up-front conference related costs)

b = variable costs per unit (related to q, the number of delegates)

p = price to delegates, assumed to be fixed and, therefore, initially eliminating the prospect of discounting.

Figure C1.1 (page 14) illustrates the simple linear case.

Break-even occurs where $R = C$

i.e.
$$pq = a + bq$$

i.e. where
$$q = \frac{a}{p - b}$$

$$\text{Break-even output} = q_1 = \frac{\text{fixed cost}}{\text{price} - \text{variable cost per unit}}$$

In order to allocate costs appropriately, realistic assumptions need to be made, but there is no single 'right' answer. Figure C1.2 details a possible cost allocation.

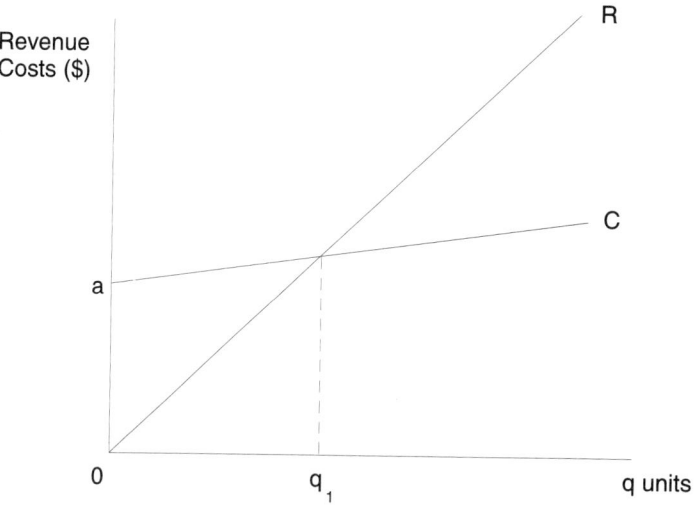

Figure C1.1: Break-even Output

Cost per delegate	£	Up-Front Pre-Conference Costs	£
Delegate rate (2 @ 30)	60.00	Speakers Fees	2900
		AUD $2000	1000
Meals: 2 @ 18;		US $2800	2000
1 @ 12; 1 @ 28	76.00		5900
		Deposit	2000
Room rate	49.50		
		Advertising	1500
Stationery	10.00		
		Mail shot: set-up	500
Confirmation letter	0.50	5000 @ 0.70	3500
Total	196.00		
		Administration	7000
		Total	20 400
		Conference Related Fixed Costs	
		Speaker Expenses	1200
		Speaker Travel (Economy)	10 800
		Total	12 000

Figure C1.2: Conference Costs for CBC

Case Study Method

A number of areas of uncertainty exist which require a sensitivity analysis to determine their impact:

- how do we treat the £2000 non-returnable deposit? It may constitute an up-front booking cost or a deposit which is lost only in the event of cancellation. In the latter instance it may be used to offset other conference related costs, and not constitute additional expense, should the conference go ahead;

- the meals combinations is assumed to constitute two lunches, but only one breakfast and one evening meal;

- double rooms are provided but it is unrealistic that we can assign two strangers to share one room;

- speakers' fees (and travel costs) need some assumptions about the exchange rates pertaining;

- speakers' travel costs require assumptions regarding the likelihood of having to meet first class/business/economy modes of travel.

These assumptions in Figure C1.2 yield:

Total Fixed Costs $\quad= 20\,400 + 12\,000 = £32\,400\ (a)$

Variable Cost per Unit $= £196.00\ (b)$

Price per Unit $\quad\quad\quad= £700\ (p)$

So that the break-even No of Delegates $= \dfrac{a}{p-b} = \dfrac{32\,400}{700-196}$

$$= \textbf{65 delegates}$$

Given that the venue can only accommodate 90 delegates in seminar style, the 65 delegate break-even is extremely high, severely limiting the potential profitability of the event (i.e. a maximum of less than £13 000 with all seats filled). Theatre style, increasing the accommodation to 150 possible delegates, therefore appears a must.

A detailed sensitivity analysis reveals that this solution is relatively robust to the uncertainties detailed above, except in one instance. The necessity of paying first-class airfares for pivotal conference speakers could cause a blow-out in travel related expenses. Costings based on economy-rate fares are probably unrealistic for all but academics! CBC might expect to pay first-class fares for several and business-class for the remainder of the speakers, seven in all, flying to the venue. Conference related fixed costs might easily double to £24 000, increasing the break-even figure to **88 delegates**.

This conference is beginning to look a little risky. Up-front expenses of £20 400, with no matching revenues, will put pressure on the overdraft facility. With realistic assumptions we cannot make a profit with a seminar-style presentation. Even with a theatre-style format we need well over one hundred delegates to make it a viable proposition.

There is a distinct possibility that we will not manage to attract delegates in these numbers at a fixed fee of £700. Other contingencies have to be examined, one of which is the cancellation option.

If we have already incurred the up-front pre-conference expenses (approximately £20 400) then we can forget about those. They are sunk costs which cannot be recovered. Of more concern is our ability to recover those costs incurred in the actual running of the event, and if possible to make a contribution which alleviates the sunk cost burden. Either way the event will result in a hefty loss, but it might be smaller than it otherwise would have been. To justify continuing to run the conference at all, on financial grounds, we must cover the fixed costs element of speaker expenses and travel:

i.e. $\dfrac{12\,000}{700 - 196} = 24$ delegates (on the economy fare assumption)

or $\dfrac{24\,000}{700 - 196} = 48$ delegates (on the first/business class assumption)

The latter result suggests that we may be struggling to justify the non-cancellation of the event on financial grounds, in that the extent of the losses may be extended past the initial £20 400 by doing so. The numerical analysis here is a great help in heightening our awareness of problems and facilitating the next stage in the process.

PROBLEM IDENTIFICATION

It is possible that the survival of the whole company might be endangered by this one event. Early cancellation would cut short the haemorrhage of funds, but at what cost to the company's reputation? If we wish to continue to be regarded as conference professionals we may have to bear the loss of this one event, making it crucial that such losses are minimised. This is the only real problem facing us: it is pointless going into great detail on peripheral issues (e.g. sensitivity analysis of obscure items) when these will matter little to the final outcome.

INVESTIGATION OF PROBLEMS

Although conference cancellation may be the best (or even only) option on financial grounds, from a strategic point of view it may be a non-starter. Cancellation of an event at a late stage will inevitably incur short-term financial costs and long-term, perhaps even insuperable, damage to reputation. The problem is, therefore, to run the event at a minimum loss, both to Profit and Loss Account and professional reputation. We therefore need to develop alternative approaches to:

- increasing the number of paying delegates (to increase revenue);

- increasing the number of non-paying delegates (to improve reputation);

- seeking other sources of revenue;

- reducing costs (fixed and variable);

- adopting accounting procedures which alleviate the losses incurred.

DEVELOPMENT OF ALTERNATIVE SOLUTIONS

A number of possibilities exist to tackle the issues itemised above:

- **Increase the number of paying delegates.** Some flexibility in the fixed price structure might be possible. The two days of the conference might be marketed separately, as might the separate sessions. Discounts might be offered for early payment and for the second and subsequent delegates from the same organisation. Price discrimination might be practised in favour of local delegates approached at the last minute.

- **Increase the number of non-paying delegates.** The reputation of the company will depend on the ambience of the conference venue and the 'feel' of the event. If there are very few paying delegates then the conference room must not look empty; a return to a seminar style, with tables, chairs and static flower displays will reduce the extent of spare space. The number of people attending may only be increased by providing free places (e.g. to colleagues, academics, friends, spouses etc). It may even be necessary to 'pay' for free places by providing lunch and afternoon tea. This strategy might backfire if the newcomers are differentiated from the paying delegates (e.g. through age or dress code) and do not conceal the circumstances of their presence.

- **Seeking other sources of revenue.** A number of alternatives exist:
  - sponsorship of the event, in whole or parts. Sponsorship of meals and cocktail parties by firms wishing to advertise their name will be relatively easy to come by and will at least reduce the costs to CBC of meals. Major sponsors, with acknowledgment in all literature and with an opportunity to speak to delegates at opening or plenary sessions, should also be sought from among members of the hardware and software industry;
  - selling space in thoroughfares of the venue to book publishers and computer companies to provide sales opportunities for them with interested delegates. Prime selling space adjacent to tea/coffee areas would command premium fees;
  - selling collected conference proceedings immediately after the event in the form of books and/or videos. A high price, though significantly discounted from the conference fee, might be charged at the outset to those unable to attend as delegates. The computer and IT industries and financial institutions might then be targeted for the sales of collected proceedings.

- **Reducing costs.** This may be difficult because quality must not be sacrificed in return for a few cents. Most delegates remember the venue, food, drink and contacts from a conference and not the content of the presentations! It is important that we do not skimp on the quality of meals, for example. It is better to try to reduce long-term costs by coming to some single-venue agreement with the hotel for future events.

- **Alternative accounting procedures.** It is doubtful whether all of the fixed costs noted in Figure C1.2 are specific to this conference. It could be that at least part of the following expenditures are attributable to other events or to the company as a whole:
  - advertising (£1500) may include fliers for future events;
  - administration (£7000) will include the establishment of a database of names/addresses for use in targeting delegates of future conferences.

Part of these could, arguably, be treated as depreciable assets rather than being expensed directly and attributed to this particular conference activity.

EVALUATION OF ALTERNATIVES

The going concern assumption relative to CBC incorporates a commitment to running this conference once it has been promoted. Any financial losses incurred must be borne in the cause of furthering the reputation of the company. The suggestions above which involve increasing revenue, increasing the number of delegates and seeking new sources for both should be explored. Great care should be taken in cost-cutting, and accounting procedural manipulation attempted only if it is essential that the financial outcome of this particular conference 'looks' better: for the company as a whole it may represent wasted effort.

CASE REPORT: CAMBRIDGE BUSINESS CONFERENCES

The presentation of the findings of the analysis for this case is relatively straight-forward. There is a single overall thrust, so that problems of integration are not apparent, and the recommendations are clear. Major difficulties may arise in the level of numeracy to be attempted in the presentation; some compromise must be reached between clarity of exposition and the detailed content of costing calculations.

Consider the approach within the **STRIPED** procedure:

SIMPLICITY

Use brief introductory overheads focusing on short-term and long-term objectives initially; similarly brief bullet-point recommendations to conclude. Figure C1.2 might be divided into two overheads (left-hand column followed by right-hand column) for maximum focus. Even so the numbers presented will not satisfy all members of the audience — especially those with different answers and/or assumptions. More detail on the overheads might, however, cause confusion and the detail must be explained in simple terms. Problems will arise here unless the rules of the game are clearly specified at the outset. Simple two or three line graphs might be used to advantage to illustrate the break-even situation in practice.

Case Study Method

TIMING

Appropriate emphasis on the timing of the different parts of the presentation is critical. The calculations are important, but less important than the strategic direction of the company. Take care to leave time to spell out the motives for alternative actions and not get bogged down on peripheral detail (e.g. different assumptions for sensitivity analysis computations).

RULES OF THE GAME

Make it clear how questions are to be dealt with. Queries regarding the detail of the calculations are inevitable and it is feasible that a member of the audience will pinpoint an error that you have made! Worse still a member of the audience will pinpoint an error that you have not made, but will argue so articulately and vehemently that you are temporarily convinced that you are wrong. The worst sort of chaos can ensue, particularly when the presenter attempts to alter all the numbers on the spot, with errors inevitably resulting. Much better to acknowledge the error (if obvious) or express doubt and the need for time for further consideration (if not) while providing an estimate of the effect of the change on the outcomes. In this case, alternative assumptions will have little effect except for the specification of travel mode. Do not get into arguments or entertain conflicts, as they will only serve to distract the audience and divert the attention of the presenter.

Make it clear up-front that there is no unique solution and that this is just one set of possible assumptions. Respond to pleas for clarity, but avoid the temptation to do any detailed recalculation.

INTEREST

Try to relate to the audience members and their experiences. Conference anecdotes will help, especially for mature audiences. David Lodge's novel *Small World* might be used as a prop, possibly with reference to some of his hilarious situations and quotations set in the context of the academic conference circuit. The cancellation option might be explored as a product-mix problem if the audience is more familiar with that context (i.e. cancellation of the event might be equated to the elimination of one non-performing product in the range).

PRACTICALITY

The audience is not interested in break-even theory, the solution of algebraic equations — and especially not calculus solutions to non-linear break even problems! A graphical exposition of the actual case situation demonstrating the robustness of the solution to alternative scenarios would be extremely useful, as long as it is not overcomplicated by the addition of multiple lines for multiple alternatives.

The case is based on an actual situation, so it should not be difficult to make the outcomes and the decision alternatives both practical and meaningful.

EYE CONTACT

Attend closely to the audience at all times to ensure that the pace is appropriate and that arguments and calculations are being followed by most audience members.

DIRECTION

Begin with a clear specification of the long-term and short-term goals of the enterprise and the approach to be taken in their analysis. The conference (including calculations) can be examined with reference to short-term objectives, with these leading back to a long-term perspective.

The IT conference as part of the product portfolio of Cambridge Business Conferences provides the vehicle for a discussion of the recommendations which will ensure that its reputation remains intact, while the financial downside is minimised. Both oral and written reports can adopt this approach; the latter has the advantage of providing an opportunity to present detailed numerical findings (of costings and sensitivity to change) in an appendix.

Chapter 2

Accounting Ethics

2.1 INTRODUCTION

The stock market crash of October 1987 indirectly sparked a renewed interest in business ethics. Its direct consequence, imminent corporate collapse for many enterprises worldwide, engendered an increase in activities, considered by many to be unacceptable, in order to secure short-term survival. When self-interest causes a shift away from 'gentlemanly behaviour', by either gender, then stricter guidelines are necessary to enforce behaviour which is in the commercial interests of the majority.

Principles of equity and justice are paramount in the ethical standards developed in ancient Egyptian civilisations. Well before the formulation of a Christian ethical doctrine, Confucius, in ancient China, used 'reciprocity' as a basis for ethical principles: 'do as you would be done by others'. The development of ethics in Anglo-Saxon based communities derives largely from ancient Greece, in the guise of the three key philosophers:

- Socrates — seeking to measure what is 'just' or 'good';

- Plato — defining the concept of 'justice'; and

- Aristotle — defining the term 'virtuous'.

In practice, an individual's business decision making will be guided by an ideology established through the influence of parents, schooling, religion and national or regional culture. There will be a perception of a natural way of the world which differentiates right from wrong. Social regulation of actions will be provided by moral laws (and the need to avoid personal guilt), social mores (and the need to avoid embarrassment and loss of face) and the requirement of conformity to the expectations of family, team or professional body. The legal framework will provide regulations which are *facilitative* (necessitating the following of strict procedures to validate transactions), *prescriptive* (in that a duty of care is demanded in personal and professional dealings) and *proscriptive* (in that rules and guidelines are in force such that non-compliance will render the subject liable to penalty).

Hunt and Vitell (1992) develop a model of the ethical decision making process, a simplified version of which appears in Figure 2.

21

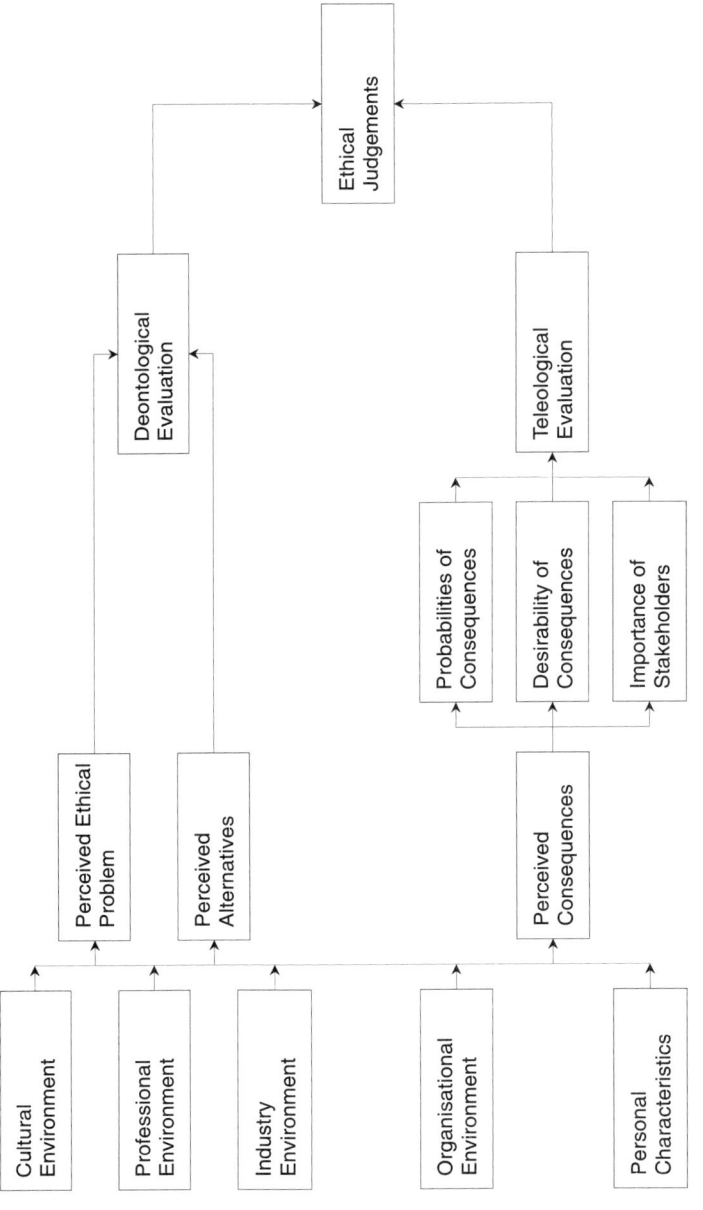

Figure 2: Model of Ethical Evaluation

Accounting Ethics

They view ethical perceptions as being determined by the cultural, professional, industrial and organisational environments as well as one's personal experiences. Thus religion, the legal and political system and personal value and belief systems would all impact on the evaluation of an ethical problem.

Ethical judgments, and subsequent actions and outcomes, are consequential upon the two major forms of ethical evaluation:

- *Deontological* — concerned with the duty that individuals have to recognise the needs of others. This form of analysis assesses the 'rightness' or 'wrongness' of alternative forms of behaviour, irrespective of their ultimate consequences.

- *Teleological* — concerned with the consequences of the behaviour and the evaluation of the 'goodness' or 'badness' of the consequences. These might be viewed, at the extreme, in utilitarian terms (satisfying the general good) or egotistical terms (satisfying individual self-interest).

Utilitarians judge actions based on their outcomes, with the objective of achieving 'the greatest good for the greatest number'. The implication of this line of thought for accounting decision making is that allocation of resources based on the optimum for individual, department, division or company might be questionable if it were not also in the interests of the community as a whole. The interests of the minority would be subservient to those of the 'greater good' and any alternative outcome deemed unethical.

The alternative approach recognises the *rights* of individuals and justifies right/wrong decisions in terms of the impact on these rights. Respect for the dignity and interests of others suggests that no one should be permitted to take actions in their own interest simply because they view those interests to be more important than all others. With these rights comes an inherent duty to respect the rights of others. Ethical dilemmas may arise in the accounting environment when interested parties have both moral rights and duties to others. The rights approach is problematical in that, in itself, it provides little guidance for the resolution of ethical conflicts.

Criteria of *justice* and fairness exist to allow a judgment to be made between the rights of individuals and those of the general community. These criteria require the clear specification, administration and communication of rules and guidelines for acceptable behaviour, and even so may be difficult to implement in practice because of uncertainty regarding the facts of the case.

Kant's normative ethics do not require a utilitarian maximisation. He emphasises human rights rather than human virtues so that actions may be judged in terms of their avoiding violations of basic moral principles. The consequences of acts are seen as much less important than the means employed to achieve the desired ends. The outcome is seen as irrelevant in evaluating the rightness or wrongness of an act, and two actions with identical consequences would be evaluated differently. The emphasis is clearly on doing 'right' because it is 'right' regardless of one's self-interest in the degree of 'rightness'.

As if the ethical theories themselves are not problematical enough, the practicalities of a given situation will present further barriers to successful implementation. These may be categorised as:

- *Systemic* — legal constraints, custom and practice

- *Organisational* — problems associated with management systems and culture

- *Individual* — information asymmetry, lethargy and mental attitudes

The above framework helps to identify the ethical issues of a case, which can then be categorised according to their relative importance from the trivial — perhaps with minor implications for one individual — to the major issues with potentially disastrous consequences for both company and community. A ranking of the ethical dilemmas under consideration may then be generated.

The codes of conduct of particular companies and the accounting profession with regard to ethical aspects provide further frameworks against which perceived ethical dilemmas can be judged. The Codes of Professional Conduct and Ethical Guidelines of the UK Accounting bodies have great similarities, leaning heavily on the requirements of members of the International Federation of Accountants (IFAC), and provide a basis for further investigation. Acceptance of responsibility to the public interest, defined as the collective well-being of the community served by the professional accountant, is the primary focus of attention. The distinguishing mark of a profession is deemed to be that its members have a duty to society as a whole and not just to their clients or employers. Duties and loyalties are owed to the community and these should not be in conflict with the interests of clients and employers.

A number of fundamental principles (the actual number varies slightly between codes) is consistent with the objective of achieving the highest possible standards of ethical conduct:

- **Integrity**. The decisions and actions of the professional accountant should be honest and straightforward. Members should not breach the trust of public, client or employer nor be a party to the falsification of records or the provision of false or misleading information. Members of the accounting profession should not engage in any activities that would prevent their practising ethically and should necessarily refuse gifts, favours or hospitality that would, actually or apparently, influence their actions.

- **Objectivity**. Members of the profession should be fair and not allow bias or prejudice to influence their actions. They must be impartial and remain free from conflicts of interest in their professional dealings. Their independence and intellectual honesty will be reflected in the fair, accurate and objective communication of information, necessarily embracing the full disclosure of all information that might reasonably be expected to be relevant to a particular scenario.

- **Competence and Due Care**. Members must carry out their professional services with due care, competence and diligence. Implicit in this is the duty to maintain their professional knowledge and technical skills at a level suitable to demonstrate competence. Professional accountants will correspondingly refrain from accepting any performance role which they are not competent to carry out directly or with the assistance of others.

- **Confidentiality**. The confidentiality of information acquired during the performance of professional services should be respected. Members must not disclose such information without prior authority unless there is a specific legal or professional duty to disclose; nor should they use such information to their own personal advantage, either ethical or illegal. Members in managerial positions have a corresponding monitoring duty to ensure that subordinates under their control similarly respect the confidentiality of the information with which they are working.

- **Professionalism**. A member must behave in a professional manner and refrain from any conduct which might bring the accounting profession into disrepute or damage the name of their professional body. Any activity which detracts from an individual's credibility as a professional with a reputation for the provision of a high quality of accounting service is deemed unethical and unprofessional. This includes engagement in a simultaneous business role regarded as undignified in a professional context.

- **Technical Standards**. The services of professional accountants should be in accordance with relevant technical and professional standards. Members must comply with statutory accounting and auditing standards of the profession. Where appropriate, they must also comply with guidance provided in other matters of a technical or professional nature.

'Integrity' and 'objectivity' are apparently the fundamental principles, each of which provides readers with plenty of ammunition through which to visualise examples of unethical behaviour. However, pursuit of the public interest appears to suggest the adoption of utilitarian principles in the resolution of conflict, in that no distinction is made between different components of 'public'. Little guidance is provided for situations where decisions might result in benefits to one component (e.g. debtholders) at the expense of others (e.g. shareholders).

The guidelines above suggest some of the areas in which unethical behaviour may occur, and some examples are given below:

- *integrity* — falsification of records for personal gain such as the achievement of a performance-related bonus;

- *objectivity* — failure to disclose harmful information which might otherwise prejudice the completion of a project generating considerable commissions to a family member;

- *competence* — lack of awareness of current developments results in the provision of unsound advice by a colleague, and you are pressured to hide the true facts to protect his career;

- *confidentiality* — disclosure of inside information to friends or family resulting in its use for personal gain;

- *professionalism* — engagement in or promotion of illegal or immoral activities as a secondary source of income;

- *technical standards* — non-compliance with professional standards and guidelines at the insistence of a superior.

Where these conflicts arise and some means is sought to resolve them then a systematic examination of the alternatives available should be undertaken. The CIMA Ethical Guidelines provide some useful advice in this respect:

- follow the established grievance policies of the organisation where these exist;

- if these are unsatisfactory or inappropriate discuss the problem with your superior;

- where the superior is at the centre of the conflict, submit the issue to the next highest level of management. Where the superior is not involved such elevation should only take place with the immediate superior's prior knowledge;

- discussion with an objective adviser to clarify the issues and identify possible courses of action, as long as such discussions do not breach duties of confidentiality;

- if a significant incidence of ethical conflict remains after exhausting all levels of review, resignation of employment may have to be considered;

- communication of information, regarding the conflict, to outsiders, or other instances constituting 'whistleblowing', should be avoided and is not considered ethically appropriate;

- legal action may be a last resort, in which case it is essential to document all steps taken to resolve the conflict throughout each stage of the process.

The development of alternative courses of action should take into account their impact on all the component groups of stakeholders, together with a consideration of the likely barriers and aids to their successful implementation.

Neither resignation nor whistleblowing should be contemplated lightly. Both may seriously influence future employment prospects and the future well-being of the company. However, if following orders proves intolerable, because of their immoral or unethical basis, and no modifications result from following the grievance procedure, then the grounds for whistleblowing must be examined and contrasted with their likely impact. Such action might be justified, either in terms of a sense of duty, i.e. the deontological approach of pursuing the moral course of action regardless of the consequences; or in terms of the satisfaction resulting from the company or manager being forced to adopt an ethically correct position, i.e. a teleological evaluation adopting the utilitarian approach of pursuing the consequences since their importance outweighs that of the necessary actions.

Evaluation of alternative courses of action with respect to their consequences, in the context of the ethical theories outlined above, will likely present no unique outcome. Different moral philosophies may lead to disagreements regarding the appropriate alternative for implementation. Such a result does not invalidate the process, since it has increased our awareness of the implications of ethical conflict and the managerial controls that might be implemented in order to reduce their incidence. However, the final step in making and justifying an ethical decision may be very difficult in practice.

Case studies revolving around accounting or business ethics require a systematic approach, just as described in Chapter 1. They differ in that the analysis achieves a new dimension, frequently concerning issues that are not directly mentioned in the case. However, as before, an analytical structure can be developed so that the facts of the case under consideration can be investigated with reference to an appropriate theoretical framework.

Let us consider how our six stage RAPIDE framework, developed in Chapter 1, might be implemented in an accounting ethics environment, using *Minicase A: Ashley-Yeats Retailing* as an example:

Murray Howell has an accounting degree and is part way through his professional examinations. He expects to qualify in 1996. He works for Ashley-Yeats, one of London's largest retailers, in their Brent Cross department store. As part of his management training Murray spends time, usually at least three months, in each of the store's divisions to learn their procedures so that he will be able to make a positive contribution to administration and internal audit. The financial services arm, of which he is currently a part, is responsible for administering the store's in-house charge card which is promoted as a means of facilitating sales. Security is strict because of the need to access the personal financial records of customers. Every employee has a target number of card openings per week, which they are required to meet in order to earn a bonus. Completed forms come to financial services for processing with the employee ID number written in so that bonus-related efforts can be recognised. Murray has noticed two types of charge card application that do not conform to the norm:

- those where the employee ID has been omitted, and

- those where a customer comes directly to financial services with the sole intention of opening a charge card (termed 'walk-up' sales).

The service-centre operatives process these cases by writing in their own ID on the forms, to help themselves reach the target for bonus awards. Furthermore, when this week's target has been reached the operatives delay any further openings to the following week by filing the forms, still unprocessed. Murray feels that such action is not in the spirit of the scheme, but is being pressured by his colleagues to cooperate fully. They expect him to write in his own ID when processing such cases and to just meet his targets. Murray has a dilemma: he is saving hard to get married and the extra bonus money would come in very useful, and he does not wish to implicate any of his workmates. In any case, the ID write-ins do not appear to do any harm; somebody else would be earning the bonus points if they had only taken the trouble to fill the forms in properly. Nobody appears to be disadvantaged.

Strategic Management Accounting

While an initial reading of the case will highlight the key facts and assumptions, a more detailed inspection is necessary to increase awareness of the potential ethical issues involved.

ANALYSE

Normative ethical theories provide a suitable starting point for the analysis of the key issues of any case. The alternative approaches and knock-on effects provide the basis of a structure for viewing ethical problems in an accounting environment.

The three-way division based on utilitarianism/rights/justice allows us to specify appropriate issues in this case:

Utilitarians would observe that the interests of a minority of participants (operatives in the service centre) are apparently being catered for in preference to those of the great majority (particularly colleagues in other departments, other bonus recipients and shareholders of Ashley-Yeats Retailing).

The different interest groups clearly receive disparate benefits. Recognition of the *rights* of individuals highlights the obligations that the operatives have to both their colleagues and their employers: in the case of Murray Howell these obligations extend to standards of professional conduct owed to his professional body.

Justice arguments highlight the unfairness in the distribution of benefits resulting from the selfish actions of the financial services operatives. Their working practices appear to be disadvantaging both their fellow workers at the store and the company in general. In this way they are likely reducing the overall extent of the bonus 'pie' and cutting a larger slice for themselves than they would otherwise deserve.

Rules and guidelines for acceptable behaviour should be in place at Ashley-Yeats, with procedures adopted to ensure efficient administration of their adoption. The different categories characterising the practicalities of any situation highlight some of the uncertainties associated with the facts of this case.

A consideration of *Systemic* factors provokes a number of questions:

- Are the actions of the service centre operatives illegal? Do they constitute stealing in the accepted sense of the term so that they could be arrested and charged for their offences?

- Are the 'write-in' practices an accepted 'perk' of the job, acknowledged by successive managers without disciplinary action?

- Are there procedures in place to govern the processing of charge card applications? Are these being contravened by the existing service centre operatives? Would such action, if more widely recognised, constitute grounds for dismissal?

An extension of focus to organisational factors questions the nature of the bonus system and the way in which it rewards the observed actions. The management systems in place are clearly inadequate to control the manipulation of the scheme, but the worst excesses might be eliminated by modifications to the scheme itself. Healy (1985) observes the self-interested actions of bonus earners in consistently 'adjusting' the timing of receipts and expenses to maximise their awards. Where the triggering of a target hurdle is sufficient to earn a bonus — and no performance related target exists beyond this trigger — we might anticipate that the recognition-manipulation activity would be increased.

A consideration of individual factors questions the morale of the organisation. Where operatives feel they have secret information regarding charge-card transactions they apparently have no compunction in maximising their own rewards. There is no appreciable team spirit or loyalty to the organisation, which might be addressed with modern management techniques.

PROBLEM IDENTIFICATION

In any particular case the ethical issues, though present, may pale into insignificance relative to non-ethical issues. It is therefore important to identify problems associated with accounting, marketing, management and MAIS together with strategic opportunities.

Evaluation of the full extent of any problem may be dependent upon an investigation of greater depth, possibly involving the use of numerical methods to quantify the impact of alternative actions. Just as we might quantify the financial benefits of investment alternatives, we can specify the costs and benefits to the various stakeholder groups resulting from alternative solutions to ethical conflicts.

In this case it should prove relatively easy to quantify the extent of the write-in activity, by referencing processing records; it will likely prove more difficult to quantify the extent of the 'shelving' of completed forms. The monetary impact on bonus earning might, therefore, be difficult to estimate without some means in existence whereby forms are dated at the time of receipt.

This scam reveals clear inadequacies in the management accounting information system. In the short term procedural changes and increased monitoring will rectify most of the manipulation opportunities; in the longer term training may modify the corporate culture and change the attitude of the erring workforce. However, without more vigilant management, customer complaint or the acquiescence of Murray Howell, in the first place, it is quite possible that this scheme could continue to operate indefinitely without coming to the attention of senior management. Professional ethics and the consequences of loss of professional status, reputation and ultimately, job, may provide the motivation for Murray Howell to initiate corrective action.

INVESTIGATION

At the investigation stage we should identify and categorise conflicts of interest, which may vary from trivia to executive level fraud or other illegal activities. Such investigations will identify the participants in the conflict and the likely impact on different stakeholder groups.

Murray Howell has obligations to himself, his professional body, his employers, his colleagues, inside financial services *and* elsewhere, not necessarily in that order. Conflicts of interest suggest that he cannot serve each of these simultaneously.

We might argue that he has the least obligation to those in the financial services section, but if he is satisfied that nothing illegal is taking place any action could be detrimental to his future.

DEVELOPMENT OF ALTERNATIVES

Murray's personal and professional integrity is being questioned. He has five major alternative courses of action to consider:

- Do nothing and cooperate with the scheme, making him as guilty as any other operative in the financial services centre.

- Do nothing but do not cooperate with the scheme. He seeks no personal gain but takes no action to eliminate the manipulative actions of others.

- Persuade his colleagues to cease their actions but fail to report past misdemeanours. This may prove a short-term solution, but one which leaves him vulnerable to subsequent audit outcomes. Further ethical dilemmas may arise if he is assigned to the audit section and authorises a cover-up.

- Report the actions to his immediate superior (provided that no evidence exists to suggest that he or she is directly involved with the scheme). This will undoubtedly irk his colleagues, whose bonus-earning excesses will be terminated, and some of whom may be sacked as a result. Some of these people may be his friends. Blowing the whistle may not improve his reputation with those colleagues that remain, if they believe he cannot be trusted

- Resign his employment if he is prepared neither to countenance the actions of others, nor bear the consequences of informing his superiors of the nature of the problem.

EVALUATION OF ALTERNATIVES

The absence of clearly documented procedures and the empowerment of individuals to take unmonitored action is at the source of the difficulty. The problem can be rectified in the medium term through tighter procedures, though these may result in customer delays and complaints that run counter to a customer focus.

In the short term, Murray's professional reputation requires that he make his superiors aware of the scheme. He might seek to accuse nobody but report that, through his own ingenuity, he has identified a number of loopholes in the existing scheme. A focus on procedures, and his suggested solutions to overcome the observed deficiencies, may save his colleagues from the sack. If not, he must learn to live with the consequences.

The case studies which follow provide a multitude of examples of ethical conflicts of interest, and an opportunity to apply the RAPIDE analytical framework.

In *Case 2 : Kambalda Manufacturing* we have an individual seeking to breach the fundamental principle of integrity by measures which also place the technical standards principle in jeopardy. In these efforts he is ably supported by his subordinates, all with the objective of personal gain, further complicating the ethical context.

In *Case 3 : SLI Holdings* we have an individual who apparently views his own personal interests as superior to the public interest, with implications for ethical conflict which vary from the immoral to the clearly illegal.

REFERENCES

CIMA Ethical Guidelines, Chartered Institute of Management Accountants, London, 1992

Cooke R A , Ethics in Business: A Perspective in Business Ethics Program, Arthur Andersen and Co, SC, 1991

Healy P M, 'The Effect of Bonus Schemes on Accounting Decisions', *Journal of Accounting and Economics*, Vol 7, 1985, pp 85–107

Hunt S and Vitell S, 'A General Theory of Marketing Ethics', *Journal of Marketing*, Vol 8, 1992, pp 5–16

Kant I, *Foundations of the Metaphysics of Morals*, (trans LW Beck), Bobbs-Merrill, Indianapolis, 1959

Madison R L, 'The New Ethical Guidelines from an International Perspective', *Management Accounting* (UK), April 1993, pp 32–37

Northcott P H, *Ethics and the Certified Practicing Accountant: Case Studies*, ASCPA, Melbourne, 1993

Parker C (ed), *Accounting Handbook* 1993, Prentice Hall, 1992, pp 1253–1348

Velasquez M G, *Business Ethics: Concepts and Cases*, 3rd ed, Prentice Hall, Englewood Cliffs, NJ, 1991

Williams J G, 'The Relevance of Ethics: A Practical Problem Analysed', *CIMA Student*, August 1992, pp 8–9

CASE 2: KAMBALDA MANUFACTURING

This case addresses the ethical issues that are raised when bonuses are awarded on the basis of accounting numbers which are capable of manipulation by the bonus recipients, potentially in a dysfunctional manner.

Kambalda Manufacturing is based in Trafford Park, Manchester and provides construction and building materials throughout the North West of England. It has a divisional organisational structure with each of the five divisions making a significant contribution to group profits. Figure C2.1 details the organisation of the group:

	Builders Materials	Corrugated Board	Plastics	Roofing	Glass
Divisional Manager (DM)	(Jim Jameson)	(Dick Richardson)	(Robin Robinson)	(Bob Robertson)	(Bill Williamson)
% Group Profits	15%	20%	35%	17%	13%
% Profit Target	10%	15%	20%	12%	10%

Figure C2.1: Kambalda Manufacturing Divisional Structure

The performance of each division is measured by reference to the profits it generates relative to its asset base. The bonus element of the Divisional Managers' compensation packages is highly geared to the achievement of a target Profits/Net Assets performance ratio. Senior managers within each division receive bonuses which are a fixed percentage of that awarded to the DM. For bonus calculation purposes:

- **Profit** is determined as the annual trading profit, excluding any extraordinary items.

- **Net Assets** is determined as the net book value of assets at the year end after netting off both cash and overdraft.

Robin Robinson, Head of the Plastics Division, has been at odds with Head Office for several years over what he sees as inequities in the distribution of bonuses. His division consistently provides the lion's share of group profitability but the nature of the business requires investment in expensive high-technology equipment, increasing the value of the asset base. He feels that he is being doubly penalised by being asked to achieve a target profit ratio significantly larger than any other division in order to earn his annual bonus.

Accounting Ethics

Now a crisis has arisen. The Divisional Management Accountant (Tony Baldrick) has alerted Robin to the likelihood of the 1996 target not being achievable. Baldrick forecasts that at 30 June 1996 trading profit will be £350 000 while net assets employed at the year end will be £1.8m resulting in a profit ratio of 19.4%, marginally below the 20% target for earning performance-related bonuses.

Robin calls on his function managers — Bob Drucker (sales and marketing), Peter Kaplan (production), Doug Lomax (personnel) — together with Baldrick, to come up with proposals which might avert a personal financial disaster. Baldrick highlights the reason for the shortfall: investment in new equipment essential for the division to remain competitive, at a cost of £100 000. The equipment is expected to result in cost savings of £25 000 per year over each of the next ten years. However, he suggests that the simple solution is to defer this expenditure to the next financial year. Lomax is unwilling to endanger the long-term competitiveness of the division and suggests a safer alternative, as long as the division is prepared to bite the bullet by retrenching a few workers. He proposes to close down the small, but profitable, Goole plant with a loss of 25 jobs.

The move would incur a disengagement payout approaching £50 000 and would reduce divisional profits by £10 000 per year. On the other hand, the sale of the plant would immediately raise £250 000 while reducing the book value of assets by £200 000.

Drucker is amazed at such Draconian measures. He suggests that a simple manipulation of creditors would provide an appropriate solution. Plastics Division owes £100 000 to Jones Brothers, a small independent manufacturer and long-standing supplier. There are plenty of alternative suppliers and Jones cannot afford to lose Plastics' business. They are vulnerable to exploitation and Drucker suggests that payment of the debt be deferred from 14 June to 2 July. A £5000 late-payment penalty would result and Jones would likely have problems meeting their own creditors. But that was not Plastics' problem. Kaplan is unhappy with the unnecessary £5000 pay-out and suggests a time-shift in the opposite direction, by bringing forward customer receipts. He suggests that by introducing an extra shift, additional overtime working and cutting a few corners, he can complete the Vulcanex project four weeks ahead of schedule (20 June instead of 18 July). Quality might suffer a little as a result, but the customer could then be invoiced in June increasing profits by £20 000, at a cost of £2500 resulting from penalty production rates.

Robin is encouraged by the creativity of his executive team, but requires guidance in choosing the most appropriate of the alternatives. After all, there is no point in implementing all of the policies. He is rewarded for beating target, not for beating target by 10%, and he does not wish to alert the Group Executive to the flexibility of his accounting procedures.

You are required to consider the relative merits of each of the proposals and to discuss any ethical issues that might be apparent.

Make recommendations to Kambalda of possible improvements that might be made to the bonus scheme for divisional managers.

CASE 3: SLI HOLDINGS

This case tells the story of one individual, his values, goals and actions in achieving success. It provides a framework for the discussion of actions of varying degrees of legality — fraudulent, unprofessional, unethical and immoral — and prompts a consideration of control mechanisms that might be initiated.

You won't have heard of Alec Smart. In fact he doesn't exist. But there are many like him today. Naturally, any resemblance that Alec has to any particular corporate cowboys is purely coincidental. Alec is interested in making money — lots of it — in a clinical manner and with as little attention to ethical considerations as possible.

From his early teens Alec single-mindedly pursued his money-making activities. He studied hard and saved any money that came his way. Books were his first priority and, just as his mother had predicted, he needed reading glasses by the time he was 13. He had no time for the beach, football or other strenuous team games. He liked cricket, but had no time for the flair of Randall or Gower, preferring the whole-hearted commitment and will-to-win of Jardine and Close.

He did well at school and went on to University, where a business degree with a practical accounting specialization followed by a relevant professional accounting qualification would get him in at the sharp end of business in double-quick time. He overloaded subjects, took extra courses at summer school and kept his head down to graduate in a little over two years. His one vice was the stockmarket, and he used the little money he earned stocking supermarket shelves at the weekend to invest in suitable shares. Like everything else, he took that seriously too, using his accounting training to spot undervalued companies from their corporate statements and public disclosures.

With his charts and reports he resembled the professional punter, working full-time on form guides and breeding records. And he made money too; not the millions he yearned for, but hundreds of pounds. He soon realised that he wanted more than share dealing: he wanted to run a business. More precisely he wanted to run down a business.

Alec was confident, arrogant almost. He was prepared to back his own judgment down to the wire and didn't mind taking a calculated risk or treading on a few toes. He could not understand those who did not make the most of their abilities. His old accounting professor was smarter than him, but prepared to spend his life divorced from reality for £40 000 a year. He was smarter but he did not have Alec's entrepreneurial commitment. Alec was prepared to go bust if he had to, in order eventually to make a fortune.

His first job was in the valuation department of the ABM merchant bank, which he had joined for the experience rather than as a career stepping stone. But fate decreed that this humble start would provide the opportunity for his first leap forward. His spare time he spent analysing companies and he had a 'Top Ten Targets' list of firms vulnerable to takeover.

When one of his targets appeared in preliminary documentation that hit his desk he knew it was time to move. He buried the documentation, eliminated all cross-references and started buying shares. It crossed his mind that what he was doing was unethical — words like 'fraud', 'dishonesty' and 'insider trading' flashed past his eyes — but he immediately dismissed such thoughts as wimpish in the extreme.

Mostly Moccasins Ltd had been a successful company up to the 1980s. Now changes in fashion had sent the company into steep decline. Its shares languished at two pence each and the founder and chief executive, Joseph Jessop, had died the previous week. His undeserving son and heir in the family business, Graham, was interested only in unloading his shareholding and departing for the warmer climate of the Carribbean. The company was making losses of £30 000 a year and its only tangible assets were £50 000 worth of obsolescent stock — that was apart from the lease on its South London property valued at £1 in the books. It was pure luck that Joseph Jessop had been making tentative enquiries of ABM regarding property revaluation.

A discrete personal loan, plus his own savings, provided Alec with the £20 000 he needed to buy 51% of the two million shares in issue. Both Alec and Graham Jessop were ecstatic with the deal; Graham with the money, Alec with the opportunity of putting into practice his AAAS — Alec's Alternative Accounting Standards. He had started with AAAS 1:

AAAS 1	Information is power.

On his first visit to the shabby premises, Alec was greeted by the family retainers, some 20 employees with over 200 years of combined service to the company. They were somewhat taken aback by the pale-faced 21 year old at the door, but thought that anything must be better than Graham Jessop. They were wrong. Alec sacked them all on his first morning. There was no union, no golden handshakes, just 20 stunned mullet's leaving the building at 11.30 am.

At 11.45 am Alec made a magnanimous gesture by donating the whole of his inventory to the Salvation Army. They were pleased. Such generosity might contribute to his knighthood a bit later on. The stock was shipped out in the afternoon, just in time for the emergency board meeting called for 5pm. The turnout was 100 per cent, the level of optimism zero per cent, given the events earlier in the day. Alec began by quietly stating the next of his alternative accounting standards:

AAAS 2	Manufacturing is for fools. Business is about buying and selling — but *never making things.*

The board resigned en masse and Alec picked up their shares at a generous one pence per share. At a price of £30 000 he now controlled the whole of a publicly quoted company and set out to make the most of its three valuable assets:

- a stock exchange quotation,
- an undervalued lease,
- and a deviously entrepreneurial chief executive.

In so doing, he adopted AAAS 3:

AAAS 3	Assets are for stripping money *out* of — never investing money *into*.

He sold the unexpired 53 year term of the South London lease to a friendly property developer for £400 000. A new era had begun.

At a stroke the asset backing of the company had risen from 2.5 pence (£50 001/2m) to 20 pence (£400 000/2m), an eight-fold increase which had an immediate and corresponding effect on the stock market. Alec was pleased he had chosen the Efficient Markets elective at university ahead of Accounting Ethics. Anonymous phone calls to the city desks of the financial papers ensured that the required rumours would result in speculation and a demand for his shares.

He disposed of just enough shares to repay his personal debts. He had higher sights for the remainder. He had shares and assets per share but no earnings. Analysts focused on earnings per share in a myopic fashion, so it was essential that he service their requirements with a suitably glowing (and growing) EPS of his own.

The 20 pence a share asset backing provided him with hard currency with which to fund expansion and diversification. He quietly tendered his resignation from his employers — he had no time for salary earning any more — and returned to his list of Top Ten Target companies. He selected No 3, Stringvests Incorporated (Mostly Moccasins had been No 2 and No 1 was out of his league at the moment). With the help of his old merchant bank colleagues he arranged a share-exchange purchase of enough of Stringvests to gain control. He promptly changed the name of Mostly Moccasins to Smart Leisure International (SLI) Holdings to reflect the newly diversified portfolio.

The Stringvests operation was going nowhere. It had been unable to respond to changes in fashion, was uncompetitive on price and unwilling to compromise on quality. Alec closed down the operation, sacked the staff and sold off the acquired property. He then turned to Stringvests' only worthwhile asset — its pension fund and accumulated surpluses. He wound up the old scheme and implemented a new one which absorbed only £1m of the £4m 'vested' in the scheme. The remainder provided the earnings he so desperately needed in the EPS quote for the group, together with a corresponding increase in the share price.

Alec then turned his attention to Trimble's Trilbies, Fashion Flairs Ltd and Movielux Home Entertainment, the only three remaining companies on his list which still remained free from the attentions of predators; Alec was not alone. He set about turning the companies around, not redirecting them in the normal sense of the phrase, but rather turning them inside out to milk them all for short-term earnings. Any division that was not generating earnings was immediately eliminated and its assets liquidated. Those making money adopted AAAS 4 in order to increase their short-term earnings.

AAAS 4	Companies should be lean, fit and mean, and poised to take advantage of any opportunity.

He made the companies leaner by cutting staff and moving into smaller, cheaper accommodation. He repeated his redevelopment property strategy wherever possible. He eliminated new product development and all investment in new capital projects. He cut, or eliminated, depreciation provisions, abolished advertising and promotion expenditures, deferred maintenance and repairs. He arranged sale and leasebacks on those properties still essential to operations and cut expenses by capitalising everything in sight. The effects on the bottom line were staggering — the earnings growth of which city analysts dream. The share price of SLI Holdings escalated to £5.30. It was certainly lean, fit and mean but the 'poise' had somehow been overlooked.

It had not escaped Alec's attention that he had no new products in the pipeline and the state of his premises was such that his earnings growth would be very short-term indeed. Fortunately AAAS 5 and AAAS 6 then came into play:

AAAS 5	Make your affairs so complicated that outsiders get tired of noseying around.

AAAS 6	Everything in life is relative, and there is always somebody worse off than you.

He surrounded himself with an empire of trusts, subsidiaries, holding companies, interlocking directorships and cross-shareholdings so it was unclear even to him to where and from where money was being channelled. Having blunted the analytical power of the snoopers he now took advantage of his inflated share price to make some ambitious acquisitions. This time it was firms with futures, and he might have paid over the odds — but so what, he was paying with his own shares anyway, not real money! He was the living proof of AAAS 7:

AAAS 7	Neglect short-term goals at your peril. Long-term strategies make you a short-term takeover victim.

Where necessary he borrowed to support his acquisitions, stripping assets and disposing of the peripheral companies in the targets in order to repay the debts.

Repeated acquisition made the share price for SLI Holdings even higher, making further acquisitions relatively even cheaper.

He created a merchant banking arm, SliBank, lending big at high rates of interest to the growing army of property developers. The security was provided by fast-growing bricks and mortar — he had no time for the manufacturing industry and their potentially obsolescent computer-aided equipment. The growth escalated, with the manufacturing sector increasingly squeezed out because property-based lending was safer and more profitable.

Alec anticipated the property market crash well in advance and was able to execute a timely departure at little cost to himself. The same could not be said of the property developers, most of whom went to the wall in a manner entirely consistent with AAAS 8.

AAAS 8	The active support of one's bankers may just as swiftly be followed by a knife between the shoulder blades.

Despite the sorry Smart-induced state of the manufacturing base he left behind, at least Alec escaped with his reputation intact; a reputation as a skilled and shrewd operator with a sharp, analytical, accountant's brain.

Alec only ever considered the short-term and he thought he needed a holiday anyway — just in case the attitude or political complexion of the government were to change overnight. He thought Hong Kong sounded good, and it was 1997, the year of unification with China. He needed time to check out the Asian markets and exchanges.

There would likely be plenty of undervalued takeover targets there too, but if conditions were not right he was prepared to wait until they were before mounting a comeback. He was confident that he would not have to wait too long!

You are required to examine the ethical aspects of Alec Smart's accounting choices and the relevance of his Alternative Accounting Standards to the realities of business practice.

Your report should consider the internal and external controls within the financial and management accounting systems which might have eliminated the worst of his excesses.

Chapter 3

Management Accounting Information Systems (MAIS)

3.1 INTRODUCTION

Executive decisions rely on information from many sources, not all of which is accounting information. The various sources might be described simply as:

- accounting/non-accounting

- financial/non-financial

- quantitative/qualitative

- internal/external

Non-accounting data might include personnel and marketing records, both essential elements in the management accountant's database for planning and control purposes. Much of this data may be external in form, concerning market share, competitiveness, industry comparisons and the impact of economic changes on the operations of the business.

Non-financial data focuses on numbers of occurrences (e.g. set-ups, complaints, errors, reworks), volumes (e.g. chemical reactions in the production process) — in fact any information to which pound units are not attached. These measures provide the basis for performance indicators (NFIs) based wholly on non-financial factors.

Qualitative sources would include informal information gathering based on rumour, gossip, normal social intercourse, or what Horngren refers to as MBWA (management by walking about!).

Non-financials are becoming increasingly important in management accounting but the major source of information is still currently the internal-quantitative-financial-accounting combination. Systems to provide this information encompass the planning and control of activities and the costing of products. Such systems would gather information from the control and monitoring mechanisms in place: inventory control, working capital management, budgeting and variance analysis.

The systems in place must be seen as *relevant*, having been based around the operation of the different processes of the organisation and providing information appropriate for support and reporting. They should not have the potential to mislead by distorting the true picture (see Cooper and Kaplan, 1987). Lack of relevance — which would normally include lack of timeliness — is perhaps the greatest potential deficiency of any management accounting information system. The nature of the systems will differ between organisations, generally being simpler when there is process manufacturing and when there are only minor fluctuations in work in progress inventories.

Smith (1990) provides examples of both kinds of NFI deficiency:

- measures of 'backlog' by time or number of jobs outstanding were manipulated by the maintenance crews being monitored, partly because it was possible — by rescheduling existing jobs or closing down jobs early so that they could reappear as new ones — and partly because the outcomes did not conform with their self-interest, since no backlog meant no overtime working.

- accounting information provided by the centralised management accounting team was seen as irrelevant at plant level, often being regarded as untimely and inaccurate. Consequently plants established their own informal systems of data gathering and internal reporting to cope with their unsatisfied decision making requirements.

For any organisation the choice of an optimum set of NFIs is inextricably linked to its goals. A given set of NFIs must provide measures consistent with the achievement of corporate goals. Where the goals change, the optimum set of NFIs will change too, and a system should be in place which is sufficiently robust to reflect these changes over time. Figure 3 illustrates just such a system.

The various processes of the operation are designated A1, A2 ... A7. An initial evaluation allows their classification into value-adding (A1,A3,A4,A5,A7) and non-value adding (A2 and A6) activities, immediately highlighting the importance of eliminating, or at least restricting, the latter where they do not constitute essential control procedures.

For each activity there is an associated group of cost drivers — a sequence of events or actions which cause costs to be incurred within that activity. For simplicity these are numbered C1, C2 ... C21, and arbitrarily allocated on a proportional basis to activities. In practice the number of cost drivers and their allocation will be dependent on the complexity of the activities.

For each cost driver we will have alternative measures of performance, usually non-financial indicators, designated F1, F2 ... There will, therefore, be a multiplicity of A-C-F combinations representing particular measures of particular cost drivers for particular activities; in practice too many to measure and monitor on a regular basis. We need to identify a subset of indicators (A-C-F combinations) and associated targets, the achievement of which is most closely congruent with corporate goals: as few as five or six such combinations may be enough. These must be monitored to measure trends in performance, and the constituent combinations changed when corporate goals change.

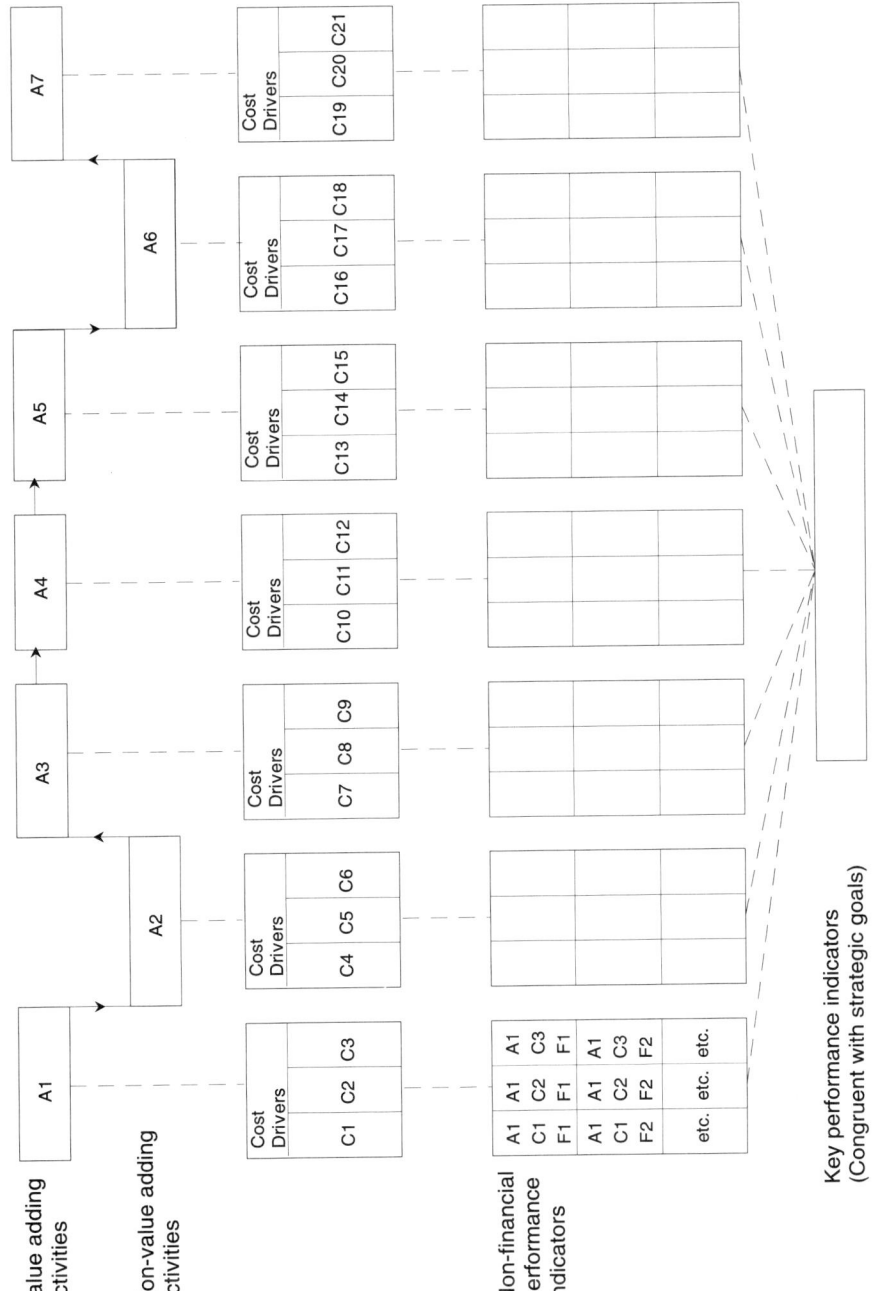

Figure 3: Measuring Process Performance

The original purpose of management accounting was to provide a decision making tool to management, with whatever data was considered relevant. But the requirements of financial accounting and external reporting have effected a retrograde change of emphasis. The direct link that exists between management accounting practices and strategic corporate goals within Japanese companies, as espoused by Hiromoto (1988), means that financial accounting constraints of inventory valuation and reporting for taxation purposes, though still in place, are not allowed to overwhelm the efficient measurement of organisational performance.

In manufacturing operations process parameters provide, usually through on-line monitoring systems, the means of exercising minute-to-minute control, performance measurement, forecasting and budget setting. The absence of comparable systems to monitor cost information is a serious deficiency, motivating the generation of alternative work effectiveness performance measures to gauge the likely impact of variations in procedure and practice.

Where management accounting systems focus entirely on the measurement of costs, then employees will likely adopt a similar focus. With a more extensive use of NFIs, especially those linked to the reward structure, then a tighter focus on strategic direction can be achieved.

3.2 INTERNAL CONTROL

Casual observation of management accounting control systems (MACS) within large, complex organisations suggests that they are all the same - a combination of short and long-term planning, budgets, variance analysis and project reporting. Closer examination reveals that the manner in which the MACS is applied varies greatly and reflects the preferences of senior management. Where, for example, management signal their perception of the importance of NFIs in interactive control systems, we might anticipate that in consequence subordinates will focus on the monitoring of these activities and the development of new measures.

The goals of MACS address four key strategic areas:

- planning — the setting of goals and an overall vision;

- control — the monitoring of external events and the measurement of internal activities to ensure a direction congruent with these goals;

- motivation — concerned with getting the best out of employees and linked to participation, empowerment and reward systems;

- performance — evaluation of individual and group performance for consistency with objectives and ethical considerations.

Following Anthony (1965) the planning and control areas have provided the traditional link between MACS and strategy. The SPAMSOAP mnemonic, so familiar to students of examinations in the management control area, designates the eight elements of the traditional system of internal control:

- Segregation of duties

- Physical safeguards

- Authorisation and approval

- Management review

- Supervision and audit

- Organisational structures

- Accounting and information systems

- Personnel arrangements

Planning and control activities rely heavily on financial and non-financial performance measures, and Chapter 8 focuses on the development of a number of planning techniques. But the internal control process goes far beyond policy manuals and audit, because it is determined by people at every level of the organisation. It is geared to the achievement of corporate goals, not just financial reporting, making it a strategic process.

Information systems and control procedures (embracing authorisation, verification, reconciliation, review and reports against budget) are necessary but insufficient features of a successful control environment. ICAEW (1993) identify additional features which contribute to our 'motivation' and 'performance' goals:

- commitment to truth and fair dealing

- commitment to quality and competence

- leadership in control by example

- communication of ethical values

Corporate integrity, culture and code of ethics are thus central to successful internal control and lead us to consider alternative managerial approaches to motivation as a means of overcoming non-goal-congruent behaviour and the exploitation of MACS gaps. The seminal work in this area is F.W. Taylor's (1911) treatise on *scientific management* in which he assumes that unskilled workers can be motivated to work only by money and close supervision. The resulting control system is one based on standard costing, budgeting and variance analysis. The natural consequences of the tight identification and planning of resource inputs, costs and variances are:

- work study, to analyse jobs and processes and find the 'best' way that unskilled labour can perform the task;

- scientific selection of personnel for the task at hand;

- minute division of labour to short specialised tasks;

- incentive schemes and targets;

- deskilling and potentially dehumanising the workforce;

- ensuring that management, and not craftsmen, control production and the speed of the production line.

Taylor's principles were widely adopted in the 1920s, most notably by Henry Ford in the mass production auto industry. Subsequent theorists have suggested alternative roles for management and supervisors in the organisation. The *human relations movement* of the late 1930s recognised that financial reward was only one aspect of what working people wanted from their employment. The importance of mutual respect, discretion and recognition of contribution to the organisation became more apparent. The implications for MACS were a focus on interpersonal relations and the monitoring and measurement of morale and job satisfaction. Since the 1950s the *human resources model* has extended the focus on individual needs to embrace working conditions and the nature of supervision. The implications of MACS have been greater employee participation in decision making, total employee involvement (TEI, see Section 5.5) and employee empowerment (see Section 7.1). Recognition that subordinates often 'know the job' better than their managers, and associated research, suggest that participation in decision making and employee empowerment will lead to greater motivation, greater job satisfaction, improved morale and greater commitment to the organisation. The human resources model blends the 'motivation' and 'performance' goals of MACS by suggesting that goal congruence will be achieved by:

- strong organisational leadership,

- satisfying work and appropriate rewards,

- opportunities for advancement, and a

- supportive work environment.

The simplistic Taylorist assumption that financial reward is the only motivator to improved performance causes distinct problems for reward systems under *scientific management:*

- a short-term focus;

- high costs associated with servicing the system (particularly with share option schemes);

- manipulation opportunities (particularly with bonus plan schemes, as in Case 2: *Kambalda Manufacturing*);

- doubts about whether the actual rewards target the most appropriate employees and whether they increase shareholder value.

The human relations movement and human resources model promote team working and reward systems associated with the contributions of individuals to the team effort. Rewards may take the form of non-cash payments (e.g. gifts, or points schemes leading to gifts). Total Quality Management (TQM, discussed in detail in Chapter 7) is one philosophy which aims to encourage teamwork and rewards participants for their co-operation in instituting organisational improvements.

Cullen *et al.* (1994) suggest that internal control failures will result from one of five eventualities:

- *Lack of integrity of top management.* This may be apparent from dishonesty, fraudulent or unethical behaviour. The resulting ethical dilemmas (see Chapter 2) will emerge in the form of conflicts between individuals and organisational values, and between an organisation's stated and practised values.

- *A weak control environment.* This may be associated with corporate culture (e.g. a culture of excessive and unrealistic risk taking). Shields and Young (1989) suggest that it will be very difficult to change organisational culture, especially in those organisations with weak leadership and no clear direction, or where internal conflict is high because of autocratic rule. They suggest that change will be resisted because of fear of the new, the cost of change in terms of both time and money, and the resulting changes in the balance of power in the organisation.

- *Inconsistent or unrealistic objectives.* For example, Smith (1995, p.4) highlights the inconsistency of pursuing a corporate goal of industry leadership through technological innovation while still allocating overheads to product costs in a manner which penalises the use of high-tech machinery.

- *Communication breakdown resulting in the pursuit of conflicting objectives.* For example, innovation in entrepreneurial firms may be constrained by the implementation of unsuitable control systems focusing on costs to the detriment of the innovation goal.

- *Inability or inflexibility to react appropriately.* This may mean that corporate inertia prevents the organisation from taking advantage of technological opportunities or responding to threats from the external economy (see Chapter 4). For example, Williams and Ashford (1994) highlight four of the changes in control systems and product costing systems that may be necessitated by new manufacturing technologies:

  (1) competitive pressures necessitating shorter product life cycles and the faster introduction of new products and services (see Chapter 5). MACS must respond with flexible management structures, project teams and new performance measures (NFIS, see Section 3.4);

  (2) emphasis on activity analysis and the supply chain. MACS must respond with much closer attention to long-term supplier alliances and investigate activity based management systems (ABM, see Section 5.5) and customer profitability analysis (CPA, see Section 5.6);

  (3) adoption of Total Quality Management (TQM, see Chapter 7). MACS must respond with an increased emphasis on NFIs, to observe internal and external failure costs, to monitor prevention costs and to measure the costs of quality;

  (4) adoption of Just in Time management (JIT, see Section 5.5). MACS must respond by making wholesale modifications to traditional systems based on labour productivities machine efficiencies, rejection and wastage rates, and inventory holdings. These will no longer be appropriate and new NFIs must place the emphasis on service to customers and speed of delivery.

Roslender (1992), Puxty (1993) and Atkinson *et al.* (1995) all provide excellent summaries of the accounting literature relating to management control, but no generally accepted view of the adequacy of existing theories in explaining organisational behaviour emerges. Researchers (e.g. Porter, 1980) agree that an 'overall cost leadership' strategy requires sophisticated cost controls, but Simons (1990), among others, suggests that otherwise such studies have been of little help in the design of MACS.

Porter's cost leadership strategy in pursuit of sustainable competitive advantage provides a grounding for much of the subsequent research in the areas of value-chain analysis and strategic management accounting. It has popularised strategic cost analysis, with its identification of a value-chain between raw materials and end-user, and the specification of cost drivers and cost reduction opportunities for each activity of the chain to effect appropriate internal management. The value-chain perspective is explored in detail by Shank and Govindarajan (1992).

Companies with different management control systems compete in different ways. Goold and Campbell (1987) identify three different strategic control styles where the degree of control from the centre is dependent on the balance between the competitive (growth) and financial (risk aversion) goals of the enterprise. Leadership, and the manner in which controls are implemented, emerges as a key distinguishing feature between companies. Future research must focus on the relationship between MACS and corporate strategy. The BCG portfolio matrix approach, discussed in Section 4.5, provides one possible explanation, but other, less simplistic approaches must be developed and tested empirically.

3.3 PERFORMANCE EVALUATION

Traditionally accounting procedures measure organisational performance on the basis of the 3 Es of evaluation:

- **Efficiency** — utilisation of equipment, and efficiency of the workforce;

- **Economy** — optimum use of materials;

- **Effectiveness** — achievement of target outcomes.

This classification is particularly helpful in the generation of non-financial indicators:

- **Efficiency (Work Performance Measures)**

    Process — efficiency, productivity, overtime, waste
    Constraints — safety, environmental impact
    Temporal — milestone dates, elapsed time.

- **Economy (Resource Measures)**

    Input levels — budget versus actual.

- **Effectiveness (Product Measures)**

    Quantity — units, percentage completion
    Quality — reliability, availability, obsolescence, safety
    Temporal — delivery.

Such measures are more concerned with the productivity of the business than with throughput. Consequently they ignore measures of the flow of materials, such as those suggested by Goldratt and Cox (1986) and Waldron and Galloway (1988). It is important to avoid a myopic focus on equipment and labour productivity to the exclusion of all else. Where productivity levels are pursued as goals in their own right, rather than being seen as tools in the achievement of higher goals, throughput can be reduced and production costs increased. Where the emphasis is on keeping both employees and machines busy at all times then work in progress will increase beyond economic levels, especially where insufficient attention is devoted to the random fluctuations and process dependencies inevitable within a manufacturing system.

In a typical manufacturing environment only five per cent of the product leadtime is concerned with adding value to the product; the great majority of the time is spent in queuing and waiting (e.g. handling, moving, picking, inspecting, counting and monitoring). McIlhattan (1987) observes that the amount of process time is less than ten per cent of the total manufacturing leadtime for many organisations. Over 90 per cent of the leadtime associated with a product adds cost but adds no value to the product.

It might be argued that some traditional accounting measures are counter-productive, in that they actually encourage the generation of waste:

- **Standard Costs** institutionalise waste and idle time within expectations.

- **Absorption Costing** encourages excess inventory by allowing production-for-stock to contribute to income.

- **Labour Efficiency Variances** encourage more output, and potentially overproduction, in the cause of productivity of the workforce.

- **Price Variances** encourage bulk-buying and unnecessarily increase inventory.

- **Machine Utilisation Rates** encourage the pursuit of equipment productivity, with consequential overproduction and over stocking.

- **Scrap Cost Rates** encourage costly reworks in order to avoid measured scrap outcomes.

Further, the continuing commitment to the traditional reporting of monthly variances to budget, even where the latter represent insignificant random fluctuations, is arguably more to meet the financial requirements of head office than the decision making requirements of management. Such an emphasis may bring about unfortunate results in that a focus on unfavourable variances may mean that wrongly trended, but favourable, variances are ignored, and that inappropriate budgets and standards result in variances being wrongly perceived as 'insignificant' or 'in control', with no action resulting.

3.4 NON-FINANCIAL INDICATORS

The declining relevance of traditional management accounting systems is attributed by Johnson and Kaplan (1987) to three failure types:

Strategic Management Accounting

1. *Use-type*, concerned with a failure to adopt flexible budgets, to evaluate discretionary expenditures or to adopt appropriate measures to control fixed costs.

2. *Relevance-type*, concerned with a failure to develop quality control and factor productivity measures or to highlight opportunity costs.

3. *Control-type*, concerned with a failure to consider non-financial factors, through undue emphasis devoted to short-term financial performance indicators and financial accounting considerations in most calculations.

Each of the three types embraces the use of non-financial indicators (NFIs) as measures which improve the decision usefulness of management accounting information and facilitate evaluation and control.

Figure 4 describes a matrix, detailing 60 NFIs drawn from the relevant literature and from observation of accounting practice in manufacturing industry. The spread of performance measures is wide-ranging, encompassing production, marketing and customer-orientation aspects.

	Focus of Measurement		Non-Financial Indicators (NFI)
Input	Quality of purchased components	1	Zero Defects
	Quantity of raw material inputs	2	Actual v target units
Work	Equipment productivity	3	Actual v standard units
	Equipment failure	4	Downtime/total time
		5	Time between failures
	Maintenance effort	6	Time between overhauls
		7	Time spent on repeat work
		8	Mean time to effect repairs
		9	Total time in backlog jobs
		10	Number of production units lost through maintenance
		11	Number of repeat jobs
		12	Number of backlog jobs
		13	Number of failures in planned jobs prior to schedule
		14	% failures: planned/unplanned jobs
		15	Preventive maintenance/total maintenance
		16	Corrective maintenance/total maintenance
		17	Breakdown maintenance/total maintenance
	Overtime	18	Overtime hours/total hours
	Waste	19	% deficit items
		20	% scrap
		21	% rework
	Throughput	22	Return per factory hour = $\frac{\text{Return}}{\text{Total Cost}} \times \frac{\text{Time available}}{\text{Time on key resource}}$
	Production flexibility	23	Set-up time
	Product complexity	24	Number of component parts
Product	Quantity of output	25	Actual units
		26	% completion: actual v target

	Focus of Measurement		Non-Financial Indicators (NFI)
	Quality of output	27	% yield
		28	Index of key product characteristics
	Safety	29	Serious industrial injury rate (SIIR)
	Reliability	30	Warranty claims/costs
	Availability	31	% stockouts
	Obsolescence	32	% shrinkage
	Commitment to quality	33	% dependence on post-inspection
		34	% conformance to quality standards
Market	Market share	35	Local/domestic/world volume
	Market leadership	36	% R & D expenditure
		37	% new production innovation
	Growth	38	% increase in market share
		39	New clients/total clients
	Strengths	40	Index of competitive value
	Competition	41	Index of vulnerability
Employees	Employee skills	42	Index of educational attainment
		43	% training costs
		44	% staff turnover lost to competitors
		45	Age/experience profiles
	Employee morale	46	% absenteeism
		47	Cost of employee downtime
		48	Leadership impact (e.g. % cancelled meetings)
		49	New staff/total staff
		50	New support staff/total staff
	Employee productivity	51	Direct labour hours per unit
		52	Managed labour hours per unit
		53	Labour effectiveness $= \dfrac{\text{Standard hours achieved}}{\text{Direct + Indirect labour hours worked}}$
		54	Output efficiency $= \dfrac{\text{Output}}{\text{Payroll Cost}}$
Customers	Customer awareness	55	% approval rating
		56	% service calls/claims
		57	Number of complaints
		58	% repeat orders
	Timeliness	59	Number of overdue deliveries
		60	Mean delivery delay

Figure 4: Matrix of Non-Financial Performance Indicators

Management will usually be highly resistant to changes in the accounting system, so that suggested improvements must have a demonstrably positive impact on outcomes. Thus while JIT (just-in-time procedures) have been quickly incorporated worldwide, there has been a much greater resistance to ABC (activity based costing) where the benefits are much less clear and convincing, and the costs of implementation much higher.

In small businesses, or those which have grown from humble beginnings, even the most basic of accounting information systems may be absent. Management decision making is then based on experience or 'hunches' and may function in the short-term, especially through inflationary periods and 'boom' economic conditions. However, downturn and recession require much closer attention to costs and if prosperity is to persist in the long-term, then basic management accounting systems must be in place to provide the information base for sound business decisions.

Cases 4 and 5 provide examples of businesses which have grown so rapidly from one-person concerns that the decision making requirements have outstripped the information provided by the management accounting information systems. Both cases are characterised by the reluctant delegation of power by the owner manager but whereas *Case 4: Inner City Cycles* has an entrenched chief executive determined to oppose any changes which might restrict his all-embracing control of the enterprise, *Case 5: Pinewall Furnishing* provides a scenario where all are aware of the need to implement new systems.

REFERENCES

Anthony R N, *Planning and Control Systems: A Framework for Analysis*, Harvard University, 1965

Atkinson A A, Banker R D, Kaplan RS and Young SM, *Management Accounting*, Prentice Hall, New Jersey, 1995

Cooper R and Kaplan R S, 'How Cost Accounting Distorts Product Costs', *Management Accounting* (US), April 1987, pp 20–27

Cooper R and Kaplan R S, *The Design of Cost Management Systems*, Prentice-Hall, Englewood Cliffs, New Jersey, 1991

Cullen J, Broadbent, J M and Gray I H, *Management Accounting Control Systems: Practical Elements*, Chartered Institute of Management Accountants, London, 1994

Goldratt E M and Cox J, *The Goal*, North River Press, New York, 1986

Goold M and Campbell, A, *Strategies and Styles: The Role of the Centre in Managing Diversified Corporations*, Blackwell, Oxford, 1987

Hiromoto T, 'Another Hidden Edge—Japanese Management Accounting', *Harvard Business Review* 66 (4) July/August 1988, pp 34–35

Horngren C T and Foster G, *Cost Accounting: A Managerial Emphasis*, 7th ed, Prentice-Hall, Englewood Cliffs, New Jersey, 1991

Management Accounting Information Systems (MAIS)

ICAEW, *Internal Control and Financial Reporting: Draft Guidelines for Directors of Listed Companies*, Institute of Chartered Accountants in England and Wales, London, October, 1993

Johnson H T and Kaplan R S, 'The Rise and Fall of Management Accounting' *Management Accounting* (US), January 1987, pp 22–30

Kaplan R S and Norton D P, 'The Balanced Scorecard—Measures that Drive Performance', *Harvard Business Review*, Jan/Feb 1992, pp 71–79

McIlhattan R D, 'How Cost Management Systems can Support the JIT Philosophy', *Management Accounting* (US), September 1987, pp 20–26

Porter M E, *Competitive Strategy: Techniques for Analysing Industries and Competitors*, Collier MacMillan, New York, 1980

Puxty A G, *The Social and Organisational Context of Management Accounting*, Chartered Institute of Management Accountants, London, 1993

Roslender R, *Sociological Perspectives on Modern Accountancy*, Routledge, London, 1992

Shank J K and Govindarajan V, 'Strategic Cost Management: The Value Chain Perspective', *Journal of Management Accounting Research*, 1992

Shields M D and Young S M, 'A Behavioral Model for Implementing Cost Management Systems', *Journal of Cost Management*, 1989

Simons R, 'The Role of Management Control Systems in Creating Competitive Advantage: New Perspectives', *Accounting, Organizations and Society*, 1990

Smith M, 'The Rise and Rise of the NFI', *Management Accounting* (UK), May 1990, pp 24–26

Smith M, 'Management Accounting for Total Quality Management', *Management Accounting* (UK), June 1990, pp 44–46

Smith M, 'New Tools for Management Accountants: Putting Activity Based Costing and Non-financial Indicators to Work', *Financial Times*, 1995

Spicer B H, 'The Resurgence of Cost and Management Accounting: A Review of Some Recent Developments in Practice, Theories and Case Research Methods', *Management Accounting Research*, Vol 3, 1992, pp 1–37

Taylor F W, *The Principles of Scientific Management*, Harper & Row, London, 1947 (first published 1911)

Waldron D and Galloway D, 'Throughput Accounting: Ranking Products Profitably', *Management Accounting* (UK), December 1988, pp 34–35

Williams J and Ashford J K, *Management Accounting Control Systems: Knowledge*, Chartered Institute of Management Accountants, London, 1994

CASE 4: INNER CITY CYCLES

This case details an all-too-familiar small business environment — the growth of a business to a point where the entrepreneur must let go some of the reins and delegate real decision making to avoid constraints on growth and potential long-term survival. With growth beyond a level suitable for one-person control come the requirements of formal planning and systematic management procedures.

Norm Bartlett started buying and selling second-hand bicycles at open-air markets when still in his early teens. He eventually graduated to rented suburban premises dealing exclusively in second-hand sales and bicycle hire before moving in 1988 to his present location close to Covent Garden, London. Lack of access to second-hand cycles initiated his development of trade in new cycles and the decline of bike hire activities, with new cycles and spares now accounting for 95 per cent of sales. Norm has always been the driving force behind the business but a rapid growth in turnover has reduced his leisurely contact with customers and caused his interest to wane. Based on an initial investment of £1500 the business has grown profitably without the need for additional borrowings or overdraft facilities.

ICC have none of the sports-shop salesmanship or department-store uniformity, but provide bespoke cycles assembled to appropriate size and gearing. All sales are strictly cash or cheque, an experiment with credit cards having been abandoned in order to maintain a ten per cent across-the-board customer discount on normal retail prices. Sales are made almost exclusively from existing stocks, with about 200 new machines stored on the premises in knock-down form ready for in-shop assembly. Additional supplies from a range of eight models each in three sizes are available at short notice, with the single supplier offering discount terms for 14 day settlement. Norm regards these terms as advantageous and follows them religiously.

A markup of 25 per cent on the cost of new cycles and 75 per cent on spares is employed, giving annual turnover in excess of £500 000 and cost of sales of only half this figure. The seasonal nature of the business makes ICC vulnerable to summer stock-outs, which Norm counters with a heavy build-up of inventory during spring. Because no detailed inventory records exist, ordering is haphazard and stock-outs of spares not uncommon. New cycle sales have recently slipped back to 25 per week on average, following a spate of inner-city accidents and calls for the introduction of mandatory cycle helmets, after peaking at 40 per week in the summer of 1991. This represents a 37.5 per cent sales decrease.

In Norm's case the search for involvement and self-fulfilment is much more important than purely monetary considerations. He may have been the driving force behind Inner City Cycles at its inception but he now lacks commitment to the business and seeks an alternative direction in which to channel his entrepreneurial flair.

Management Accounting Information Systems (MAIS)

The ownership of a thriving and highly profitable business is not sufficient to motivate him — he could sell more bikes but this is not the sole objective of the enterprise. He encourages the haphazard organisation of the business and obstructs its efficient running by his mere presence. His control of the business revolves around his being there — the only man to create order from chaos in the absence of a management information system or a logical separation of duties. He needs the customer contact and extends it beyond that time normally needed to secure a sale: he needs to get to know the potential customer and to ensure that his bicycle is going to a good home. In this respect he may be likened to a collector rather than a businessman — every sale has a bit of him in it — and every contract is concluded reluctantly. He is unwilling to extend his local advertising because he does not want to attract 'the riff-raff': he is proud of his middle-class clientele and this is more important to him than the sale of more bikes as mere objects of purchase.

Norm gives the impression of a confused man, desperately trying to cling on to what he has created and what he knows, while also trying to convince himself of the need to move on in new directions. Norm's confusion is transformed to anxiety among the rest of his team. Figure C4.1 illustrates the organisation at ICC.

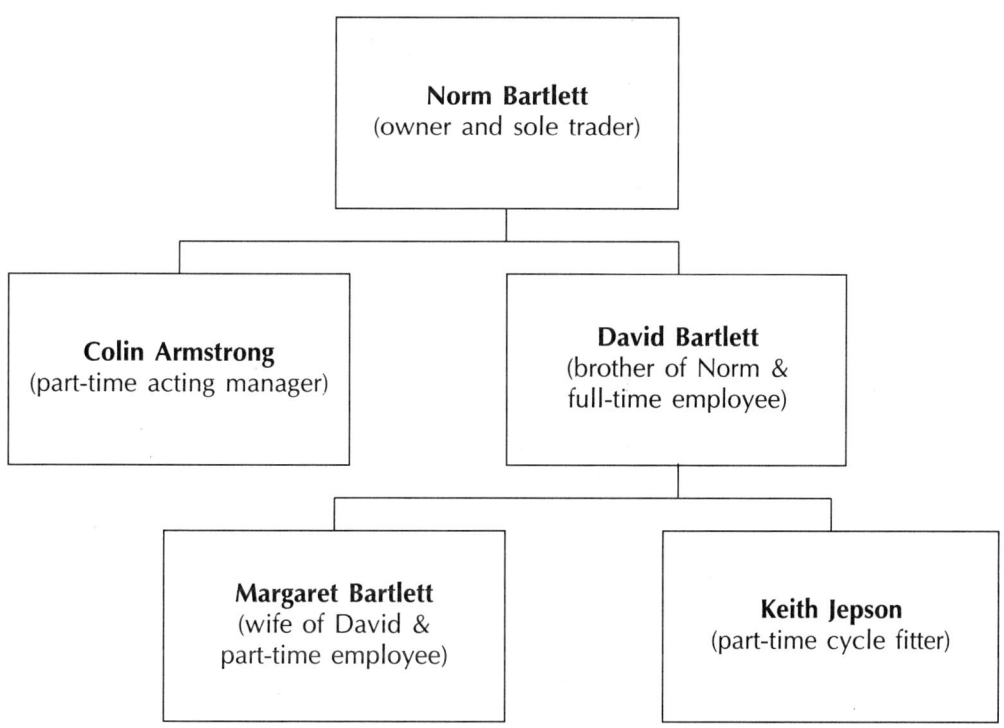

Figure C4.1: Organisational Structure Chart

David is being groomed to take over the business eventually but to do so he must be allowed to develop his management expertise, with Margaret's help if necessary, through a familiarity with financial and inventory control procedures. Mere experience of the day-to-day running of the bike business is not enough. Colin has the opportunity and authority to act as a change agent by introducing new procedures with the approval of the remaining staff. Reorganisation may necessitate some evening and weekend work and it is unlikely to sell more bikes — but it may sell more spares and a more efficient operating environment should help to relieve tensions.

While Norm's impetus is responsible for the formation of a thriving business and a successful team, he needs to move on, but is unwilling to let go. The haphazard organisation of Inner City Cycles suits his purposes admirably; staff are made to operate on the basis of limited information, chaotic job separation and without standard operating procedures. The result is that by 'being there' Norm is able to exert the control over the business that would be unnecessary with better organisation. The poor display and layout provide Norm with ample opportunity to mind everyone's business.

By logging sales and keeping precise checks on inventory levels a database would be provided to explain past movements and project future trends. Bookkeeping, accounts, financial reports and stock control procedures could provide a management information system which would make Norm's physical presence superfluous. Therefore it is not surprising that, although such a system is necessary in the long run, especially if the business is to grow, Norm will obstruct its introduction.We cannot expect Norman to take the initiative in introducing change: it must be internally generated by the rest of the team, who recognise the deficiencies of the present system.

Norm points to the current financial structure (Figure C4.2) and estimates of performance (Figure C4.3) as evidence that nothing drastic needs to be done.

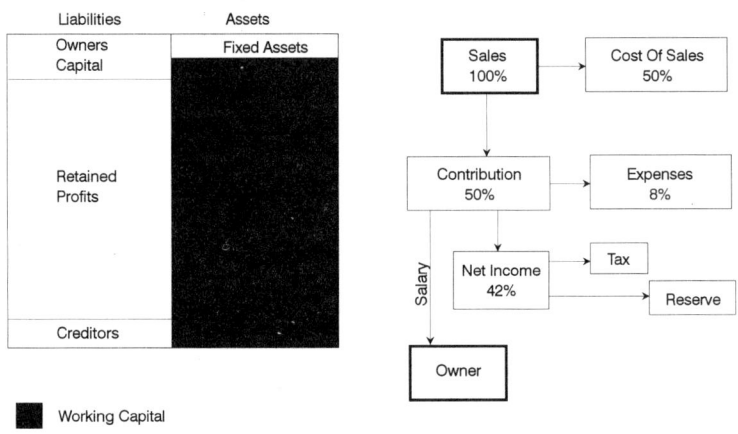

Figure C4.2: Financial Structure of ICC

Management Accounting Information Systems (MAIS)

	£	£	£	£
PROFIT & LOSS ACCOUNT				
Sales	520 000			
Cost of Sales	260 000			
CONTRIBUTION		260 000		
Rent, Rates, Utilities	122 000			
Advertisements	2000			
Accountants' Fees	1200			
Wages & Salaries	40 000			
Expenses	4800			
EXPENDITURE		170 000		
NET INCOME			90 000	
Tax			37 800	
NET PROFIT				52 200
BALANCE SHEET				
Non-Current Assets	2000			
Current Assets: Inventory	50 000			
Bank/Cash	13 600			
TOTAL ASSETS		65 600		
Current Liabilities: Creditors	4000			
Owners' Equity	1600			
Retained Earnings	60 000			
		65 600		

Figure C4.3: Estimated Current Financial Position

Space is at a premium in the shop and the clutter makes things worse. The existing entrance is too narrow and impedes access. There are no purpose-built vertical

55

racks and bikes are everywhere! The situation is made worse by ad hoc repairs taking place close to the entrance. Display and demonstration are difficult because of the absence of easy location of bikes by size and type. Selection and replacement from the basement storage area are made more difficult because it always needs tidying. Colin has suggested the use of the simple stock control procedure of Figure C4.4 in the basement, but neither Norm nor David has shown any enthusiasm. Norm is convinced that a regular stock-count is the only sure way of knowing what you have — and haven't — got.

Colin's attempt to introduce the continuous logging of sales at the till point with his simple sales form (Figure C4.5) has been rejected by everyone else. They claim they have no time to fill in forms while serving customers. Colin suggests it is the only way to keep track of what is being sold. Norm thinks he can remember each and every one of his 'children' in detail.

Colin has ambitious expansion plans for the business and has projected a doubling of sales turnover (detailed in Figure C4.6) despite the extent of the competition (detailed in Figure C4.7). Frustration of this plan may cause him to depart to add to the competition. It is uncertain whether ICC can survive without both Colin and Norm.

Norm frequently absents himself from the business for weeks at a time, searching for pastures new and fresh opportunities. When he returns he disturbs what he has left behind, unsettling staff and lowering morale. Colin has shown that he can exercise leadership in Norm's absence and he has more flair than David, the heir apparent. Norm has built an uneasy alliance of family and friendship into a business enterprise. The existing bonds are not appropriate and some of the relationships are unclear. Expansion means that Norm must do something about it.

You are required to make recommendations to improve existing operations and reduce the future vulnerability of ICC. Your findings should encompass the implementation of management accounting controls and the examination of alternative expansion scenarios.

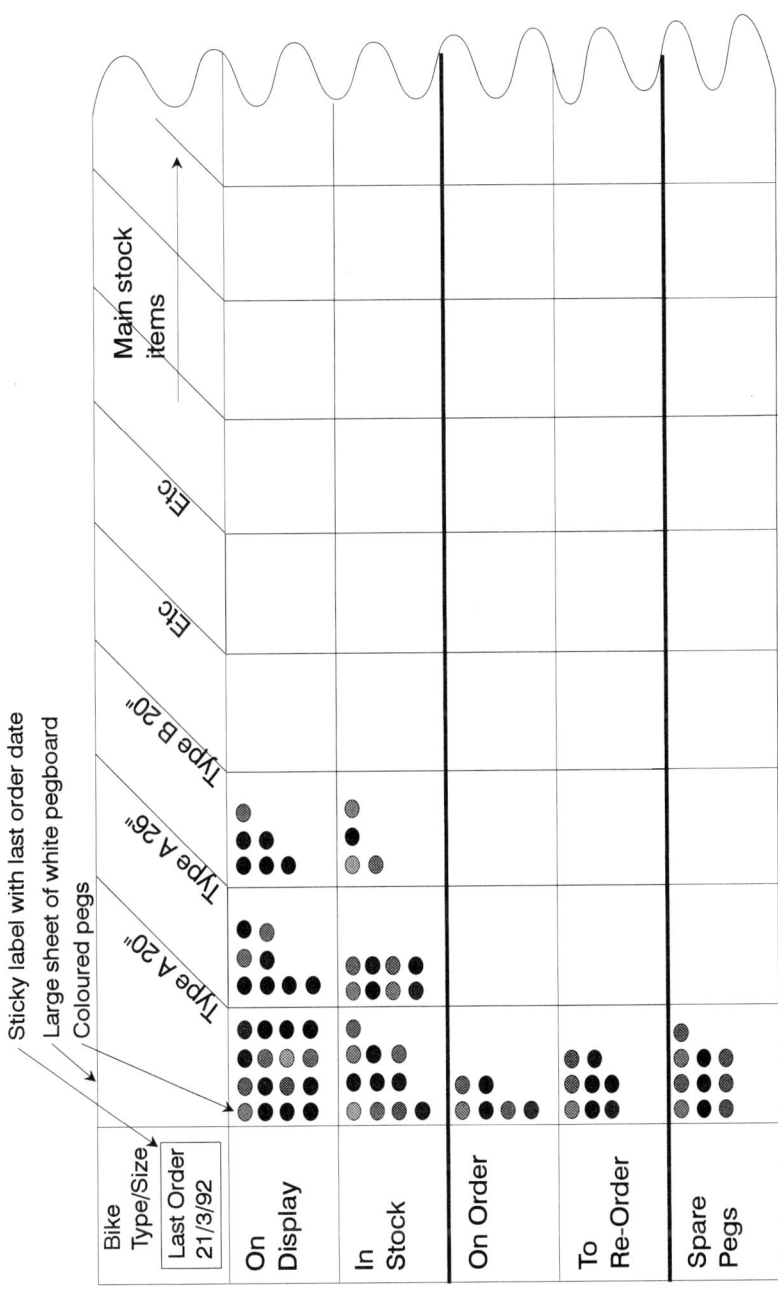

Figure C4.4: Bikes On Order and In Hand

Notes: 1) Colour of pegs = Colour of Bike
2) Bikes Received   : Pegs moved from 'On Order' to 'In Stock'
3) Bikes Made-up   : Coloured peg moved from 'In Stock' to 'On Display'
4) Bike Sold   : Coloured peg from 'On Display' to 'To Reorder'
5) Bikes Reordered : Pegs moved from 'To Reorder' to 'On Order'

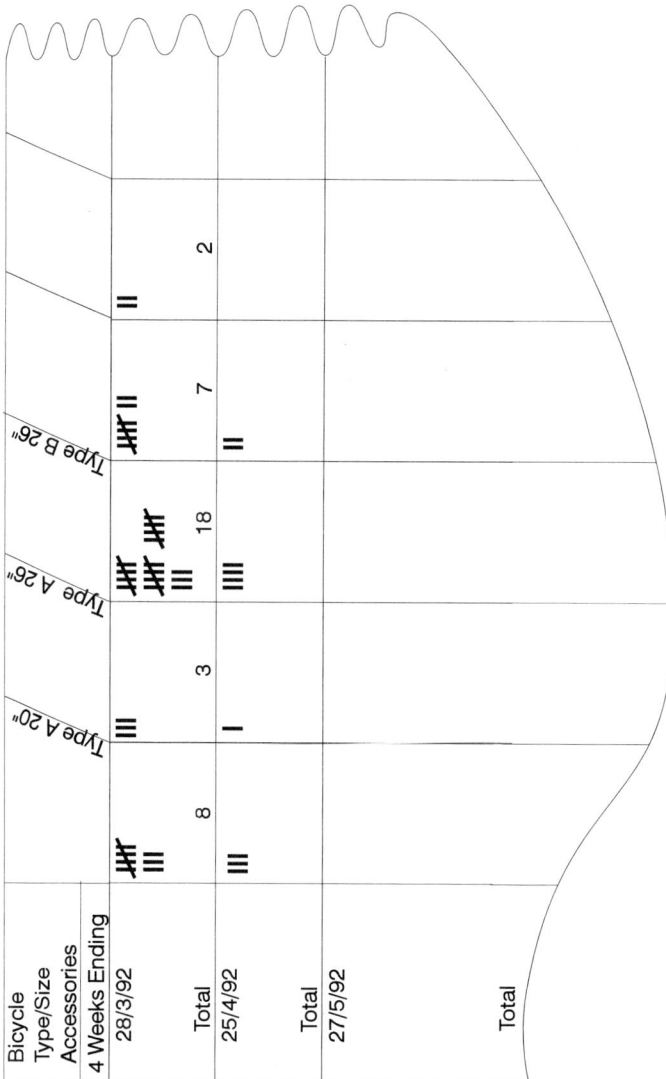

Figure C4.5: Till Point Sales Record

	£	£	£	£
PROFIT & LOSS ACCOUNT				
Sales	1 040 000			
Cost of Sales	<u>520 000</u>			
CONTRIBUTION		520 000		
Rent, Rates, Utilities	148 000			
Advertisements	2400			
Accountants' Fees	2400			
Wages and Salaries	60 000			
Expenses	<u>11 200</u>			
EXPENDITURE		<u>224 000</u>		
NET INCOME			296 000	
Tax			<u>124 320</u>	
NET PROFIT				171 680
APPROPRIATION:				
Reserves			80 880	
Owners' Drawings			<u>90 800</u>	<u>171 680</u>
BALANCE SHEET				
Non-Current Assets	12 000			
Current Assets: Stocks	150 000			
Bank/Cash	<u>8000</u>			
TOTAL ASSETS		170 000		
Current Liabilities: Creditors	12 000			
Owners' Equity	1600			
Retained Earnings	<u>156 400</u>			
		<u>170 000</u>		

Figure C4.6: Projected Financial Position on Expansion

IMMEDIATE COMPETITION (within 1 km)	
Ardross Cycles	Shogun/Orion/Mountain Bikes/Family/ Lightweight/Spares/Helmets
Attadale Cycles	Mountain & Racing Bikes/Family/Triathlon
Canning Bridge Cycles	New and Used/Mountain Bikes/Family and Racing
Churchill Cycles	New/Racing/Professional
Re-cycle Cycles	Used/Trade-ins
Ace Cyclery	New and Used/Mountain/Racing/Touring
Ambassador Cycles	New and Used/Touring/Family/Trade-in/Layby
Bicycle World	New/Racing/Professional
Action Bikes	Mountain/Racing/Touring Helmets
Cycle Circuit	Trade-ins/Accessories/Repairs
The Cycleman	New and Used/Marathon/Triathlon
George's Bike Shop	New and Used/Repairs/Accessories
Gordonson Cycles	Top Brands/Competitive Prices

Figure C4.7: Competitors for Inner City Cycles

CASE 5: PINEWALL FURNISHINGS

This case provides a focus for familiar management problems associated with growth without delegation. Organisational, marketing and accounting deficiencies are all apparent, each needing attention if appropriate managerial control is to be exercised.

Neil Berry and his wife Anne own and run Pinewall Furnishings, a manufacturer of quality storage units for living rooms, kitchens, bathrooms, family rooms and studies. Neil is concerned that his product costing system is not all that it should be; he seems to be spending all of his time preparing quotes and tendering for business that the company fails to win. He knows the company is competitive and the product of high quality so he fears that the product costings must be inaccurate.

The business has grown from a one-person operation in Neil's South Yorkshire garage to one where Neil now employs 13 people at a Hillsborough factory, in addition to himself and his wife. Figure C5.1 shows Pinewall's organisation chart, together with the actual lines of communication.

Pinewall operates in four major areas:

- a factory retail service manufacturing to order for private individuals (20 per cent of annual sales turnover);

- manufacturing standard wall units to a required design for Jackson Furniture, a major UK retailer (45 per cent);

- manufacturing furniture for builders for particular jobs, usually fitted kitchens and bathrooms (20 per cent);

- manufacturing custom-designed Hi-Fi equipment installations for Farmer Electronics, a major Sheffield retailer (15 per cent).

Both Jackson and Farmer are reliable, established enterprises, neither of whom relies on Pinewall for the whole of its furnishing manufacturing requirements.

The private factory sales are particularly demanding on Neil because he has to do the design work here too. They remain attractive because they are financially rewarding, yielding a 35 per cent markup on direct costs and overhead allowance. Neil wants to expand this side of the business, but is conscious of the need for a proper showroom facility and more widespread advertising. His current marketing ploy is to take potential customers to the homes of previous customers to display and demonstrate the product. Neil undertakes all such 'guided tours' himself, at an enormous cost in lost time.

The corresponding markup on the builders' kitchens is lower at 15 per cent since this area is more competitive, but there is rarely the need for new cupboard designs. Pinewall does not actively seek new work in this area but receives contracts on a regular basis from the three builders with whom they work.

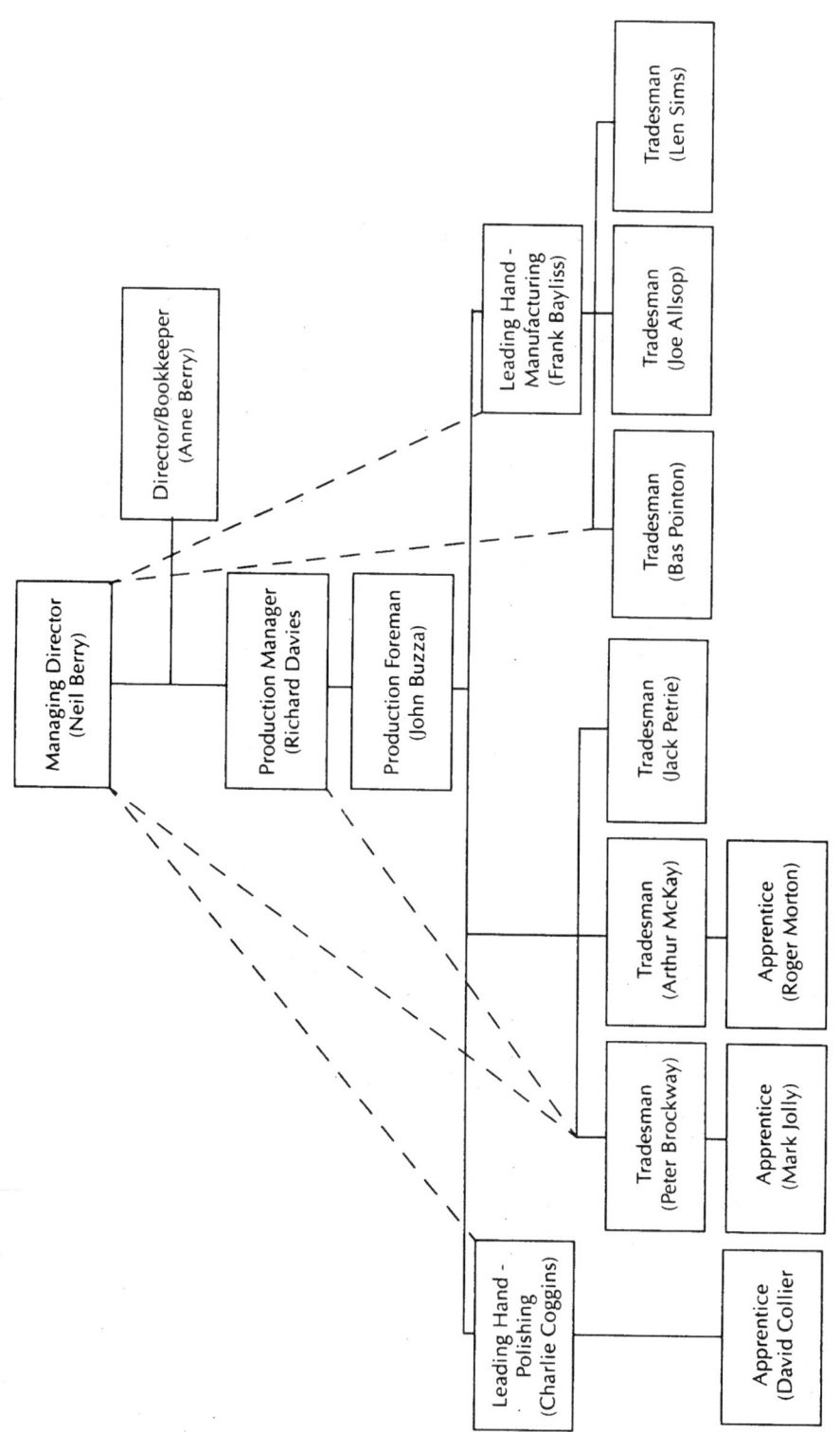

Figure C5.1: Theoretical Organisation Chart (and Actual Reporting Lines – – –)

Management Accounting Information Systems (MAIS)

The wall units for Jackson Furniture are based on a modular concept which Pinewall helped to develop. Pricing is based on standard costing, fixed for a period of six months, and provides a 25 per cent markup on the direct cost of labour and materials.

The electronic sound equipment supplies provide a 20 per cent markup on direct costs in a market which is quite restricted and showing no signs of growth. Increased penetration in this area is thought to be totally dependent on Farmer Electronics' marketing efforts. There is no advertising requirement on Pinewall for its products with either Jackson or Farmer.

The business has grown rapidly since 1988 and Neil no longer feels that he is totally in control. He has experienced periods of anxiety and stress associated with the variability of workflows. He has no worries regarding the quality standards, but deliveries are always behind schedule.

Bottlenecks at the quotation and design stage, for which Neil is largely person- ally responsible, mean that enquiries are not turned into jobs and delays occur on jobs that are won. Workflow difficulties at Pinewall have already caused Jackson Furniture to seek a second source for the manufacture of their wall units.

Systems for the recording and control of physical workflows are in Neil's hands. Each of the four types of work undertaken utilises a different control system but Neil controls the progress of all jobs from quote to supply. Pressure of work has already shown, in the past few months, that the existing systems provide no guaran- tee that any job will be effectively documented through all stages from quotation to delivery and invoicing. Richard Davies and John Buzza have recently been promoted from leading hand positions to Production Manager and Production Foreman respectively to take some of the pressure off Neil. But delegation of responsibility has not been made; all lines of communication pass through Neil and he is involved in the control of every aspect of the management, manufacturing and administration of the company. Neil sees this as the only way he can be sure of identifying any process or person not performing to standard. Both Davies and Buzza are frustrated that they have been stripped of their technical responsibilities without the compensation of appropriate managerial responsibilities; Buzza has asked to return to his duties as a leading hand.

Difficulties with the tradesmen are assuming increasing importance and are usually associated with three aspects of production:

- use of raw materials, in particular growing wastage levels;
- lines of authority and the recognition of responsibilities;
- bottlenecks in the production process.

Until now Neil has never considered production scheduling to be an issue, so no system exists which indicates the likely start and completion dates/times for jobs in progress. Staff keep worksheets of the time spent on a job, but this is used more for determining wages than for product costing. Neil has always managed to monitor slack time and fit new jobs into the system, but now he doubts his ability to do either efficiently. The growth of production has not been accompanied by a change in production layout. Neil fears that this might increasingly become a problem, but has assigned it to the 'too hard' and 'too big' baskets. Figure C5.2 (see page 65) illustrates the current layout of the factory.

There is no agreed timetable for the training of apprentices and no one is in control of their progress. Consequently they are frequently regarded as gophers rather than being encouraged to develop as tradesmen. This is particularly apparent in the polishing area where Charlie Coggins, the leading hand, rules supreme and guards his position and reputation jealously.

Bottlenecks are associated with the lack of scheduling and capacity planning. The final processing area, polishing, is under intense pressure and increasingly inadequate for the workflow demanded of it. The tradesman in polishing effectively controls output from the factory by determining job priority. No system exists to monitor his output and management exercises no control over flows from the rest of the factory into the polishing area. Figure 5.3 shows the flow of work and associated responsibilities for each of the four systems/product types involved.

Anne Berry recognises that the needs of the business have outgrown her bookkeeping skills and has brought in Matthew Riggs, an independent accountant, to review the accounting systems and computerise the budgeting and financial planning. There are no plans at present to extend the system to management accounting: Neil will continue to cost all jobs, for which standard costs do not exist, on a one-off basis.

No systems exist to allow the comparison of actual with standard costs and there is no means of tracking the issue of raw materials to particular jobs. Orders for raw materials are rarely in writing and no sequential numbering system for orders exists. No system exists for the issue of raw materials from store.

Direct labour costing is based on an hourly rate charged at £15 per hour. Factory overhead is estimated to be £20 per direct labour hour, based more on what the market will bear than actual costs. There is no variation in the allocation of overhead to jobs dependent on their type or the number of production processes to which they are subject. Neither is there any difference in the charge-out rate recognised for different grades of tradesmen used on a job.

The scheduling of tradesmen to particular jobs is based on ability, and polishing is the only area in which flexibility for employee-switching does not exist. Otherwise tradesmen are capable of working in all product areas.

Neil is conscious that changes have to be made. The personal costs to him of running the business are high and his marriage is suffering in consequence. Resistance to change from the tradesmen is inevitable since they have never been accountable before and fear that tighter control will allow management to point fingers at bludgers. Neil is willing to learn and change but desperately needs direction.

You are required to examine the strategic directions available to Neil and Anne in directing the future of Pinewall. Your report should analyse the degree to which product costing is Pinewall's real problem and suggest appropriate changes to the management accounting system.

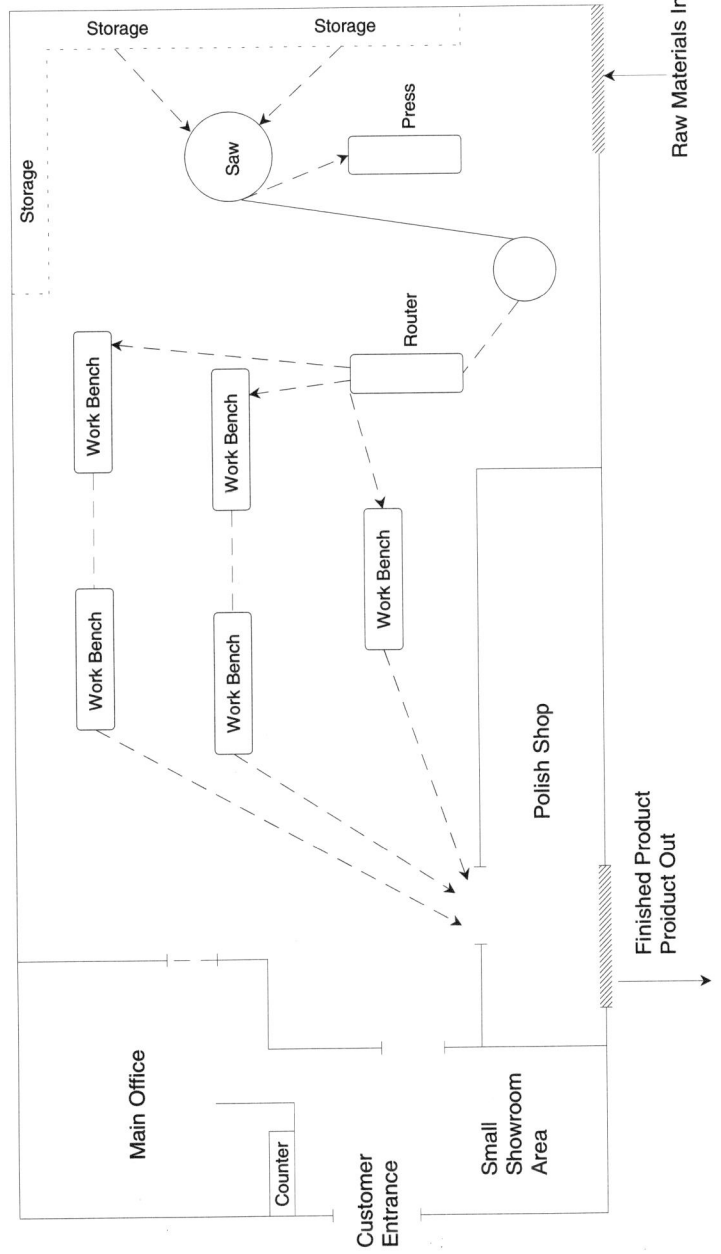

Figure C5.2: Current Factory Layout (And Workflows – – –)

Storage

Storage

Storage

Saw

Press

Router

Work Bench

Work Bench

Work Bench

Work Bench

Work Bench

Work Bench

Polish Shop

Main Office

Counter

Customer Entrance

Small Showroom Area

Raw Materials In

Finished Product
Proiduct Out

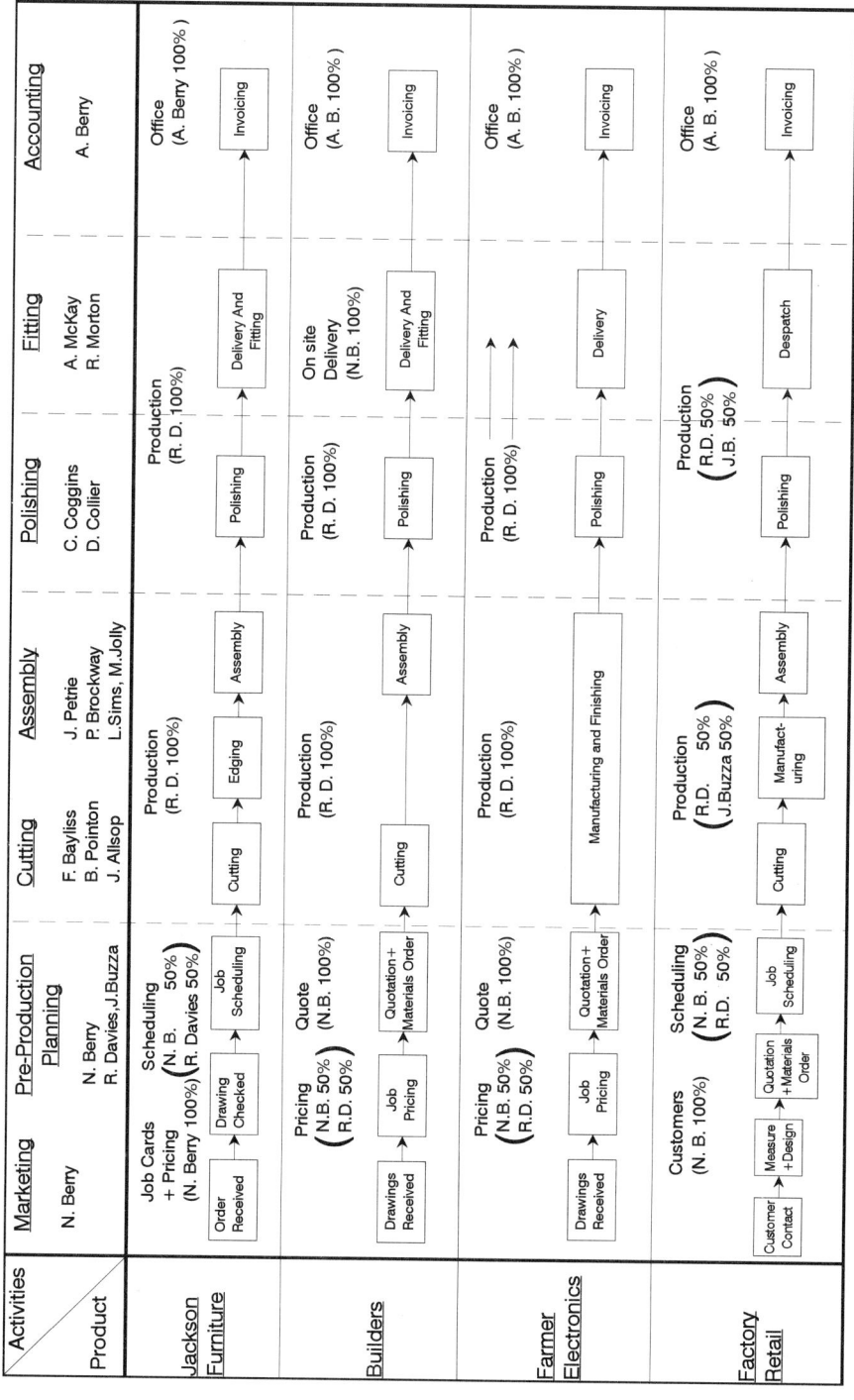

Figure C5.3: Job Flows and Responsibilities

Chapter 4

Strategic Management Accounting (SMA)

4.1 INTRODUCTION

Strategic decisions are required in three fundamental business areas, where a number of questions arise:

- corporate strategy

  what business do we *think* we are in?
  what business *should* we be in?

- competitiveness

  who are our current/future competitors?
  how do we compete with them efficiently?

- operational strategy

  how do we pursue our corporate goals?
  what internal organisation allows the marketing, human resources management, finance, accounting and information technology functions to achieve corporate objectives?

Strategic management accounting focuses on the goals of the enterprise and revolves around the creation and maintenance of a decision support system which provides the information necessary to allow decision makers to pursue corporate goals effectively. A notable feature of this system is 'performance measurement', with the requirement that the management accounting information system (MAIS) encompasses appropriate, accurate and timely indicators of performance at all levels.

Figure 5 (page 68) illustrates the different stages of the process that must be examined in adopting a strategic management accounting approach. We will consider each of these in turn.

4.2 CORPORATE OBJECTIVES

A commitment to a corporate mission, together with a strategic plan for its achievement, should come from the top of the organisation. A succession of 'milestones' to monitor achievement and performance indicators for processes at all levels are an integral part of the plan.

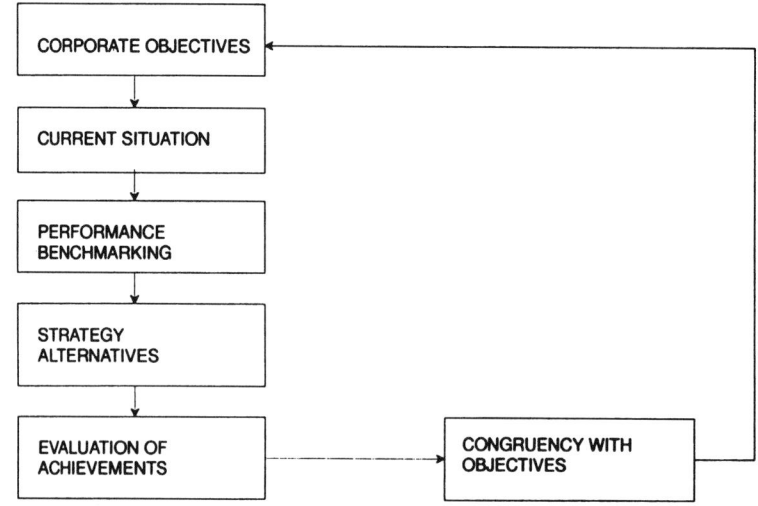

Figure 5: The Strategic Management Accounting Approach

Goals and objectives should be implemented across all processes and articulated across the organisation in order to evaluate their impact on customers. Hiromoto (1988) emphasises the direct link between strategic corporate goals and management accounting practice in Japan: rather than establishing a 'right' way of doing things, a proactive approach is taken to the choice of accounting procedures so that they support the chosen corporate goals.

4.3 CURRENT SITUATION ANALYSIS

A strategic approach to future development demands that we are aware of our precise current position; in particular, a knowledge of our current performance relative to our own previous performance, to that of our competitors and to that of the rest of the industry. A SWOT analysis — detailing the strengths, weaknesses, opportunities and threats of the organisation — is an extremely useful marketing tool which provides a starting point to case analysis. A matrix of the kind illustrated in Figure 6 can be developed to highlight the vulnerability of the organisation and improve awareness of a potentially precarious position.

The left-hand side of the matrix emphasises positive features, the right-hand side negative features. The SWOT analysis can be conducted for several different perspectives — e.g division, product, competitors — to give an overall view of the current position. All of the cases in this chapter, and many elsewhere, provide opportunities for the application of the SWOT methodology. *Case 9: Easton Printing* is a particularly good example.

Strengths	Weaknesses
• • • •	• • • •
Opportunities	Threats
• • • •	• • • •

Figure 6: SWOT Analysis

There are four fundamental issues that the SWOT analysis must address:

• financial performance;

• competitiveness;

• market impact; and

• environmental factors.

In each case, as well as evaluating our current position, we wish to identify our future direction and the costs and benefits of not implementing the appropriate change strategies.

Financial performance appraisal allows us to assess our current position relative to standards for comparison (e.g ourselves, competitors, industry means, performance yardsticks) as well as to highlight the dangers of insolvency and vulnerability to takeover. Financial ratios in five different areas of performance, constructed from the Profit and Loss Account and Balance Sheet, can provide useful insights, especially where we have a comparative base:

• **Profitability**, measured, for example, by:

$$\frac{\text{Profit Before Tax}}{\text{Total Tangible Assets}}$$

Relative performance on this measure will be highly industry dependent, but a 10 per cent yardstick for acceptable performance is often a useful start for manufacturing companies.

- **Gearing**, indicating the extent of the debt burden and measured as, for example:

$$\frac{\text{Funded Debt}}{\text{Shareholders' Funds}}$$

A 50 per cent yardstick is often sought, but may give a misleading impression since debt on which interest does not accrue is not included. Some current liabilities, particularly trade creditors, will therefore be ignored, consequently underestimating the extent of dependence. Where this impact is serious, an alternative ratio Total Liabilities/Total Assets including all liabilities may be preferred, and a 100 per cent yardstick sought.

- **Liquidity**, measured, for example, as:

$$\frac{\text{Current Assets}}{\text{Current Liabilities}}$$

A 150 per cent yardstick usually applies but, again, may mislead since current assets include inventory, which may be extensive, non-liquid and/or obsolescent. The Quick Assets Ratio (using current assets less inventory) is therefore often preferred, and a yardstick of the order of 70 per cent implemented.

- **Working capital**, indicating the future growth potential of the business through the availability of current funds to finance investment. Often measured as:

$$\frac{\text{Current Assets} - \text{Current Liabilities}}{\text{Net Capital Employed}}$$

- **Internal efficiency**, giving indications of operating performance and its impact on current assets and current liabilities, might be measured by:

$$\text{stock turnover} = \frac{\text{sales}}{\text{inventory}} \quad \text{measuring inventory holding procedures}$$

$$\text{debtors turnover} = \frac{\text{sales}}{\text{debtors}} \quad \text{measuring debt collection procedures, and}$$

$$\text{creditors turnover} = \frac{\text{sales}}{\text{creditors}} \quad \text{measuring the integrity of credit extension procedures}$$

A useful measure of overall financial performance is given by the computation of an expression combining three of the above ratios:

$$\frac{\text{PBT}}{\text{TA}} + \frac{\text{QA}}{\text{CL}} - \frac{\text{TL}}{\text{TA}}$$

$$= \frac{\text{Profit before Tax}}{\text{Total Assets}} + \frac{\text{Quick Assets}}{\text{Current Liabilities}} - \frac{\text{Total Liabilities}}{\text{Total Assets}}$$

Despite the simplicity of this linear, unweighted expression it can be surprisingly robust in a variety of circumstances. A negative value for the overall measure is a good first indicator of a company which is not performing satisfactorily and which is potentially subject to financial distress. In Chapter 8 we explore in more detail the choice of an optimum ratio-variable set, together with appropriate weightings. This facilitates the use of financial ratio analysis in *Case 25: Whittlesford Hardware* and *Case 26: British Motors*.

An appraisal of competitiveness centres on a consideration of those non-financial factors which allow a company both to resist competitive pressure and to apply such pressure successfully to others. Loss of markets, financial failure and susceptibility to unwelcome takeover predators are all potential outcomes of lack of competitiveness.

Adoption of one of the three Porter (1980) strategies with respect to competitive position gives a firm indicator of the ability to thwart the pressure exerted by others:

- **Industry leadership** — characterised by a cost-conscious approach to operations, pursuit of the technological edge and acknowledged lowest costs in the industry. This is often combined with economies of large scale production and a reputation for the highest quality.

  These factors allow the firm to resist competitive pressures through price cutting, and because the competition cannot match the technological expertise that has been created.

- **Product differentiation** — characterised by the manufacture of multiple products, each branded and fiercely promoted. Competitors are forced to compete simultaneously on many fronts, rather than attacking a single product, and must overcome the established brand loyalty through price cutting.

- **Niche marketing** — by targeting niche markets, ignored by larger and less flexible operators, the company can steal a march on the competition. Focus on cost or quality and responding to customer needs in a restricted market will lead to supernormal profits in the short-term, even though they may be eroded eventually by imitators.

The choice of generic strategy will often dictate the *operational strategy* necessary to meet consumer demand. Capacity planning offers three alternatives:

- **demand matching** (i.e. production = demand), with a consequent impact on the efficient use of resources, equipment and labour;

- **operation smoothing** (i.e. production = average demand), with a consequent impact on the inventory holding necessary to meet variations;

- **subcontracting** (i.e. buy not make), with a consequent impact on the power the company exerts to control its own destiny.

The focus on capacity considerations highlights the importance of product cycle time, bottlenecks and delivery reliability, and the consequent need for innovative measures of operating performance. The intricacies of job scheduling and the time variations inherent in production set-ups and operations sequences foreshadow complexities which may lead to substantial operating delays and outcomes inconsistent with corporate strategy.

Case 7: Geelong Textiles illustrates the impact of both capacity planning and production bottlenecks on strategic direction.

An appraisal of the relative *market* position will include market share, share price and the structure of shareholdings. A company should have developed both offensive strategies (e.g. product or market diversification) and defensive strategies (e.g. horizontal or vertical integration) to reduce vulnerability. Figure 7 illustrates the scope of such activities.

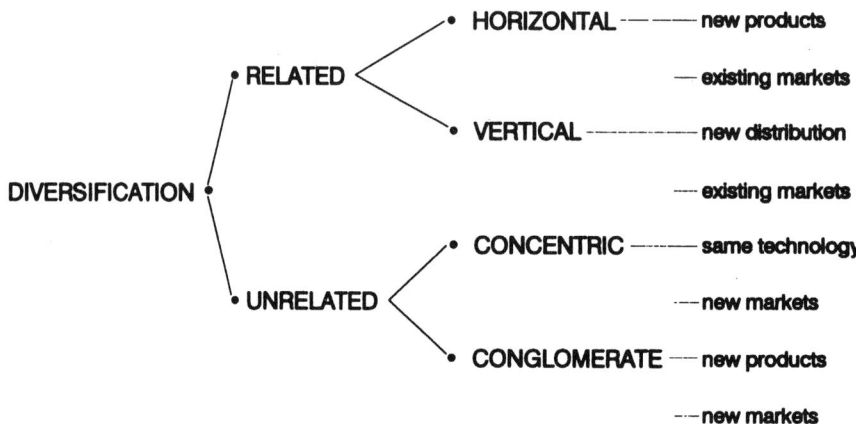

Figure 7: Alternative Market Diversifications

Of all the alternatives the conglomerate diversification is perhaps the riskiest because it represents a step into the unknown. It has the potential to reap the rewards of new and exciting markets by spreading risks and turning around underperforming assets. On the other hand, it will stretch management strength to the limit in areas of little experience and perhaps no expertise. *Case 6: Vertex Printing Group* illustrates the dual problem of diversification accompanied by an underperforming subsidiary.

Many of the arguments and methods applied to market analysis for groups can also be applied to their individual subsidiary companies and separate products. Two further marketing tools, the product life cycle (PLC) and Boston Consulting Group (BCG) portfolio matrix, are useful for an understanding of the corporate impact of product and subsidiary strengths/weaknesses.

4.4 THE PRODUCT LIFE CYCLE (PLC)

The Product Life Cycle (PLC) provides a useful framework for the consideration of alternative product strategies and for alerting management to the dynamics of the market and the consequences of inaction.

Figure 8 illustrates the five stages of the basic cycle:

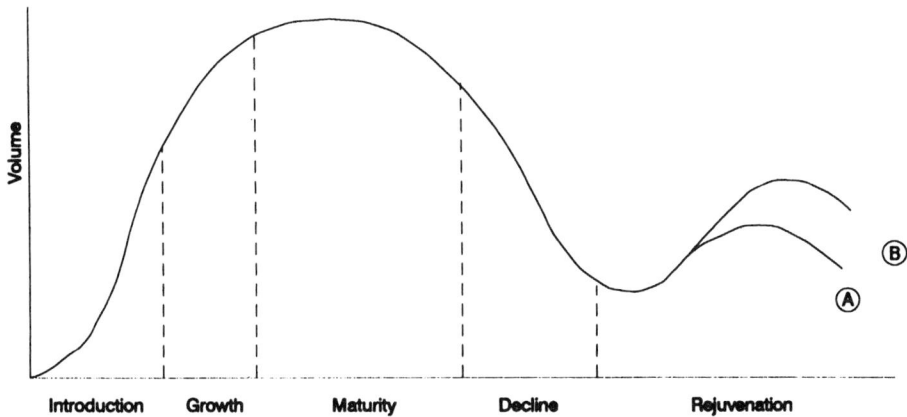

Figure 8: The Product Life Cycle

INTRODUCTION

Some new products diffuse very slowly into their potential market while others virtually ignore this stage, taking a swift trajectory into rapid growth. A number of factors can contribute to a slow product take-up:

- lack of comparative advantage on price or quality with existing products;

- uncertainty about the longevity of the product, such that consumers perceive a potential risk of, say, failure or technical obsolescence;

- lack of availability of product information or the product itself.

Producers must invest in promotion (to improve consumer awareness) and distribution (to ensure that the product is on the shelf and available for trial). Warranties and demonstrable after-sales service will reduce the perceived risk of purchase, but may not eliminate it in areas of rapid technological advancement.

GROWTH

The transition to rapid growth will be characterised by one or more of three factors:

- a changed relationship with substitute products so that consumers perceive the existence of distinct price and/or quality advantages;

- reduced uncertainty surrounding the likely success of the product so that it gains widespread acceptance and imitators attempt to enter the market;

- repeat buyers as an element of brand loyalty develops.

Producers must invest in increased capacity to meet demand, expanding both distribution channels and inventory holdings. Product extensions might be added to the basic line.

MATURITY

The growth rate will slow as the target market reaches saturation point. Producers will seek to attract new users while retaining their existing ones. As products become more familiar buyers become more price sensitive and less responsive to advertising, so that producers must focus on quality continuity and competitive pricing, at a time when competitors are likely reacting in a similar manner.

DECLINE

The onset of decline may be rapid (if attributable to changes in fashion) or may be more gradual if it results from technological change. Producers will attempt to slow down the decline by focusing on sub-groups of customers and by restricting the product line, aiming to stabilise sales at a level below the original, but still acceptable. The rate of decline will depend on the comparative price/quality advantages of emerging products.

REJUVENATION

Producers will attempt to prolong the life-cycle through product and user innovation, corresponding to positions A and B in Figure 8:

A — make major product improvements;
— reposition the product with regard to customer perception;

B — seek new distribution outlets, possibly through exports;
— establish new uses for the same product.

Only when rejuvenation strategies have failed to arrest the decline and the product is no longer profitable should product withdrawal be contemplated.

The major problem of applying the Product Life Cycle in practice is the difficulty of establishing exactly what stage product development has reached. The position will be product and industry dependent and cannot be forecast simply on the basis of past sales. A product may be designated 'mature' when in practice it has reached only a temporary plateau midway through the 'growth' stage.

4.5 BOSTON CONSULTING GROUP (BCG) PORTFOLIO MATRIX

The BCG model and other portfolio planning methods have revolutionised strategic planning over the past 20 years, helping management to understand how each of its businesses contributes to the whole, and clarifying the overall picture. They have provided an information source to facilitate the elimination of weak businesses and shift resources into those with more promise. Overall they have provided the data to improve the level of analysis in the strategic planning process.

The Boston Consulting Group (BCG) portfolio matrix provides a useful framework for the analysis of a whole into the sum of its component parts, to determine the extent of the synergy existing in the whole. Such analysis is most often of the form:

- **Group Performance** in terms of the relative performance of SUBSIDIARIES;

- **Market Performance** in terms of the relative positioning of PRODUCTS;

- **Sales Performance** in terms of the relative profitability of CUSTOMERS.

By allocating subsidiaries/products/customers into the categories of Figure 9 we can clarify overall group strategies or highlight the impact of changes in the product or customer mix. On the vertical axis the market growth rate provides a measure of market attractiveness, while on the horizontal, relative market share measures the competitive strength in the market.

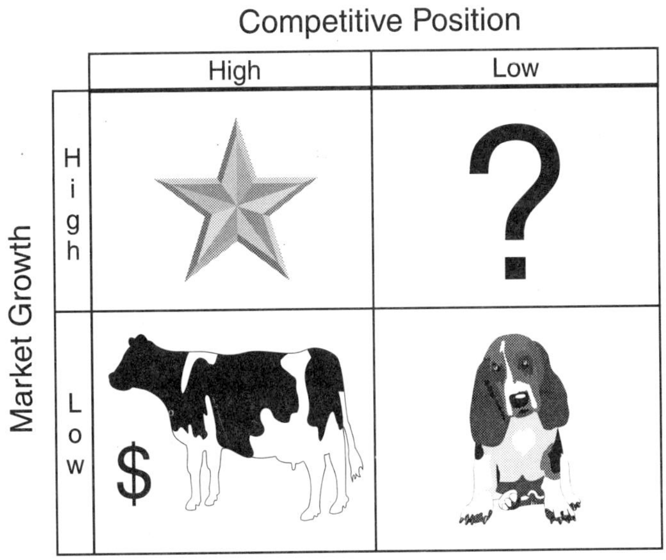

Figure 9: BCG Portfolio Matrix

A market growth rate in the range 0 to 20 per cent would be normal. A market growth rate for any individual product/company in excess of 10 per cent is high, and 10 per cent is therefore normally used as the cut-off point between the upper and lower quadrants.

The relative market share measures the company's strength relative to that of the largest competitor. A log scale is normally used on this horizontal axis so that equal distances represent the same percentage increases. A value of 1.0 is used as the divider of the quadrants into left and right-hand sides. Values less than one (right-hand side) demonstrate low market share, while those greater than one (left-hand side) demonstrate high market share.

By positioning subsidiary companies (for example) on a map graphing competitive position against market growth we can classify them as:

- **Cash Cows** — in a mature market in which they are strongly positioned so that few investment resources are needed but consistent cash outflows are generated. Cash cows are market leaders despite an annual market growth rate below 10 per cent. They enjoy economies of scale and high profit, but these might be drained by supporting the rest of the group.

- **Stars** — the market leaders in the portfolio; profitable and high growth businesses but still requiring extensive injections of investment and promotional expenditures to maintain their position and reputation. Eventually their growth will slow and they will be turned into cash cows.

- **Dogs** — uncompetitive in static markets. No further promotional or investment expenditure is justified and elimination might be considered unless they occupy a strategic role in the portfolio. They may earn sufficient cash to maintain themselves, but little more.

- **?** — competitive operations but yet to make a significant market impact. Barely profitable at present they have the potential to become stars but require large-scale investment to do so. A question mark hangs over their future such that if their market penetration is insufficient to justify such further investment in the future they will decline to a dog position.

An unbalanced portfolio would have:

- too many 'dogs' and 'question marks';

- too few 'stars' and 'cash cows'.

Four basic strategies emerge from the matrix:

- **Build** — increase market share, even at the expense of short-term profits (e.g. turn question marks into stars);

- **Hold** — preserve market share (e.g. ensure a cash cow remains a cash cow);

- **Harvest** — increase short-term cash flow, often without adequate regard to its long-term effects (e.g. use cash cows to fund other businesses);

- **Divest** — eliminate those businesses whose use of resources is inefficient and which are sufficiently peripheral to the rest of the group to merit abandonment (e.g. under-performing dogs and question marks).

Smith (1994) uses the international electronics group Thorn EMI to illustrate how the BCG matrix might operate in practice. He identifies subsidiaries that might be categorised as:

- Stars (in defence electronics and music);

- Cash cows (in electrical components and TV rental);

- Question marks (in films, entertainment and satellite broadcasting);

- Dogs (in white/brown goods, lighting and heating);

Their balanced portfolio of the mid 1980s lends itself to the building of the question marks through harvesting the cash cows, while holding the stars and abandoning the under-performing dogs, a strategy which subsequently came undone only because the cash cows were unable to supply the resource needs of the question marks, resulting in the disposal of the latter.

The adoption of a group perspective to the matrix would seek a balanced portfolio by shifting funds between the component companies. This is illustrated in Figure 10:

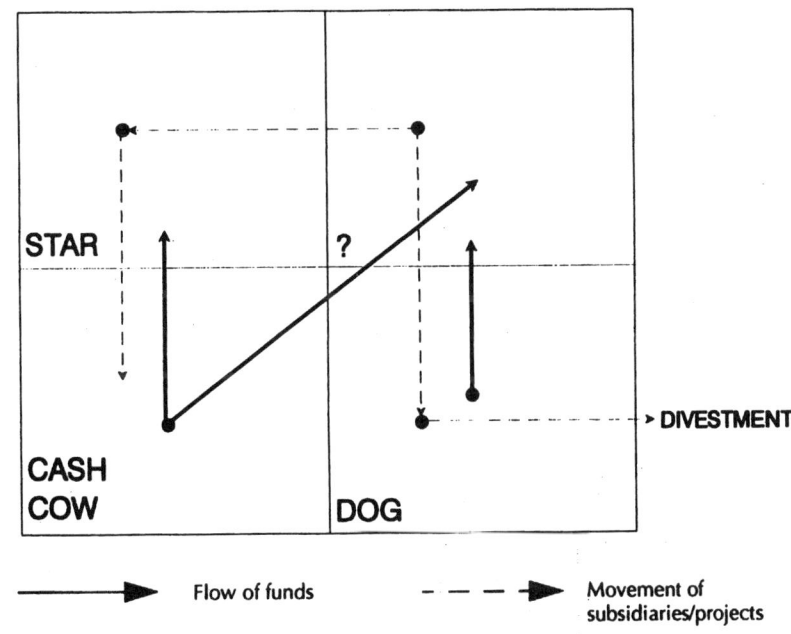

Figure 10: Strategy Outcomes in BCG Portfolio

- use of funds made available by the cash cows to promote both the star performers and those with the potential to become stars;

- management of dogs to ensure that they are not a cash drain; unless they generate even marginal positive cash flows, divestment must be considered an option;

- the nurturing and support of the stars to maintain their market prominence may eventually be rewarded with cash cow status — market leadership in a mature sector;

- the portfolio must always have its '?' quadrant as a feeder for the future. Star performers will emerge here but will require careful management and an eye for strategic withdrawal if the profits and market penetration required do not arise.

However, such models are not without their limitations. They can be costly and time consuming to construct and implement. Data collection may be difficult and subject to manipulation so that the assignment of companies to cells is somewhat arbitrary. They focus on the present, rather than the future so that managerial judgment is still required to make innovations and resource movements. A blink-ered approach to the development of a 'balanced portfolio' based on market-share growth may have unfortunate consequences, such as:

- diversification into areas/industries of which the group has no experience or expertise;

- over-milking of cash cows to finance the rest of the business, so that they are unable to maintain market leadership without reinvestment;

- the abandonment of healthy mature businesses still capable of recovery or of continuing to make a positive contribution to the group;

- neglect of the management of current businesses;

- neglect of inter-business relationships, so that each business is appraised separately without reference to the services it provides to other better-perform-ing businesses;

- making unwise investments in dogs in the hope of securing recovery in what turn out to be hopeless cases;

- maintenance of too many question marks in the portfolio, so that it proves impossible to fund them all adequately.

The portfolio matrix is simple, perhaps too simple, in design. We may have to make assumptions about the classification of some components. Their precise positioning in the matrix will be even more difficult since it requires some quantification and ranking. Despite the difficulties, the BCG matrix does allow an overview of group activities and avoids a blinkered focus on the individual components. *Case 14: Derrick's Confectionery* provides an opportunity to apply the BCG matrix in a scenario concerned with the relative profitability of the different customers of a group.

4.6 ENVIRONMENTAL ANALYSIS

The *environment* is the fourth major area that must be addressed in the SWOT analysis. Companies should be able to predict, and wherever possible, quantify the impact of environmental changes on their products and markets. In many aspects, changes in the UK will follow closely those occurring in the US and the rest of Europe, so that both warning and leadtime are available. Other instances will be uniquely British! The five major factors for consideration are:

- **Technological**
- **Demographic**
- **Legal**
- **Economic**

It is instructive to consider each of these factors briefly, focusing on the final two in more depth to investigate models developed to assist management decision making.

TECHNOLOGICAL FACTORS

Companies must be aware of technological changes regarding their own and related products so that they can respond appropriately and eliminate, or at least minimise, their impact on markets. They must not focus on technological wizardry to the exclusion of all else, when it is not the major factor in determining customer purchase patterns. For example, Sony's Betamax may have been technically the more advanced video recorder, but the superior marketing efforts of JVC ensured that VHS became the industry standard.

Technical advances in machine tools and operating technology will impact on manufacturing capability with the potential to create instant obsolescence. The advances in computer aided manufacturing and design through desktop publishing, for example, have changed the face of the print and newspaper industries. Those companies unable to foreshadow and respond to the changes have departed the scene.

Technological change increases customer expectations in individual products (e.g. safety features in motor vehicles) so that producers have to be flexible enough to respond to remain competitive. Companies that fail to respond to such changes will soon find their product outdated and will miss new product opportunities.

DEMOGRAPHIC FACTORS

These might be categorised as geographical (concerning, for example, the effects of climatic variation and the incidence of natural resources) and true demographics (concerning changes in population, age distribution and their impact on consumer demand). Of these the latter category is of interest to all companies and a vital feature of any marketing plan. The density, location, age, gender, race, ethnic diversity and occupation of target consumer groups will determine the nature of the product, the public's attitude towards the product and the manner in which it is marketed. The ageing of the population, attributable to declining birth rates since the 1960s and greater life expectancy, has brought a response from companies in the form of different marketing strategies and new products to cater for a changed lifestyle. However, the 'baby boom' population group will cease to be dominant soon after the turn of the century and companies must be flexible enough to respond to the increased geographical mobility, earning potential and unrealised product preferences of a new dominant group.

LEGAL FACTORS

Companies must closely monitor trends in legislation worldwide to give an early indication of likely changes, so that their impact on the business can be gauged in time to take appropriate action. Some products may have to conform to national legislation while also following international guidelines. Regulations which protect consumers (e.g. product liability and misleading advertising) will constrain the way a product is made and sold; regulations which protect employees (e.g. health and safety, employment law) will impact on the profitability of the workplace; regulations which protect companies from each other (e.g. patents, licences, anti-trust legislation) may impact on a company's acquisition or diversification strategy; and regulations which protect society (e.g. heritage listings) may force companies to take a longer-term perspective than would otherwise be the case. Changes in any of these areas could have a critical effect on product planning and business survival.

ECONOMIC FACTORS

Companies must be aware of the extent to which the key economic indicators will impact on their business and the likely direction of change in the future. Changes in interest rates will impact quickly on those in the construction industry and all companies reliant on short-term debt; changes in exchange rates will impact on those trading in overseas export markets or who rely on overseas raw material or component sources; the rate of inflation and the growth rate of the economy will impact heavily on the spending power of consumers. Changes in government policy, particularly the use of deflationary policies, will have a similarly negative effect on the availability of discretionary expenditure. For companies highly exposed overseas and whose export markets and investments are vulnerable to changed economic circumstances, economic risk analysis is vital in the evaluation of trading partners. Commercially available economic risk indicators monitor the risks associated with doing business overseas, and are particularly useful when the trading partners are less developed countries or unstable political regimes. The economic risks would include the following (many of which cannot be divorced from political factors):

- deteriorating trading conditions;

- lack of demand through a shortage of foreign exchange;

- imposition of import controls or tariff barriers;

- default on payment;

- punitive measures for foreign investors;

- restrictions on the repatriation of profits.

Publicly available information can give a good indication of trading partners whose economies are not sufficiently robust to ward off short-term difficulties. These are frequently those associated with:

- susceptibility to adverse climatic conditions;

- vulnerability to swings in basic commodity prices;

- single commodity export economies;

- single export-target countries, increasing vulnerability to protectionism;

- incidence of political unrest.

Close monitoring of the balance of payments situation and the foreign debt position over time can be very revealing. Taffler and Abassi (1984) detail a discriminant model measuring economic risk, in terms of likelihood of debt rescheduling, as a function of wealth, external indebtedness, rate of price inflation and monetary policy. They suggest the model:

$$Z = a + b \star X_1 + C \star X_2 + d \star X_3 + e \star X_4$$

where $Z < 0$ indicates an economy exhibiting signs of distress through a profile resembling previous cases of debt rescheduling, and

$$X_1 = \frac{\text{Loan Commitment}}{\text{Population}}$$

$$X_2 = \frac{\text{Debt}}{\text{Exports}}$$

$$X_3 = \text{Consumer Price Index}$$

$$X_4 = \frac{\text{Domestic Credit}}{\text{Gross Domestic Product}}$$

The model works well, particularly for less well-developed countries, although less well than the equivalent models based on company failure (detailed in Chapter 8). They do not reflect instability due to either political unrest or single commodity economies, and we might speculate on their being improved by the inclusion of political risk analysis variables.

POLITICAL FACTORS

Companies need to be aware of the impact that a change of government, or political policy, would have on their products or customers, as well as the more indirect impact of the machinations of environmental pressure groups. The imposition of new regulations (e.g. exhaust gases for motor manufacturers, or CFC emissions for refrigeration and airconditioning producers, and lower acceptable levels of smoke-stack pollution in response to well-orchestrated protests), will change both product and customer attitudes. For companies highly exposed to export markets or with overseas subsidiaries, governmental changes have the potential to threaten foreign investments and disrupt income streams. Many of the political changes at home, and their environmental consequences, are predictable; those overseas might present nasty surprises unless some form of political risk analysis is undertaken.

The modelling of political outcomes on the basis of alternative risk scenarios is well established commercially and indicates the level of risk associated with particular overseas trading partners. If political developments are not taken into account they can bear heavily on a company's ability to conclude a contract on time and in profit. Political or social conflict can lead to political instability and politically motivated violence directed against personnel and/or facilities. These might include acts of destruction, bomb extortion or product contamination (targeting physical assets) or kidnap and intimidation (targeting key personnel). Such acts may be perpetrated to prevent contracts being completed, impacting upon all those who are part of the investment cycle.

While it is difficult to make absolute predictions about eventualities it is possible to assess the probabilities of change and their likely impact on a business. The evaluation and forecasting of investment decisions in dangerous locations must include an analysis of the risk of adverse political actions. This ensures that managers make decisions in the full knowledge of such risks and their potential consequences.

The extent of the environmental modelling conducted has been limited, but scenario-based studies of economic and political risk have received the greatest exposure and have at least increased awareness of best/worst positions and their likelihood.

4.7 PERFORMANCE BENCHMARKING

Relative performance, at company or departmental level, can be measured internally or externally: internally, by comparing current performance with one's own previous performance or by reference to traditionally accepted performance norms; externally, with reference to industry yardsticks, the performance of competitors or accepted exhibitors of 'best practice' within an industry. This last example of external referencing has become known as 'performance benchmarking'.

Benchmarking provides an opportunity to compare company performance with that of others engaged in similar operations to give an indication of relative performance. The comparison, provided that it includes industry lenders, will highlight areas of deficiency and improvement opportunities. It may earmark areas for action and identify the factors underpinning the success of industry leaders.

If benchmarking is to be successful confidentiality must be guaranteed. Herein lies one of the great advantages of inter-company comparison schemes run by independent external agencies to which each company contributes operating information. Mutual benefits can be made available from benchmarking on non-contentious issues — i.e. moving away from the financials to common problems of an organisational or technological nature. Avoiding competitors, but cooperating with manufacturers or service providers of a similar size and nature, can bring positive results.

Smith (1994) highlights two factors that increase the likelihood of success in benchmarking exercises:

- collaboration with companies in similar fields and with like processes, but operating in different markets;

- avoiding sensitive areas like financial outcomes, R&D and key results to focus on operations.

Consistent with these suggestions, he reports on an Australian benchmarking exercise of the management accounting function which reveals insights in the areas of:

- accounting systems — notably the compatibility and friendliness of computer hardware and software;

- internal reporting — notably the timing, content and format of performance reports relative to different target users.

The results highlight alarming differences between apparently similar companies in the following areas:

- the existence of centralised database systems;

- the reliance on manual systems;

- the ability of mainframe and PC to interface successfully;

- the use of executive level information systems;

- the clarity and coherence of corporate strategies;

- the appropriate targeting of reports; and

- the integration of financial and non-financial information.

While exposing weaknesses and identifying the superiority of systems elsewhere, the benchmarking exercise also provided encouragement for the management accounting team through the recognition of good performance and motivated them towards further improvement.

As well as providing relativities which assist the SWOT process, the benchmarking process will provide strategic insights from the directions being pursued by other companies. It forms an essential component of successful Total Quality Management (TQM) implementation, as indicated in Chapter 7. *Case 8: Harston Exploration* provides an example of benchmarking in action, with respect to the provision of management accounting services.

4.8 STRATEGY ALTERNATIVES

One of the major advances in management accounting in recent years has been the focus on customers and employees. Recognition of them as external and internal recipients of a 'quality' initiative has meant more attention devoted to their needs and abilities. Use of the creative potential of the workforce is essential to the generation of ideas and alternatives in the search for optimum strategies.

The primary aim must be to avoid jumping to quick-fix solutions, which are implemented without a detailed consideration of either alternative approaches or the potential consequences of action taken. Figure 11, distilled from an observed manufacturing problem, illustrates the dangers of jumping in the wrong direction.

A team approach and structured group decision-making, following a systematic process, allows the creative thinking patterns of De Bono (1970) to generate creative solutions which may be preferable to the 'obvious' one. Brainstorming and lateral thinking are among the most well-used methods in the search for new ideas. They demonstrate that the creative potential of individuals can be improved with practice. Common simple guidelines underpin such techniques:

- a team approach and group commitment to the process;

- the encouragement of individual contributions to the group effort by collecting ideas without discussion, criticism or evaluation;

- the encouragement of 'wild' or 'way-out' suggestions, since these may provide the spark which generates an optimum-sensible alternative;

- the grouping of like ideas so that the preferred grouping has team commitment and no individual stigma attaches to rejected suggestions;

- the assignment of selected alternatives to sub-groups for the development of action plans and implementation strategies.

The best solution may still be the 'obvious' one, but at least alternatives have been aired and the process provides the opportunity for superior options to emerge.

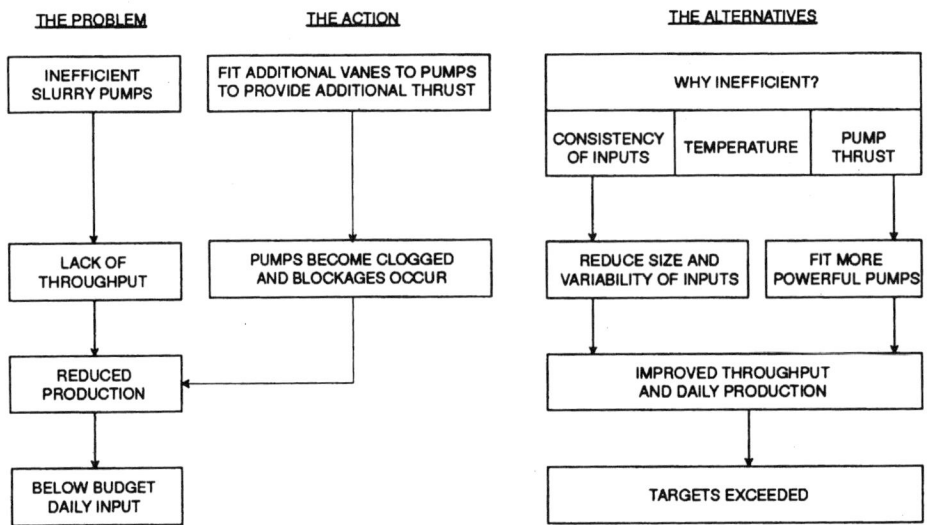

Figure 11: Solving the Throughput Problem

4.9 EVALUATION OF ACHIEVEMENTS

Outcomes resulting from the implementation of new strategies can be measured with appropriate non-financial indicators. A standard for comparison is provided by the traditional 3 Es of evaluation:

- efficiency — are the resources employed used in an appropriate fashion?

- effectiveness — is the outcome produced that which is desired?

- economy — are absolute resource requirements minimised?

Ultimately the success of achievements can only be judged by reference back to corporate goals. Outcomes must be congruent with goals, otherwise we must recirculate the loop, changing goals, outcomes, or both. It is quite conceivable that the evaluation stage will reveal conflicts between corporate strategy and the performance measurement actually guiding decisions. Such conflicts will often revolve around:

- differing priorities accorded to goals (e.g. financials v non-financials), illustrated by a preference for cost considerations rather than customer satisfaction, or

- the pursuit of performance relative to differing time horizons, often short-term v long-term.

Such differences may lead to the pursuit of short-term targets (e.g. labour and equipment productivities) resulting in outcomes inconsistent with long-term goals.

REFERENCES

Argenti J, *Corporate Collapse*, McGraw-Hill, London, 1976

Bellis-Jones R, 'Customer Profitability Analysis', *Management Accounting* (UK), February 1989, pp 26–28

De Bono E, *Lateral Thinking: A Textbook of Creativity*, Penguin Books, London, 1970

Hazell M and Morrow M, 'Performance Measurement and Benchmarking', *Management Accounting* (UK), December 1992, pp 44–45

Henderson B, 'The Product Portfolio' , *Perspectives* No 66, Boston Consulting Group, Boston, Mass, 1970

Howell R and Soucy S, 'Customer Profitability: As Critical as Product Profitability', *Management Accounting* (US), October 1990, pp 43–47

Kaplan R S and Norton D, 'The Balanced Scorecard — Measures that Drive Performance', *Harvard Business Review*, January–February 1992, pp 71–79

Kotler P, *Marketing Management: Analysis, Implementation and Control*, 8th ed, Prentice-Hall, Englewood Cliffs, New Jersey, 1994.

Porter M, *Competitive Strategy: Techniques for Analyzing Industries and Competitors*, Collier MacMillan, New York, 1980.

Smith M, 'Failure Prediction: Some Misconceptions Corrected', *Management Accounting* (UK), December 1992, pp 40–42

Smith M, 'Customer Profitability Analysis Revisited', *Management Accounting* (UK), October 1993, pp 26–28

Strategic Management Accounting

Smith M, *New Tools for Management Accountants*, Longman, Melbourne, 1994

Smith M, 'Benchmarking in Practice: Some Australian Evidence', *Managerial Auditing*, Vol 9 No 3, 1994, pp 19–22

Taffler R J and Abassi B, 'Country Risk: A Model for Predicting Debt Servicing Problems in Developing Countries', *Journal of the Royal Statistical Society* (Series A), Vol 147, Pt 4, 1984, pp 541–568

Ward K, *Strategic Management Accounting*, Butterworth-Heinemann, Oxford, 1992

CASE 6: VERTEX PRINTING GROUP

This case is concerned with the development of a strategic direction for a group in which diversification from its traditional role is evolving. The case addresses the issues of underperforming subsidiaries and franchising as an alternative means of conducting business.

The Vertex Printing Group is a family owned enterprise operating throughout the UK. There are six regional head offices with binding facilities but group headquarters are located in central Birmingham. The group has grown from modest beginnings in the early part of the century at its Nuneaton base, in the West Midlands and still the site of the Nuneaton Division. Since the early 1960s the major source of growth has been in an instant printing service provided by the Royal Printing arm of the group, and within this division franchise operations have provided the major impetus since 1980.

Royal Printing is concerned mainly with short run jobs: business cards, letterheads, envelopes, leaflets, invoices, forms and photocopying; while the Nuneaton Division handles all the more complex jobs: commercial printing, annual reports, calendars, multi-colour printing, glossies, graphic design and computerised typesetting.

Now the group has reached a watershed when it must determine its strategic direction. The plant at the Nuneaton Division is old and uncompetitive and its product contributes only five per cent of group profit. The remaining 95 per cent is attributable to Royal Printing with over half of that coming from the franchise operations. The position of the Nuneaton Division has become marginal, but in its present condition it is virtually unsaleable. Without investment it will deteriorate further and become even less competitive. Bert Palmer, chief executive and grandson of the original founder of the business, is reluctant to close down the Nuneaton Division altogether because of its central role in the reputation of printing within the state. He is concerned that without Nuneaton, Vertex will become a firm of corner shop printers competing with the cowboy operators and will relinquish its prestigious central role in 'quality' printing.

Royal Printing operates almost entirely on a half-cash half-credit basis, and its bad debts are negligible. Inventory control is not a problem due to the relatively low value of inventories held, mainly blank paper stocks. The maximum value of stock held in any shop at any time is of the order of £4000. Reliable sourcing arrangements with suppliers result in annual contracts and daily deliveries of paper. These arrangements have been extended to the franchise operations. Figure C6.1 shows the structure of the group and Figure C6.2 the distribution of the Royal Printing outlets. The final price charged per printing job is influenced by what competitors charge and by what the market will bear, but prices generally conform to the pattern displayed in Figure C6.3.

Variable costs are all estimated as a percentage of sales using the above guidelines (i.e. materials 22 per cent and labour 27 per cent of sales). Budgeted staff requirements are then determined from the sales forecasts.

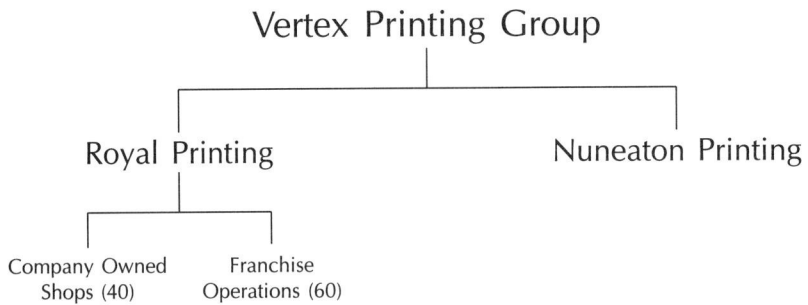

Figure C6.1: Divisional Structure

	Midlands (Birmingham)	South East (London)	North West (Manchester)	South West (Bristol)	North East (Newcastle)	Scotland (Glasgow)
Company Owned Retail Outlets (40)	10	10	10	4	2	4
Franchise Operations (60)	10	30	10	6	2	2
Totals (100)	20	40	20	10	4	6

Figure C6.2: Royal Printing — Distribution of Outlets

	%	
Materials	22	paper, ink, printing plates, wastage
Labour	27	time-based job costing, salaries
Variable overheads (shop)	7	salaries, maintenance, electricity
Fixed overheads (shop)	13	depreciation, insurance
Regional overheads	5	rent, rates, telephone
Group overheads	7	
Contribution to profit	19	
PRICE	100%	

Figure C6.3: Royal Printing Pricing Policy

The franchise outlets each contribute an up-front fee of £40 000 in the first year of operation, with a royalty of five per cent on first year sales rising to seven per cent thereafter. Franchise owners also each make a contribution to the national advertising budget of a further three per cent levy on sales. The growth of the franchise activity has been rapid so that new shop openings are now nearly 100 per cent franchises. This switch has been hastened by the superior profitability to the group of franchise outlets compared to company owned shops, with the average annual turnover for franchises at around £400 000 being 10 per cent better than that for company owned shops.

The success of the franchise operations has undoubtedly been due to very fierce scrutiny by Royal of prospective applicants and rigid adherence to the initial capital requirements — £80 000 for equipment costs and £20 000 working capital in addition to stock costs and the franchise fee. This initial scrutiny is then extended to the monitoring of monthly accounting records to ensure adherence to Royal's methods and minimum performance requirements. In return Royal provides its franchisees with an initial training package, guidance on site selection and equipment installation assistance. Advertising, accounting and technical assistance are provided on a continuous basis to support the outlets. Royal's market research uses demographic surveys to analyse all potential businesses in different locations to determine sales potential and the most appropriate product mix for each franchisee.

The Nuneaton Division, though part of the Vertex Printing Group, is effectively run by its production managers. Product costing rigidly adheres to industry guidelines and is based on rates determined from the previous year's budget with an appropriate inflation adjustment. Monthly budgets incorporate time-trend estimates of expected wastage costs, but accountants have little input. Wastage records are analysed monthly and are far in excess of those experienced by Royal Printing. Cash sales are rare at Nuneaton (less than 10 per cent) and bad debts have become an increasing problem over the last two years. All of the jobs at Nuneaton pass through three clearly identifiable stages:

1. Preparation — composing, artwork and paste-up, platemaking

2. Machining — cylinder/offset (jobs may require either or both types of machine)

3. Binding — guillotine, handwork.

The first and third stages are highly labour intensive; the second uses skilled operatives on complex machinery. Competitors have begun to use computer aided manufacturing and design procedures to streamline stages one and two, but these have not yet been extended to Nuneaton. The age of the equipment at Nuneaton frequently contributes to the spoilage rates and breakdowns cause bottlenecks to occur on key machines. Equipment upgrades are under consideration, the details of which are supplied in Figure C6.4. The cost variance problem is exacerbated by the idle time resulting in dependent processes because of machine failure. Such variances are rarely allocated to the client whose jobs are being processed.

Sales forecasting methods at Nuneaton are archaic and the historic budgeted sales + consumer price index method is entrenched, however inappropriate it may be. Market research is currently non-existent and sales budgets do not reflect the impact, if any, of advertising campaigns. Figure C6.5 illustrates how job costs are currently calculated at Nuneaton.

The production team at Nuneaton, despite its efforts, has been unable to convince the group of the economic viability of investment in new equipment. They have not used discounted cash flow procedures but have evaluated new projects in terms of their impact on the Profit and Loss Statement and the pay-back period. Most capital expenditure initiations are rejected by the group because they fail to recover the initial investment within the required five year period.

You are required to evaluate the alternative strategies available to Vertex and make recommendations for the most appropriate course of action.

TYPESETTING SECTION	£	£
2 × Lan Desktop Publishers	44 000	
1 × Varityper	46 000	
1 × Flat Bed Scanner (secondhand)	5000	
SUB TOTAL		95 000
PRINTING SECTION		
Retain Existing M/C Cylinder		
1 ×2 Colour Offset Printer	800 000	
1 ×6 Colour Offset Printer	1 500 000	
Platemaker Paper (secondhand)	10 000	
Platemaker Metal (secondhand)	15 000	
SUB TOTAL		2 325 000
FINISHING SECTION		
Electronic Guillotine	40 000	
Photocopier with 12 station collator	7000	
Collating machine	3000	
Folding Machine	2000	
Shrink Wrap Machine	2000	
Strapping Machine	1000	
Maintain existing Stapling Machine		
Maintain existing Jogger Machine		
SUB TOTAL		55 000
Total Machinery Costs		2 475 000
Installation & Factory Modification Costs		25 000
TOTAL UPGRADE COSTS		2 500 000

Figure C6.4: Equipment Requirements and Costings for Nuneaton Upgrade

	Source of Information	Basis of Allocation	Production Operations						Total
			Composing	Artist	M/C Cylinder	M/C Offset	Guillotine	Handwork	
1 No of Operators	Direct Labour Budget	2	1	2	2	2	4	13	
2 Budgeted Hours	Direct Labour Budget		2 100	1 300	3 000	3 000	3 000	6 400	18 800
3 Direct Labour Cost	Direct Labour Budget		20 000	9 000	20 000	20 000	22 000	30 000	121 000
4 Plant Depreciation		Value of Plant	400	600	3 000	–	3 500	–	7 500
5 Plant Leasing		Cost of Lease	–	–	–	6 000	–	–	6 000
6 Factory Overhead		Direct Labour Hours	7 000	5 000	10 000	10 000	10 000	4 000	46 000
7 Selling Overhead		Direct Labour Hours	5 300	3 300	8 000	8 000	8 000	16 000	48 600
8 Administration Overhead		Direct Labour Hours	8 000	5 000	12 000	12 000	12 000	25 000	74 000
9 Total			40 700	22 900	53 000	56 000	55 500	75 000	303 100
10 Cost Rate (£)			19.38	17.62	17.67	18.67	18.50	11.72	16.12

Figure C6.5: Nuneaton Division — Cost Rate Calculation

CASE 7: GEELONG TEXTILES

This case highlights difficulties associated with bottlenecks and capacity planning which can only be solved with reference to a clearly stated strategic direction. Where goals and planning are inadequate, behavioural, organisational and transfer pricing issues are also in evidence.

Geelong Textiles was founded in 1952. Michael Wiggins purchased a site in Burnley from which to operate the business and take advantage of the post-war recovery in manufacturing. Michael's son, Roy, took over the running of the company on Michael's death in 1981. Previously, Roy, though a director, had little influence over the company. His father's autocratic style had not endeared Geelong to Roy nor given him much in the way of management experience. Roy had inherited a run-down company, in need of investment in fixtures, fittings and machinery, but without the capital base to fund a reorganisation. Roy had a 52 per cent shareholding and his three fellow directors, Messrs Archer, Pycroft and Barnes, 16 per cent each. Together they controlled the two manufacturing arms of the company: the Cobden Division managed by Brian Flynn, and the Rochford Division managed by Steve Duffy. Figure C7.1 illustrates the organisation of the company.

In 1981, when Roy took over, the business had 50 employees and produced 1000 garments a week. Now, in 1992, the workforce has 88 employees and the combined output of the two divisions to external markets averages 5000 garments per week. The two divisions have totally separate markets: Cobden supplies own-brand clothing to tight specifications to a number of supermarket chains; Rochford sells fashion clothing directly from concessions in a number of specialist retail outlets.

The source raw materials for both types of customer are the same. Top quality fabrics using man-made fibres are imported directly from Italy, since local suppliers have been found to be inconsistent in both quality of product and reliability of delivery. The basic operations for both product types are undertaken at Cobden with the unsophisticated garments transferred to Rochford for customising and repackaging. Figure 7.2 shows the flow of production and anticipated time lags.

The speciality line of the Rochford division originally began as a 'good idea' for a diversification which did not require huge investment. It was so successful in the period following 1981 that it quickly provided the majority of Geelong's turnover and profits. Lack of investment in the Cobden plant has severely constrained the growth of direct sales through Rochford. Production bottlenecks in the cutting and pressing departments have caused long delays and given Rochford the unfortunate reputation of an unreliable supplier. Steve Duffy is particularly upset since he feels that the consequent lost orders and sales reflect on him as a manager. He has urged Roy Wiggins, so far without success, to allow him to source outside of the company for the basic Rochford materials.

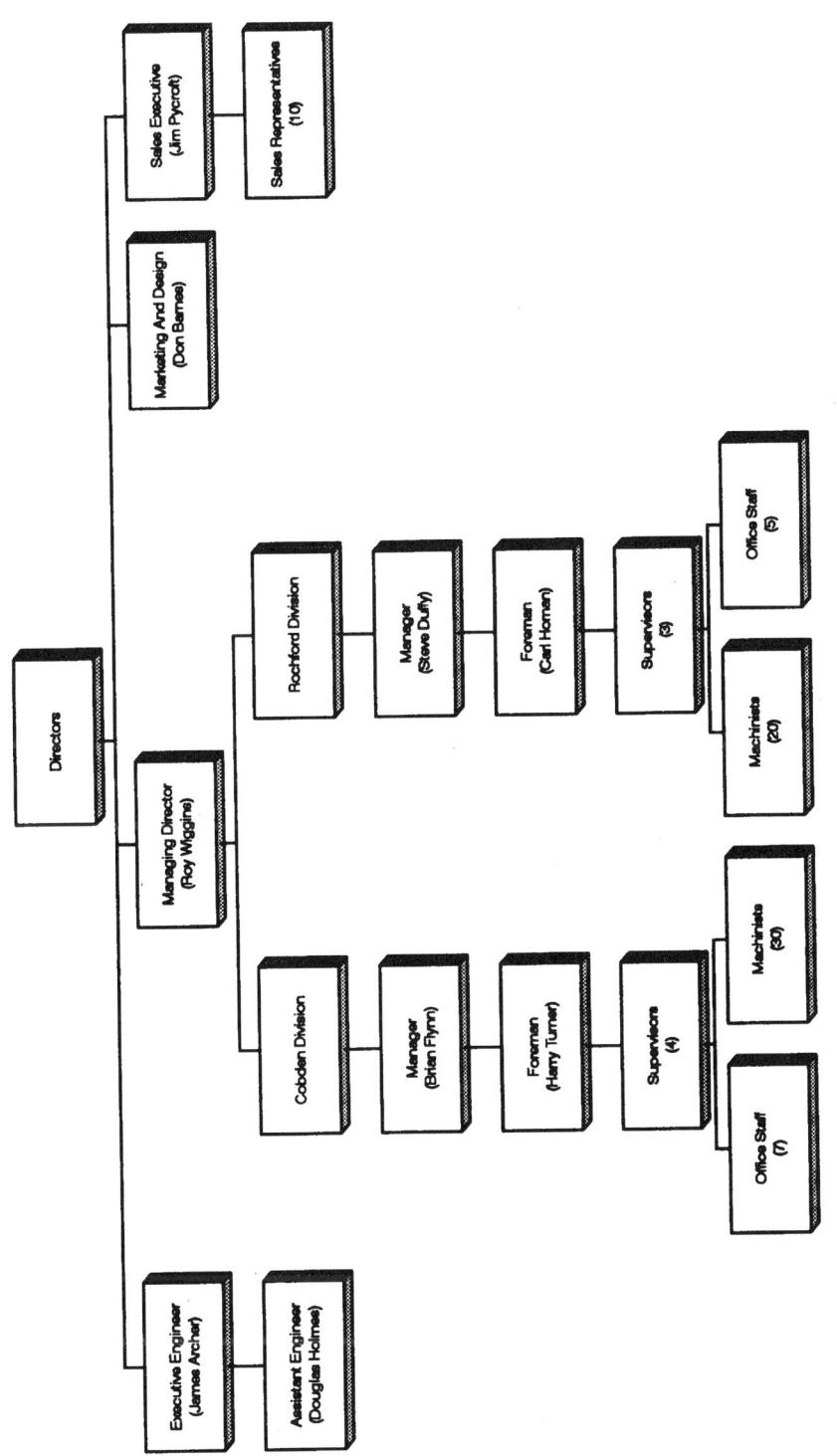

Figure C7.1: Geelong Textiles — Organisation Chart 1992

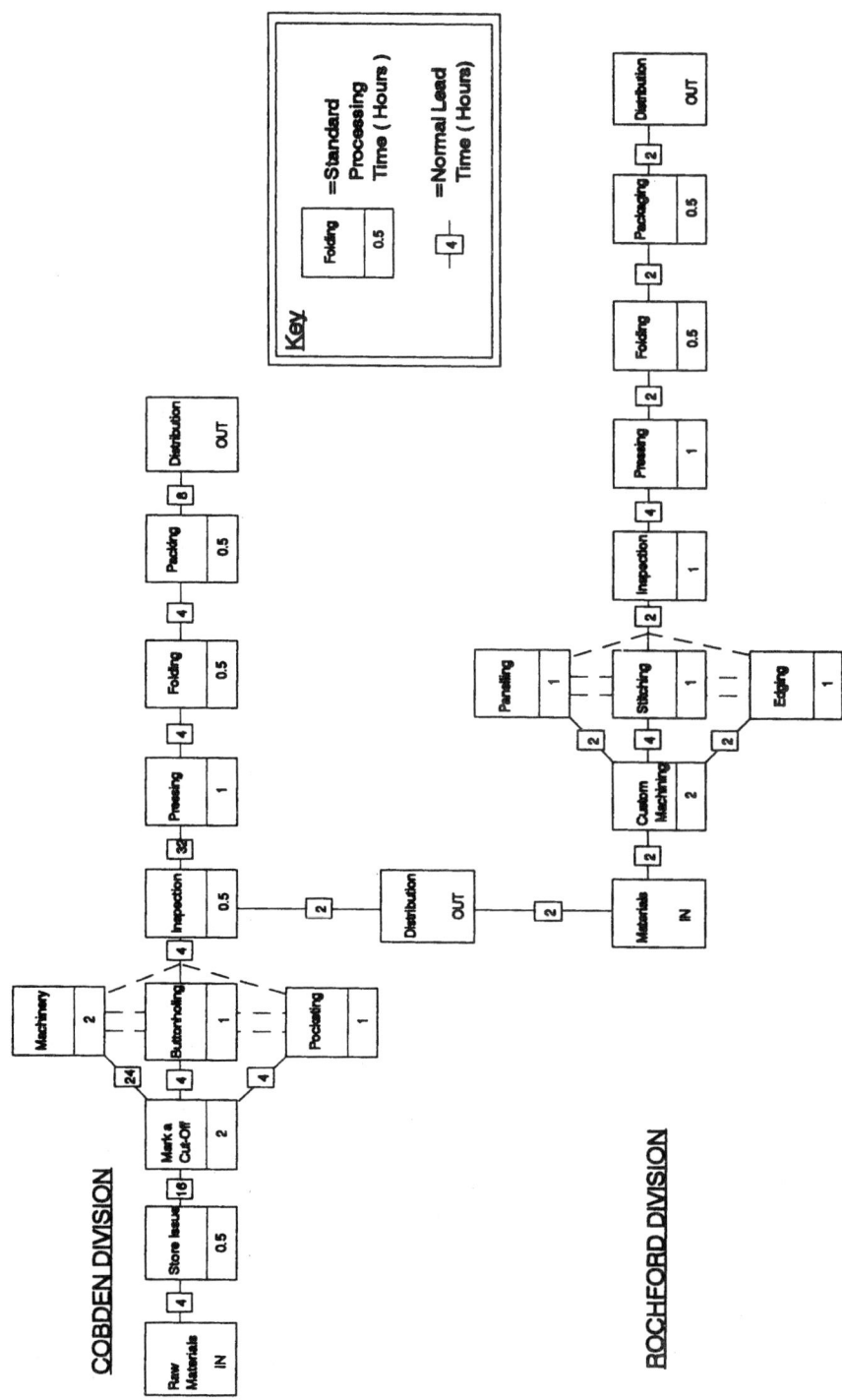

Figure C7.2: Production Flows at Geelong Textiles

Strategic Management Accounting (SMA)

The problem has been exacerbated since 1991, when Don Barnes initiated an aggressive marketing policy designed to increase Geelong's penetration in the supermarket end of the business. The success of this marketing ploy has seen Geelong gear up for bigger orders to more end-users of the basic Cobden product. In consequence, Duffy and Rochford have received a falling percentage share of the Cobden product, which has prevented Rochford from growing similarly despite the apparent demand. Steve is frustrated and Figure C7.3 details why.

	1987	1988	1989	1990	1991	1992
TURNOVER (£m)	2.0	2.8	3.2	4.4	7.0	8.5
% TURNOVER:						
Direct Sales (Rochford)	70	60	55	40	30	25
Supermarkets (Cobden)	30	40	45	60	70	75
PRE-TAX PROFIT (£m)	0.08	0.11	0.12	0.15	0.20	0.23
% PROFIT:						
Direct Sales (Rochford)	80	75	65	55	45	40
Supermarkets (Cobden)	20	25	35	45	55	60

Figure C7.3: Revenue and Earnings Trends

A system of transfer pricing operates between the divisions, governing the price of material inputs to the Rochford division for the purpose of internal profit calculation. Rochford currently pays a transfer price of £23 per garment, a figure which Steve Duffy considers too high and far higher than he would have to pay for outside sourcing. Brian Flynn justifies the figure on the basis of his costs and points to the evidence provided in Figure C7.4 (see page 96).

Steve Duffy argues that neither overheads nor Cobden markup should appear in the transfer price, while Brian Flynn is adamant that the existing overhead allocation is way below what is appropriate. Roy Wiggins has so far been reluctant to intervene in the dispute, but is aware that Steve feels his profit related bonus is inequitable.

You are required to examine alternative strategies for the future direction of Geelong and make recommendations for appropriate action. Your report should include the financial position of the company and its divisions, as well as issues of internal control.

AVERAGE COSTS PER GARMENT (£)			
COBDEN DIVISION		**ROCHFORD DIVISION**	
Raw Materials	3.00	Transfer In	23.00
DLH (7 @ £2)	14.00	DLH (8 @ £2)	16.00
Machine Time (4 @ £1)	4.00	Machine Time (6 @ £1)	6.00
Overheads	1.00	Overheads	1.00
Markup	1.00	Markup	4.00
Transfer Price to Rochford	23.00	Price to Retailers	50.00
Additional Raw Materials	1.00		
DLH (2 @ £2)	4.00		
Machine Time (1 @ £1)	1.00		
Overheads	1.00		
Markup	1.00		
Price to Supermarkets	31.00		

Figure C7.4: Cost Structure

CASE 8: HARSTON EXPLORATION

This case provides the opportunity of conducting a 'benchmarking' exercise, by comparing the performance of one company, Harston Exploration, with that of four others. The focus of the comparison is the service provided by the management accounting function in each company.

Jeff Lacey heads up the Management Accounting function of Harston Exploration from its headquarters at St George's Terrace, Perth. The company is engaged in the extractive industry, the greater part of its income coming from detecting and mining precious metals in the north-west of Western Australia (WA).

Jeff is conscious that his own management accounting systems form part of a 'fortress mentality' within Harston, such that ideas and new procedures rarely cross divisions let alone companies. He wants to initiate a new strategy within WA which will foster an attitude of cooperation among like-minded management accountants in similar process-based companies. His objective is to obtain a clearer indication of what constitutes 'industry best practice' so that he can implement improvement strategies at Harston Exploration. Though not dissatisfied with the present arrangements at Hartson, he feels that he may be in the dark about some of the latest developments in management accounting, and particularly the potential for implementing ABC, ABM and TQM procedures.

His first impulse is to get in contact with Bernie Shearer, his opposite number with Mildenhall Metals, Harston's major competitor. But Rex Rogers, the Chief Executive at Harston, cautions Jeff against such a move on the grounds of confidentiality. While supporting the benchmarking initiative he feels that Harston will get the most out of cooperation where none of the parties involved feels threatened. Jeff agrees and thinks again: he wants to work with companies who are willing to divulge information which is not publicly available and in an atmosphere of mutual respect, so that all concerned can gain from a discussion of common issues and problems.

He therefore aims to identify firms of a similar size to Harston and in the extractive/mining/refining industries, but not those who are direct competitors in the precious metals area. By doing so and focusing on relatively insensitive areas of the organisation for comparisons, he feels that Harston can make real gains. In looking at the organisation of the management accounting function he is, therefore, looking more at how they do things rather than the financial commitment and key results.

He therefore targets the chief management accountant at each of four companies:

- Bryan Munro   Holcroft Diamonds
- Harvey Cooper   Sheepcote Mining
- David Carstairs   Bolton Extractive
- Rodney Mahon   Burwell Minerals

All agree to collaborate without hesitation, and recognise that a free two-way transfer of information will be to their mutual benefit. Jeff is ecstatic, since he feels that by setting the agenda for discussions Harston will likely gain more than anyone. As an initial move he asks each of the above to supply some ball-park numerical information which can be used as a base for discussions. These have been assembled in Figure C8.1.

Next he establishes an agenda for discussion and gives each of his opposite numbers advance indication of his intention to address the six wide-ranging areas below:

- **Accounting Organisation** — the number, location and responsibilities of accountants.

- **Systems** — accounting systems and computer facilities; hardware and software — compatibility and friendliness.

- **Reporting** — the timing, content, format and targeting of performance reports.

- **Planning** — the incidence, frequency and detail of short-term budgeting and forecasting, and long-term strategic planning.

- **Cost Control** — the measurement and management of physical parameters and financial outcomes in key result areas.

- **Analysis** — the evaluation of business impact, performance analysis, commitment to the new management technologies.

As a preliminary to discussions with the other companies Jeff sketches out the main points of his own responses in each of these areas. He is gloomy at the outcome, concerned about the inadequacies of his own systems and convinced that his management accountants can do better. He is acutely aware that he might be exposed by the sophistication of the procedures employed elsewhere. Jeff's main points are set out in Figure C8.2.

Over the next two weeks he separately visits each of his fellow management accountants and spends 60–90 minutes discussing his agenda over coffee. In each instance both parties are happy that they have significantly gained from the interaction and promise to keep in touch, with the hope of making the cooperation a permanent feature. Jeff is much less gloomy than earlier as a result; he feels that Harston has not come out of the comparison too badly although significant areas needing improvement have been identified. Figures C8.3–C8.6 detail the responses of the other four companies.

You are required to compare Harston Exploration's performance with that of the four other companies chosen for the benchmarking exercise. Your report should recognise both those areas where Harston demonstrates superiority and those where it is clearly deficient. The latter instances should prompt a discussion of improvement strategies, where appropriate.

Company	Chief Management Accountant	Annual Group Turnover ($m)	No of Locations	No of Accountants	No of Clerical Support Staff	Leadtime for Generation of Routine Reports (Days)
HARSTON EXPLORATION	Jeff Lacey	2.8	7	23	41	5
HOLCROFT DIAMONDS	Bryan Munro	2.5	5	17	30	12
SHEEPCOTE MINING	Harvey Cooper	3.3	10	28	51	7
BOLTON EXTRACTIVE	David Carstairs	3.0	4	20	42	9
BURWELL MINERALS	Rodney Mahon	2.3	4	22	28	10

Figure C8.1: Numerical Responses for Five Companies

- **Accounting Organisation**

  This includes a significant head office presence (10 accountants) but with at least two accountants located at each of the remote minesites. At remote locations the accounting team are not separated from operations but positioned in offices immediately adjacent to the production controller so that they are available to provide immediate assistance.

- **Accounting Systems**

  Compatibility is the keyword in the development of accounting systems. All systems are developed in-house by the Information Technology team to ensure internal consistency. Even where off-the-shelf products are available their use is forbidden, and an acknowledged need must join the queue of projects awaiting consideration. The resulting software is extremely user-unfriendly but it is entirely compatible with existing software and hardware. Consequently the system is not accessed by senior executives — they rely on the friendlier technical operating system and its output of non-financial control data.

- **Reporting**

  Reporting is a combination of regular (usually monthly) routine reports and ad hoc reports to meet specific needs. The reports are generally timely but often not targeted accurately to user needs: users will frequently search a report for the one paragraph they consider relevant and then dispose of the rest. Few reports are available on-line but many appear on the widely detested lined computer paper, rather than the preferred laser print.

- **Planning**

  Planning is an on-going activity with monthly adjustments to forecasts and their impact communicated to all locations. Budgeting is conducted in the June-September period, annually, and remains fixed once established.

- **Cost Control**

  Cost control is only practised rigorously when commodity prices are depressed, and revenues are not increasing. Then efficiency and control of discretionary costs become more important. Otherwise production is the only focus and cost awareness is low.

- **Analysis**

  Analysis of performance is a prime focus. Value-adding activities and cost drivers are specified together with non-financial indicators in all areas of performance. Production and safety are the critical performance measures. Total Quality Management (TQM) principles have been adopted in the production areas and are under examination in the administrative areas.

Figure C8.2: Harston Exploration — Benchmarking Outcomes

- **Accounting Organisation**
  All accountants (17) are located at head office, none in remote locations. There are clerical support staff (maximum two) at each remote location in order to collect and communicate data to head office. All analysis is undertaken at head office, making some delays in feedback inevitable, but they are not considered to be serious.

- **Accounting Systems**
  There are separate on-line systems displaying, respectively, financial and non-financial information. But there is no integration of the two systems at present. Absence of PCs at remote locations necessitates extensive use of manual logs and diaries. There is poor integration between the mainframe and PCs for graphics purposes, the result of a ramshackle assortment of incompatible hardware and software.

- **Reporting**
  There is an absence of reporting in a downward direction, so that all levels below that of 'manager' have no clear perception of objectives, expectations or even past achievements. Executive access to technical reports is only via on-line systems; accounting reports are rarely addressed directly, word-of-mouth from the accounting team being preferred. There is differential reporting where considered appropriate.

- **Planning**
  Fixed annual budgets are in place, but only considered useful to give an overview of operations. Out-of-budget expenditure is considered essential to maintain the availability of equipment, so little attention is paid to production variances whether the system is in or out of control.

- **Cost Control**
  The emphasis is on long-term costs associated with maintaining production without running equipment into the ground. There is close control and monitoring of purchased services and hired equipment, but no cost priorities and there is no focus on the reduction of waste. Training schemes are in place to promote cost awareness at the shop floor level.

- **Analysis**
  No post-project audits are done to evaluate the costs and benefits of capital expenditures. No feasibility studies are done either: there is generally a preference for quick-fix solutions to observed sore thumbs. No progress reports on existing projects are routinely available.

Figure C8.3: Holcroft Diamonds — Benchmarking Outcomes

101

- **Accounting Organisation**
  There is a large head office team of 20 handling all of the computer based systems. Those accountants assigned to remote locations (one or two each) are responsible for the maintenance of manual systems on site, but must confer with head office for the solution of any problems requiring a detailed analysis.

- **Accounting Systems**
  The accounting system consists of unlinked manual procedures without any integrated on-line information system. The inflexible systems frequently necessitate the manual downloading of information from mainframe to PC in order to generate reports. All software packages are 'store-bought', often making inter-linking either laborious or impossible. Extensive manual operations are necessary to pull together diverse information items; card-based systems for ordering requirements are common.

- **Reporting**
  Hand-drawn graphs and diagrams are a feature, with no PC graphics support. There is no clear executive statement on corporate strategy, so no focus of management reporting in the pursuit of coherent goals. There is an emphasis on reporting upwards to departmental and divisional management.

- **Planning**
  Short-term planning dominates, together with the scheduling of services and maintenance requirements. Sub-optimal production is accepted (to give socially acceptable work rosters) and work-in-process is of a sub-optimal standard because of the focus on labour and equipment productivities. There is no strategic plan in evidence.

- **Cost Control**
  Decision-making is based almost exclusively on non-financial indicators. There is little awareness of costs at the shop floor level; there is no control of discretionary costs. The emphasis is on production 'at all costs'. Overtime costs are calculated on 'average' rather than 'actuals' because the systems are inadequate, resulting in massive monthly adjustments.

- **Analysis**
  No inter-site or inter-department performance comparisons are conducted, even in areas where they would clearly be appropriate. No post-project audits of capital expenditures are conducted. They have never heard of TQM.

Figure C8.4: Sheepcote Mining — Benchmarking Outcomes

- **Accounting Organisation**
  There is a large head office team of 11, but each of the remote locations has a team of three accountants. These form a cohesive group positioned in air-conditioned offices at least half a kilometre from the mining operations. Communications with production are generally by phone, e-mail or messenger. Accountants are rarely seen on site.

- **Accounting Systems**
  There is an integrated accounts package incorporating costs/budgeting/ payroll/supply/accounts payable and variance analysis. All packages are 'homegrown' to ensure compatibility, but procedures are complex, so that access by non-accounting executives is neither common nor encouraged.

- **Reporting**
  Multi-column general purpose reports, paying no attention to the differing needs of the various recipients, are produced. Internal reporting is generally regarded as redundant, providing historical documents where more timely sources are available elsewhere. The emphasis is on responsibility accounting in the manner in which internal reports are communicated. There is increasing use of on-line reporting in the accounting areas — the aim is to phase out hard copy reports completely in 12 months. Reporting is flexible in order to meet the requirements of the corporate strategic direction.

- **Planning**
  Budgets are tight, with forecasts every ten days to ensure their reality. A group-wide strategic plan is in evidence and regularly referenced to ensure the actions of divisions are consistent with it. A system of empowerment is in place to push responsibility down to lower levels and free up senior management for strategic planning purposes.

- **Cost Control**
  A detailed cost reduction mechanism is in place, targeting five separate areas for improvement: (i) discretionary fixed costs; (ii) improved equipment/labour/ materials productivities; (iii) rationalisation of operations; (iv) value engineering at the design stage; and (v) value analysis to correct faults at plant or product level. All expenditure proposals are evaluated in detail to ensure that returns exceed plan.

- **Analysis**
  Cross-site statistics relating to production levels, overtime and accidents are collected, disseminated and widely referenced, despite observed differences in technological complexity between sites. Post-audits are conducted for projects involving outlays of more than $20 000.

Figure C8.5: Bolton Extractive — Benchmarking Outcomes

- **Accounting Organisation**
There is a relatively small head office team of eight, but it carries out all the detailed group-wide analysis. All of the location-based analysis and reporting is conducted on-site through small teams of accountants comprising three to five people. The accountants are close to the mineral workings and wear safety gear at all times to ensure their ready availability for call out.

- **Accounting Systems**
A sophisticated executive information system (EIS) is in place, allowing the MD to access the accounting systems directly and retrieve key financial indicators and trends of key results. The computer system security is widely perceived to be a joke because of the ease of guessing IDs, or the total absence of passwords, which allows almost unconstrained access to different sectors, including payroll.

- **Reporting**
A profusion of pretty, glossy reports is prepared, but often for nobody in particular. Many routine reports have no apparent target audience and little impact on decision-making. Detailed reporting follows traditional variance analysis, even where this is inappropriate or irrelevant because of the nature of the fluctuations involved. Monthly variance to plan assumes monolithic proportions, with all outside budget items exceeding $1000 investigated.

- **Planning**
An annual budget with monthly targets is prepared. The participatory budget setting system is widely respected throughout the organisation. There is strict control of capital budgets to 'encourage' expenses through the operating budget. Teamworking initiated in order to conform to TQM cell requirements.

- **Cost Control**
Focus on the control of process costs and operations maintenance costs. Strict delineation of the maintenance cycle to allow work to be performed prior to failure, with consequential control of preventive/corrective/breakdown maintenance costs. Capital/Expense categorisation tightly controlled in order to minimise both income and the tax bill and to reduce the likelihood of unwelcome media attention.

- **Analysis**
No assessment of the risk attached to different projects, but all projects involving an initial outlay of greater than $250 000 are post-audited internally after one year's duration. Vague standards for performance measurement in the maintenance function make it a problem area.

Figure C8.6: Burwell Minerals — Benchmarking Outcomes

CASE 9: EASTON PRINTING SERVICES

This case concerns the development of a strategic direction for a family company which simultaneously faces problems of succession. It provides an opportunity for identifying the strengths and weaknesses of the firm's current position, diversification opportunities and threats to its long-term survival.

Stephen Easton founded his printing company over 30 years ago and has proudly maintained the family ownership since. Now he is in ill health and knows that he must soon release the reins of the company he so cherishes. Worse, none of his three children shows the slightest interest in involvement in the business so that it seems his successor must be an 'outsider'. He recognises that the problem is of his own making because his autocratic control, decision-making without consultation and refusal to take on debt to fund the growth of the company have not endeared him to senior management.

Nevertheless, the workforce idolises him and most are on first name terms. Many have been with him for over 20 years and have seen the business grow to the largest in the North West of England. Their loyalty is not in question, neither is the technical competence of senior management, but they have rarely had the opportunity to 'manage' in any real sense.

The isolation of a Cumbria-based enterprise has always aided the growth of the company because competition from the South has been negligible. Now the situation is reversed because continued growth and diversification are largely dependent upon increased penetration of the bigger markets in South East England and East Anglia.

Stephen is well aware of the challenges and opportunities currently facing the company (e.g the environmental edge possible with recycling and diversification into computer software) and of likely threats to its stability (e.g. the spread of street corner 'cowboy' franchisees, wayward internal communications, the need to import expensive new technology to stay competitive and worse, the possibility of government intervention if market share is perceived to be too great).

Lately he has begun to pay more attention to internal efficiency and improving the bottom line even if sales growth proves impossible. He has focused on four key areas of internal efficiency:

1. **Process improvement** — by balancing cost and quality in determining optimum machine speed; by eliminating non-productive downtime.

2. **Plant layout** — by seeking a more efficient design.

3. **Information systems** — by computerising the primitive manual operations control for costing and scheduling so that quotations can be nearer the mark both on cost and time.

105

4. **Client education** — by establishing a 'quality' goal which makes the inferior product and service of competitors unsatisfactory.

Performance appraisal is currently undertaken with the help of a set of financial and non-financial indicators detailed below:

Financials	Non-Financials
1. Profitability (Return on Assets)	1. Customer Complaints (registered and resolved)
2. Sales revenue	2. Spoilage rates
3. Gross Margins	3. % Successful quotations
4. Gearing	4. Direct labour productivity
5. Days debtors outstanding	5. % Cost variation (actual v quotation)

Despite the availability of existing control data Stephen feels that much of the management effort is misdirected and that new initiatives are essential if meaningful improvements are to be achieved.

You are required to identify alternative strategies for the future direction of Easton which capitalise on priority improvement opportunities while reducing its vulnerability to outside influences. Your report should include an outline strategy for the implementation of new initiatives.

Chapter 5

Product and Customer Profitability

5.1 INTRODUCTION

A number of recent surveys have suggested that manufacturers are unaware of the relative profitability attributable to individual products and customers because they have unreliable information relating to the costs of manufacturing and distributing their product.

The implication is that the existing information base makes cost control difficult and decisions on pricing and mix unsound. Chapter 3 has already demonstrated the usefulness of marketing tools (e.g. SWOT, PLC and BCG) in the analysis of the product portfolio and associated profits. The simple linear analysis of Chapter 1, employed in *Case 1: Cambridge Business Conferences*, may be extended to facilitate a discussion of optimum product mix and relative profitability.

5.2 PRODUCT MIX

The simple two-dimensional graphical format of break-even analysis can be adapted to solve product mix problems based on a maximum of two products, but with no limit on the number of resource constraints. Three product problems are also a possibility, except that the necessary three-dimensional diagram can become complex; any more products than this demand a SIMPLEX solution, preferably employing computer software developed specifically for the purpose. All problems can (and should) be solved by computer to ensure the accuracy of solutions. The great benefit provided by a diagram, where this is feasible (even in sketch form), is the indication of the sensitivity of the chosen solution and of how robust the optimum is to changing circumstances. There are many simple PC-based programs to provide SIMPLEX solutions and some spreadsheet packages (e.g. EXCEL's 'Solver' function) will solve small problems. The algorithms all work in a similar manner:

- constraints are specified as inequalities — either maxima which must not be exceeded or minima which must not be violated;

- the simultaneous consideration of all constraints provides a 'feasible region' — an area including all possible production combinations;

- the production-possibility boundary of this region (upper bound for maximisation problems, lower bound for minimisation problems) will contain the 'corner points', that subset of product mix combinations which contains the optimum;

- a check of resource use will reveal those constraints which are binding (and where the purchase of additional capacity would increase profits/reduce costs) and those where slack already exists;

- a sensitivity analysis will show how robust the optimum solution is by revealing by how much costs and prices must change before we shift from one corner point to another.

The linear programming method can cope with very large and complex problems once the initial matrix of constraints has been specified. It can optimise through maximising profits or through minimising costs. In graphical terms the two procedures are similar. In the maximisation problem the objective function is positioned as far from the origin as possible, at the limit of the upper bounds, while in the minimisation problem the constraints represent *lower bounds* and the objective function must be brought *inwards* to finish as *close* to the origin as possible. *Minicase B: Bakewise* provides a worked solution to a maximisation problem focusing on bottleneck aspects of resource capacity. *Case 11: Esau Creek Winery* and *Case 12: Subiaco Technology* provide opportunities to apply the linear programming technique to practical multi-product scenarios, involving both financial and non-financial constraints, in, respectively, minimisation and maximisation situations.

5.3 ACTIVITY-BASED COSTING

While wishing to avoid the worst-case scenario of applying rigid rules for the allocation of overhead costs to product, which results in profitable products being eliminated from the mix and unprofitable products remaining undercosted, we do need some assignment of overheads to products in order to have a complete picture of cost occurrence. Direct material and direct labour costs can easily be traced to jobs and processes, but manufacturing overhead may bear no obvious relationship to individual units of product. Assignments of overhead made through a volume-based activity base (or cost driver), attempt to ensure that products which cause large amounts of overhead costs correspond with those which require large amounts of the cost driver. Such an ideal ignores any strategic considerations and is based on a 'right' or 'fairest' way of doing things, contrary to that advocated by Hiromoto (1988). In practice many different overhead allocation bases are possible, usually non-financially based on numbers, areas, volumes, or hours.

Traditional absorption costing methods attribute production overheads to units of output without attempting to allocate administration, selling or distribution overheads. Many activities are not directly related to production volume (e.g. ordering, delivery, transportation, equipment set-up, machining and administration). These require non-volume based cost drivers if costs are to be appropriately traced and provide the motivation for the development of activity based costing (ABC) systems.

Product and Customer Profitability

ABC has been promoted by Johnson (1988), Kaplan (1988) and Cooper (1988), among others, as a means of improving the quality of management accounting information when traditional methods of allocating overhead costs might be misleading to the users of product cost information. ABC recognises that many significant overheads are related to activities which are independent of volume and identifies those cost drivers which consume resources to determine process and product costs. The fundamentals of ABC can be illustrated by reference to the one mental arithmetic problem all students need to master — how to average a restaurant bill while maintaining equity among the participants! Figure 12 illustrates the magnitude of the problem.

	Management Accountant's Luncheon				
	Starter (£)	Main Course (£)	Dessert (£)	Drinks (£)	Total (£)
Tom	10	15	7	4	36
Robert	0	12	8	8	28
Robin	15	12	0	14	41
Bill	14	14	9	13	50
Anthony	21	17	16	11	65
Total	£60	£70	£40	£50	£220
Mean	£12	£14	£8	£10	£44

Figure 12: Four Activities and Five Products

Averaging across both individuals and courses highlights how some individuals (products) are undercosted while there are significant differences in the consumption of resources by different courses (activities). Averages smooth out the very variations which we must recognise if we are to cost products properly and be aware of the differing demands they make on various activities.

Kaplan (1990) suggests that design, engineering, servicing, production, distribution, marketing and after-sales service are all relevant activities for product costing. Only excess capacity costs and R & D costs are ignored on the grounds that their inclusion would distort product costs. Many overheads (e.g. purchasing, scheduling and set-up costs) typically classified as fixed costs under a traditional system are treated as variable, responding to activity based changes.

Rather than taking the traditional approach of allocating overhead costs to production departments and then to product lines via volume-based overhead rates, ABC introduces intermediary cost pools. The revised system is still a two-stage one but ABC charges overhead costs to activity-based cost pools and onto product lines via rates based on cost drivers. Figure 13 illustrates the stages.

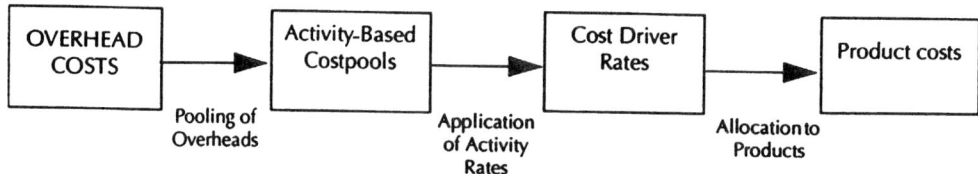

Figure 13: Activity Based Costing of Products

The three fundamental characteristics are therefore:

1. the choice of cost pools — based on the identification of the major activities which cause overhead cost (e.g. maintenance, purchasing, supply, processing);

2. the allocation of overhead costs to the cost pools — based on some indication of the significance of each major activity in the incurring of overhead costs;

3. the choice of cost driver for each activity based cost pool — which will require judgement regarding the homogeneity of the activity and the representativeness of the cost drivers.

In the US and Australia, for example, long distances make physical distribution costs a major factor of internal operations, impacting significantly on performance measurement. The application of ABC principles in tracking marketing costs to products, with the adoption of a number of possible cost drivers for each sphere of activity, should have serious consequences for costing and pricing.

A survey of organisations with respect to the benefits they expect to achieve from implementing ABC in their operations reveals five key areas:

- different ranking of product costings reflecting a correction of the benefits previously accruing to low-volume products;

- an improved awareness of the activities which are driving overhead costs so that improved cost control may result

- the use of non-financial indicators to measure cost drivers provides measures of performance of greater credibility;

- the identification of non-value adding activities;

- a new perspective for the examination of cost behaviour and the subsequent cost analysis required in planning and budgeting.

On the downside, despite its apparent sophistication an ABC system is still essentially an 'historic cost' system. Far from eliminating arbitrary overhead cost allocation, an ABC system may actually increase the number of such apportionments which we undertake. Decision rules for the pooling of common overheads into separate cost pools and common cost drivers into separate activities must be determined. A single cost driver may not be entirely representative in explaining the cost behaviour of a whole cost pool. A combination of cost drivers may provide a better means of explaining cost behaviour.

The alternative Hiromoto approach is to adopt a strategic focus in the choice of cost drivers. By choosing drivers which are consistent with strategic goals, rather than 'correct' in some sense, we can deliberately penalise certain parts of the production process whose operation is not congruent with corporate goals.

To justify the sophistication and potential complexity of ABC, efficient data collection systems are essential. Accurate, speedy and reliable measurement of the non-financials employed as cost drivers must be implemented across the whole system. Similar problems to those that exist with the financials under traditional cost systems will be present with regard to timeliness and opportunities for data manipulation. Data collection costs cannot be underestimated.

The following non-financial measures give an indication of activity costs and may assist in the choice of activity drivers.

Area	Measure
quantity of raw material inputs	actual v target number
equipment productivity	actual v standard units
maintenance efforts	number of production units lost through maintenance
	number of production units lost through failure
	number of failures prior to schedule
overtime costs	overtime hours/total hours
product complexity	number of component parts
quantity of output	actual v target completion
product obsolescence	% shrinkage
employees	% staff turnover
employee productivity	direct labour hours per unit
customer focus	% service calls; % claims

5.4 IMPLEMENTING ABC

The motives for pursuing an ABC implementation, or at least of investigating its feasibility, must be established at the outset. Most commonly these will be:

•   to improve product costing where a belief exists that existing methods under-cost some products and overcost others, or

- to identify non-value adding activities in the production process which might be a suitable focus for attention or elimination.

In practice, the former is the most quoted goal, even though the latter may be more appropriate. This is especially so for firms which are highly labour intensive and which do not have a great diversity of products in their range — here allocation of overhead based on direct labour hours may already function efficiently.

Direct costs, like materials and direct labour, are easily assigned directly to products. Some indirect costs, particularly those selling costs which are product specific (e.g. advertising), may also be directly assigned to the product. The remaining indirect costs are those which are problematic and provide the focus for ABC, with resource costs indirectly assigned to the cost object via cost pools and activity drivers. A number of distinct stages in the ABC implementation exist:

- **Staff Training** — the cooperation of the workforce members is critical to the successful implementation of ABC. They are closest to the process and most aware of its nuances. Staff training should be, as far as possible, jargon free, and create an awareness of the purpose of ABC. It should be non-threatening in nature, stressing that increased efficiencies resulting from a successful implementation will mean rewards not retrenchments. The need for the cooperation of staff in a concerted team effort, for mutual benefit, must be emphasised throughout the training activity.

- **Process Specification** — informal but structured interviews with key members of personnel will identify the different stages of the production process, the commitment of resources to each, processing times and bottlenecks. The interviews will yield a list of transactions which may, or may not, be defined as 'activities' at a subsequent stage, but in any case provide a feel for the scope of the process in its entirety.

- **Activity Definition** — the problem must be kept manageable at this stage, despite the possibility of being overwhelmed with data, much of it in need of codification. The listed transactions must be rationalised in order to aggregate those in similar categories and eliminate those deemed immaterial. The resultant cost pools will likely have a number of different events, or drivers, associated with their incurrence.

- **Activity Driver Selection** — a single driver covering all of the transactions grouped together in an 'activity' probably does not exist. Multiple driver models could be developed if the data were available, but cost benefit analysis has not shown these to be desirable. The inter-correlation of potential activity drivers will probably be so strong as to suggest that it really does not matter which one is selected. This argument might be employed to avoid the costly collection of data items not otherwise monitored or easily accessible.

- **Costing** — a single representative activity driver can be used to assign costs from the activity pools to the cost objects. If, for example, the number of engineering set-ups has been identified as a driver of process costs and the total set-up cost is £40 000 for a company producing four products (A, B, C, D) then the number of set-ups per product can be used to assign these costs. If product A requires 2 set-ups; B, 4 set-ups; C, 24 and D, 10, then the average cost per set-up of 40 000/40 = £1000, a misleading figure, which does not imply the different demands of the set-up resource made by the different products. However, total set-up costs can be distributed to product groups in proportion to use, i.e. A: £2000; B: £4000; C:£24 000 and D: £10 000 and then assigned to individual units of product in proportion to the total level of output. Thus if 20 000 units of A were being produced each would attract 10 pence of costs attributable to set-ups. This procedure can then be repeated for all material activities. The existing literature suggests that the likely outcome will be a demonstration of costing errors of varying degrees — notably the undercosting of low-volume products and the overcosting of high-volume products.

The onerous nature of this re-costing exercise should not be underestimated and may make it advisable to concentrate on the most important products in the range. Thus for a 100 product firm a focus, at least initially, on the most prominent 20 products, say, could yield the outcomes desired. The question of how to use the revised costings resulting from the ABC implementation is more problematic. It may show that some products are unprofitable at current price levels, so that a financial analysis suggests that they should be dropped from the product mix. Such a decision should not be made without reference to inter-product implications and to non-financial considerations concerning the overall impact of the product concerned.

The emergence of ABC has undoubtedly forced management accountants to reappraise their costing systems and to identify improvement opportunities. Clear advantages have been demonstrated in particular working environments, notably in multi-product organisations. *Case 15: Pitcairn Electronics* provides such an example. However, equally clear doubts have been expressed about the costs of changing to an ABC system, especially when there have been few conclusive studies suggesting that ABC generates bottom line improvements in profitability.

5.5 ACTIVITY-BASED MANAGEMENT

The evidence suggests that it will be impossible to eliminate arbitrary allocations of overhead totally, even under an ABC system, so we must look beyond product costing to a more appropriate emphasis on process management. ABC may be a useful starting point, but we are management accountants not just cost accountants.

The key to the extension of ABC into ABM is a wider appreciation of the concept of 'drivers'. We can no longer focus on cost drivers alone but must investigate the manner in which resources are consumed in non-dollar areas. Customers have perceived needs in at least four areas, all of which require simultaneous satisfaction:

- lower costs
- higher quality
- faster response times
- greater innovation.

Management information systems must therefore encompass drivers across each of the areas of Figure 14, focusing on all without giving undue emphasis to any one. In addition to costs we are concerned with quality/time/innovation, coincidentally the three elements of Value Added Management (VAM) detailed in Figure 15.

COST	cost behaviour
QUALITY	factors inhibiting performance
TIME	bottlenecks and inertia
INNOVATION	new product flexibility

Figure 14: The Drivers of Activity-Based Management

	METHOD	OBJECTIVES
QUALITY	Total Quality Control (TQC)	Zero defects; no scrap or rework
TIME	Just-in-Time (JIT)	Reduced lead times, job queues and work-in-progress
INNOVATION	Total Employee Involvement (TEI)	Creative thinking; new ideas from the shop floor

Figure 15: Aspects of Value Added Management (VAM)

The success, or otherwise, of an activity based management system will largely be determined by the depth and efficiency of its non-financial database. Extensive data collection of non-financial indicators will be necessary in each of the cost/quality/time/innovation areas.

Three common issues of concern will exist across each of the four strands:

• considerable demands on the time of those involved, necessitating widespread cooperation and total organisational involvement;

• commitment to change must come from the top, especially if a non-receptive corporate culture must be overcome in the process;

• suitable documentation and data will likely not exist, so that key drivers and non-financial indicators need to be determined and measured.

Let us consider each of the three new elements in turn, in each case referencing appropriate activity drivers. Smith (1990), referred to in Chapter 3, surveys the range of NFIs in common use. This approach can be adapted to give an indication of the type of non-financials that would be useful in each area.

QUALITY

The pursuit of quality demands that we identify all non-value adding waste in the manufacturing process, and implement procedures to eliminate, or at least reduce, such activities. This implies better production planning to limit overproduction and excessive inventory, and improved product and plant design to eliminate wasteful movement and handling. Sub-standard items will be eliminated and a changed attitude reinforced which is customer focused and adopts 'the next person on the production line is my customer' approach.

The cost of quality is a potentially important component of management accounting systems which may facilitate the implementation of total quality management. The classification of quality costs is useful in order to allow a closer examination of the drivers of quality. The costs of *prevention, appraisal* and *failure* are all aspects of the cost of quality.

Prevention Costs include the costs of plant, product and process planning, preventive maintenance, training and the implementation of statistical process control systems. *Appraisal Costs* include the costs of inspection and testing of both incoming and outgoing materials, and the cost of maintaining and administering appraisal systems and equipment. *Failure Costs* include, at the internal level, costs of scrap, rework, redesign and safety stocks necessary to provide a buffer against such failure, and at the external level, the cost of repairs, customer returns, warranty claims, investigations and losses associated with customers, goodwill and reputation. Analysis of the costs of external failure is increasingly becoming the focus of attention in this area, reflecting the renewed customer orientation of management accounting. The following measures should prove useful in the analysis of particular aspects of quality:

Area	Measure
quality of purchased components	zero defects
equipment failure	downtime/total time
maintenance effort	breakdown maintenance/total maintenance
waste	% defects; % scrap; % rework
quality of output	% yield
safety	serious industrial injury rate
reliability	% warranty claims
quality commitment	% dependence on post-inspection % conformance to quality standards
employee morale	% absenteeism
leadership impact	% cancelled meetings
customer awareness	% repeat orders; number of complaints

TIME

The amount of process time is often less than 10 per cent of total manufacturing leadtime for many organisations. The other 90 per cent is associated with the addition of costs but not value. Just-in-Time (JIT) procedures are concerned with increasing throughput and reducing leadtimes by:

- reducing inventory, through closer supplier relationships;

- implementing shorter set-ups and minimal batch sizes;

- eliminating wasteful inspecting, checking, monitoring and progress chasing;

- minimising the leadtime between innovation and the marketing of the finished product.

We might anticipate that the following non-financial measures would prove useful in the analysis of time-related factors:

Area	Measure
equipment failure	time between failures
maintenance effort	time spent on repeat work
throughput	processing time/total time per unit
production flexibility	set-up time
availability	% stockouts
labour effectiveness	standard hours achieved/total hours worked
customer impact	number of overdue deliveries mean delivery delay

Surveys of manufacturing executives of large successful companies in Europe, the US and Japan consistently rank three time-based characteristics among their top five competitive priorities:

- dependable delivery

- fast delivery

- rapid design changes.

A time-based focus has a number of positive implications for the management accountant in designing improved management information systems which:

- ensure that decision making is linked to an appropriate time horizon by the matching of short-run/long-run costs with decisions with corresponding time implications;

116

Product and Customer Profitability

- monitor customer feedback regarding the reliability of delivery and develop new indicators to measure delivery and distribution performance;

- focus on product cycle time and use of throughput time as a measure of performance;

- focus on bottlenecks in the production/service process with a more appropriate emphasis on activities which improve bottlenecks.

A focus on product cycle time, throughput time, bottlenecks and delivery reliability highlights the need for new measures of operating performance and better indicators of delivery performance and the degree of operations' interdependence.

One of the major benefits of the focus on activity based relationships has therefore been the development of new non-financial measures. These may have been employed as cost drivers in activity-based costing but have a potentially wider application when they also impact on the quality/time/innovation dimensions.

The use of some measure of set-ups provides a useful illustration. Set-up times as a cost driver will inevitably penalise small batches and encourage larger batches. While set-up cost can be reduced through shorter set-up times it can be more easily lowered by fewer set-ups, larger batches and consequently higher inventory levels. Reducing set-up times to make more set-ups possible provides a flexibility facilitating the meeting of customer requirements. But more product lines and smaller batches mean more non-productive set-up time. The congruence of production objectives and measurement implications must be ensured. Set-up times tend to ignore the question of dependence, both in terms of the way jobs are sequenced and backlogs generated, and in the way that set-up is a variable subject to the impact of special causes (e.g. unpredictable external factors) and common causes (e.g. random fluctuations within otherwise stable systems).

Just as the focus on the efficiency of machines may not be particularly useful in a sequence of operations, set-up times may not always be a useful focus. Increasing the efficiency of non-bottleneck operations incurs expense but also creates spare capacity and unnecessary units of production. Similarly the consequences of a set-up on a bottleneck operation, with the generation of idle time in a constraining activity, will far outweigh that on a non-bottleneck activity.

Recognition of the existence of a bottleneck where demand exceeds supply for a resource, and the focus is on processing time, leads naturally to a consideration of throughput, and throughput accounting. Throughput accounting represents a movement away from ABC, since it is not concerned with overhead costs, and represents a movement towards ABM, the time taken to generate profits and the rate at which raw materials are turned into sales. It identifies selling price, sales volume and material cost as the three key variables determining profitability and focuses on product flow, by treating overheads and labour costs as fixed in the short term. As with the linear programming approach to the solution of product mix problems, throughput focuses on scarce resources and the relative contribution per unit of such resources for each product. As a result a single bottleneck activity will usually become the focus of attention. Other binding constraints will exist, but these will only become bottlenecks, in the future, as a result of successful investment in overcoming prior bottlenecks. A number of consequences of throughput focus quickly become apparent:

- it is pointless investing resources in order to increase the efficiency of non-bottleneck resources. This will not improve throughput until the bottleneck activity has first been attacked;

- queues will develop in front of bottlenecks which increase production leadtime. Such inventory does however provide an essential buffer to eliminate the possibility of idle time in the bottlenecks;

- throughput will reduce inventory and work-in-process making efficient JIT procedures and reliable supplier relationships essential;

- lower inventory will mean fewer overheads available for carrying forward under absorption costing and a likely negative impact on short-term profits.

Let us consider a simple numerical example, *Minicase B: Bakewise Holdings*.

Bakewise Holdings produces two varieties of catering size pie — meat (X) and vegetarian (Y). Each type of pie undergoes six separate operations in the production process, using the same equipment resources but requiring different amounts of time in each resource. Resource capacity, material costs, selling price and operating time are all detailed below. These figures allow the calculation of relative contribution per unit for each of the products.

	Operations Time (Hours per unit)						Total (hours)
Products	1	2	3	4	5	6	
X	0.10	0.30	0.15	0.20	0.40	0.10	1.25
Y	0.20	0.15	0.30	0.25	0.30	0.20	1.40
Capacity	6500	6000	9600	8000	9600	7000	

	Material Cost ($£$)	Labour Cost ($£$/hr)	Selling Price ($£$)	Direct Costs (Material & Labour)	Contribution ($£$/unit)
Products					
X	5	12	25	20	5.00
Y	5	12	25	21.80	3.20

A linear programming problem for the determination of optimum product mix of the two pies will maximise contribution (π) subject to the operating constraints.

Product and Customer Profitability

Objective Function: $\pi = 5X + 3.20Y$

Constraints

1.	$0.10X + 0.20Y$	$\leqslant 6500$
2.	$0.30X + 0.15Y$	$\leqslant 6000$
3.	$0.15X + 0.30Y$	$\leqslant 9600$
4.	$0.20X + 0.25Y$	$\leqslant 8000$
5.	$0.40X + 0.30Y$	$\leqslant 9600$
6.	$0.10X + 0.20Y$	$\leqslant 7000$

With non-negativity constraints of $X \leqslant 0$ and $Y \leqslant 0$ the above matrix yields only two binding constraints (operations 2 and 5) and three potential optimum combinations as corner points on the feasible region:

A: where $X = 0$ and $Y = 32\,000$
B: where $X = 12\,000$ and $Y = 16\,000$
C: where $X = 20\,000$ and $Y = 0$

Examination of the objective function reveals the total contribution from the three alternatives to be:

A: £102 400
B: £111 200
C: £100 000

So the L-P solution suggests that the optimum product-mix is $X = 12\,000$ and $Y = 16\,000$; total production of 28 000 units per time period.

A closer inspection of the maximum possible throughput of product for the sequence of operation reveals:

	Operations					
Product	**1**	**2**	**3**	**4**	**5**	**6**
X	65 000	20 000	64 000	40 000	24 000	70 000
Y	32 000	40 000	32 000	32 000	32 000	35 000

Only operations 2 and 5 are used to capacity, providing an effective constraint on production. Considerable excess capacity exists in each of the remaining operations. Operation 2 is the production bottleneck, restricting the throughput of product X to the marketplace to a maximum of 20 000 units per period.

Although product X has a superior contribution to product Y, and a combination of X and Y yields a greater contribution per batch than producing Y alone, it is possible to bring more of product Y to the marketplace than of X and Y together. Sales revenue would be optimised by producing/selling 32 000 units of Y (yielding

£800 000) rather than the optimum X, Y combination (revenue of £700 000). We can process twice as many units of Y (40 000) through the bottleneck operation 2 compared to X (20 000). But the constraints in successive operations restrict the output per period to only 32 000. A throughput approach would justify a switch to product Y if the faster processing allowed more units to be marketed and sold, despite the lower contribution per unit. The approach is, therefore, more cash than profit based, seeking to focus on the rate at which the product contributes money.

Linear programming yields a static solution based on several inflexible assumptions. It ignores set-up times between operations, variation in the time taken to complete operations and the intricacies of job scheduling. Scheduling complexities may lead to substantial operating delays, especially where we have more than two products relying on the same equipment resources and competing for processing time. Each batch (32 000 of Y) or (16 000 of Y with 12 000 of X) will take a total of 9600 hours to process but delays will occur at operations 2 and 5, the effective constraints on production. The mixed product, within the batch, can be brought to the market quicker through an X followed by Y sequence (1.65 hours) compared to 1.7 hours for two of product Y, as illustrated by Figure 16.

The mixed product (X,Y) system has material queuing in front of the binding constraints (operations 2 and 5) whereas the single product (Y,Y) system has idle time in the bottleneck resource (operation 2).

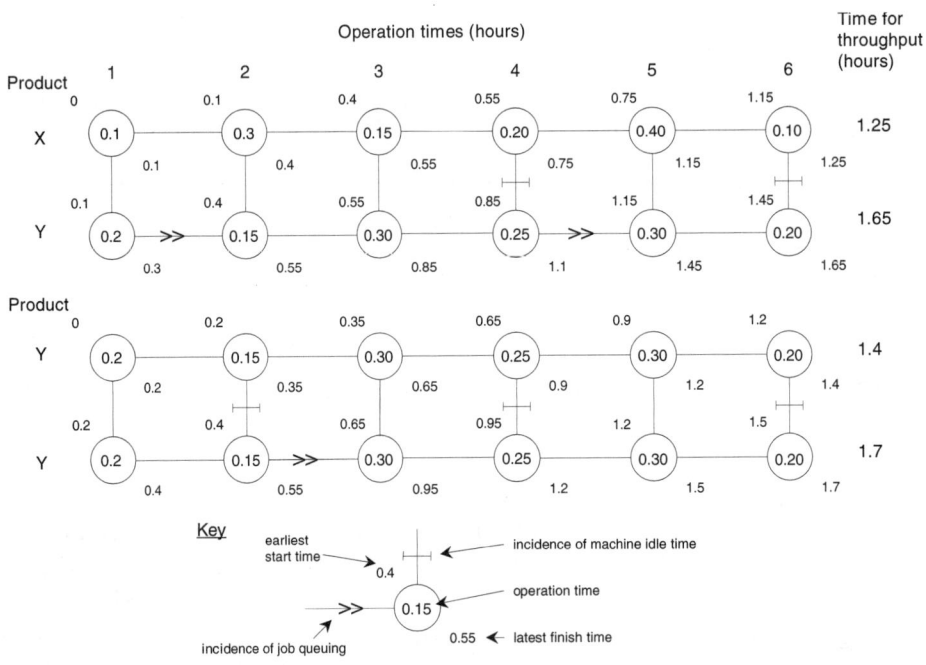

Figure 16: Alternative Product Scheduling Systems

Product and Customer Profitability

If we had treated the production of products X and Y as multiple events, instances of fluctuation in operating time might have averaged out. But where, as here, one event cannot take place until the completion of another, the fluctuations will accumulate. With product queuing for machine availability, and enforced machine idle time, inventory will increase and throughput will be reduced. Even with a balanced system, random fluctuations will cause the variation of operating time to be determined by the maximum variation of the preceding operations. Interdependence will continue to increase inventory levels and reduce throughput unless we:

- reduce the level of variation applicable to particular operations, or

- create idle time by stopping that non-bottleneck part of the line in which the inventory build-up is occurring, to allow the bottleneck activities to catch up.

Knowledge of the process and the statistical implications of operation dependencies is essential if bottlenecks are to be managed effectively. *Case 10: Willingham Furniture* illustrates the problems arising from the lack of clearly defined goals when associated with inappropriate accounting information and control systems, and inadequate capacity planning.

INNOVATION

The creative powers of the workforce must be harnessed in order to encourage innovation at all levels. Total Employee Involvement (TEI) encourages the creative involvement of the workforce by developing responsible attitudes and ensuring that ideas from the shop floor are listened to and wherever possible acted upon. By making the best use of the experience and intellect of those closest to the work processes innovative solutions may be developed in identified problem areas.

Innovation may embrace pure and applied research, developmental applications, new product development, operational and process development and cost reduction techniques. Innovation is essential to the long-term survival of an enterprise and its maintenance of market share and competitive advantage. The uncertainty associated with innovation may make traditional management accounting systems inappropriate for a number of reasons.

The focus on short-term financial performance will have an adverse effect on products or processes at the early stages of their life cycle, while measurement indicators suitable for mature products and processes may emphasise cost minimisation to an unsuitable extent. Similarly, the assessment of managerial performance on the basis of success in implementing cost reduction strategies may have negative consequences on managers' creativity and innovation. The special requirements of innovation necessitate the development of a new range of NFIs (see page 122).

Recognition of the importance of non-financial indicators in their own right, and in complementing financial indicators, is essential if a relevant and integrated management accounting information system is to be developed. *Case 13: Fibro Ltd* provides an example illustrating the relative importance of NFIs in a decision-support system.

Area	Measure
the ability to introduce new products	% product obsolescence number of new products launched number of patents secured time to launch new products
flexibility to accommodate change	number of new processes implemented number of new process modifications
reputation for innovation	media recognition for leadership expert assessment of competence demonstrable competitive advantage

The overlapping of the requirements and corresponding measures of cost/quality/ time/innovation is inevitable as instanced by the development of new accounting measures to monitor the effectiveness of companies in bringing new products to the market promptly. New product strategies must focus on the cost of leadtimes in bringing new product concepts to the market, in conjunction with the time taken to recover R & D and marketing expenditures from the projected sales of a quality product.

5.6 CUSTOMER PROFITABILITY ANALYSIS

Many recent innovations in management accounting have emphasised the need to remain competitive by focusing on customer requirements. Such developments may have overlooked the profitability requirement in that customers should also satisfy the strategic needs of the supplier. Customer profitability analysis (CPA) is a useful tool for the evaluation of the portfolio of customer profiles.

A detailed analysis of customers and differential costs of providing the service may be justified, provided that the cost of obtaining and maintaining information is not excessive and the information obtained is useful for making strategic decisions.

Analysis of the revenue streams generated by customers, relative to their service costs, may lead to some customers being eliminated from the business. The problem is a similar one to that dealt with in the preceding section on product mix, except that rather than product profitability and product mix, we are interested in customer profitability and customer mix.

Kaplan (1992) discusses three types of customer that might be retained despite the absence of current profits:

1. new and growing customers, who promise profitable business in the future and who may facilitate the penetration of lucrative new markets;

2. customers providing qualitative rather than financial benefits (e.g. those at the leading edge of technological or marketing developments);

3. customers with a reputation and status in the field, where an association would increase customer credibility.

In each instance the potential strategic advantage of a trading relationship must be balanced against the quantifiable future benefits and the inherent risks of failure.

We must avoid any attempt to apportion total costs over all customer groups, where the effects of so doing would cause us to drop a customer and respread costs over the remaining customers. We could find ourselves in the position of continuing to drop customers and respread costs until no customers remain, in the same manner as that discussed by Robin Cooper (1985) in his classic 'Camelback Communications' case study on product profitability.

A diverse customer base will consume resources and current management accounting practice will usually be to classify customer-related costs as period expenses. Even ABC systems will rarely analyse cost drivers in these areas, despite the likelihood of their not being volume dependent. The analysis of non-value adding customer-related expenses might be approached by comparing customer types and expense types. We wish to identify customer-specific expenses and to do so we must identify those which are necessarily linked to particular markets or particular distribution channels. We may not be able to avoid these by eliminating a particular customer.

Customer-driven activities and associated expenses can conveniently be examined in some detail under a number of expense categories, following an approach originally suggested by Howell and Soucy (1990):

- **Purchasing patterns**
  cost of volume discounts
  size of agents' commissions
  cost of field service to maintain products distributed by customers
  cost of sales support

- **Delivery policy**
  distribution expenses
  shipping frequencies
  freight fleet requirements

- **Accounting procedures**
  sales credits
  settlement discount costs
  debtor collection support
  order processing

- **Inventory carrying**
  inventory support
  distribution support
  holding requirements

Relative Profitability

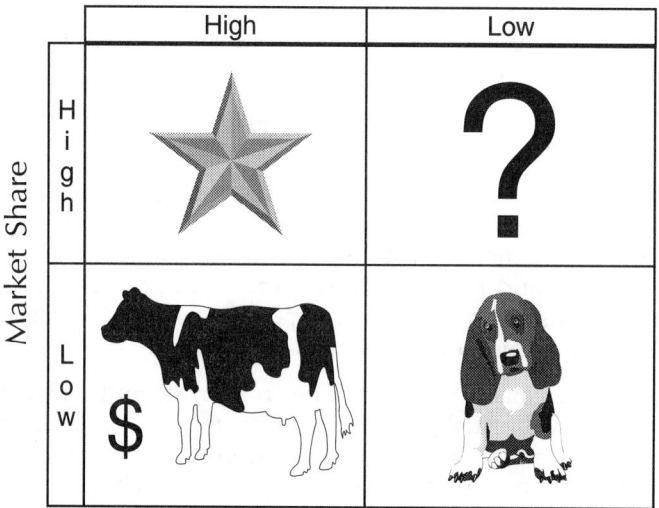

Figure 17: Customer Portfolio Matrix

Whereas product profitability analysis emphasises the impact of undercosted products resulting from low volumes, high wastage and high levels of rework, customer profitability analysis wishes to pinpoint low volume/low margin customers who consume more than proportionate time and expense in servicing orders. We wish to identify the problem customers and eliminate or modify the service provided to the unprofitable ones. Conventional accounting methods will rarely reveal such differences, but a fundamental analysis of customers will provide the information base to support strategic decisions relating to the customer base. The BCG Portfolio Matrix approach (described in detail in Chapter 4) can be adapted to great effect in order to highlight customer differences. Figure 17 illustrates the grid that might be employed in order to plot both relative profitability and relative customer importance together.

Case 14: Derrick's Confectionery provides the opportunity of applying customer profitability analysis in a realistic scenario.

REFERENCES

Bhimani A and Pigott D, 'Implementing ABC: A case study of organisational and behavioural consequences', *Management Accounting Research*, Vol 3,1992, pp 119–132

Cooper R, 'Camelback Communications Inc', *HBS Case Services*, Harvard Business School, Boston, Mass, 1985

Product and Customer Profitability

Cooper R, 'Does your Company need a New Cost System?', *Journal of Cost Management*, Spring 1987, pp 45–9

Cooper R, 'The Rise of Activity Based Costing—Part One: What is an Activity-Based Cost System?', *Journal of Cost Management*, Summer 1988, pp 45–54

Coughlan P and Darlington J, 'As Fast as the Slowest Operation: The Theory of Constraints', *Management Accounting* (UK), June 1993, pp 14–17

Darlington J, Innes J, Mitchell F and Woodward J. (1992), 'Throughput Accounting: The Garret Automotive Experience', *Management Accounting* (UK), 1992, pp 32–38

Galloway D and Waldron D, 'Throughput Accounting: The Need for a New Language in Manufacturing', *Management Accounting* (UK), November 1988, pp 34–5

Gietzmann M, 'Implementation issues associated with the construction of an activity-based costing system in an engineering components manufacturer', *Management Accounting Research*, Vol 2, 1991, pp 189–199

Goldratt E M and Cox J, *The Goal : A Process of Ongoing Improvement*, Gower Publishing, Aldershot, 1989.

Hiromoto T, 'Another Hidden Edge: Japanese Management Accounting', *Harvard Business Review*, July–August 1988, pp 22–26

Howell R A and Soucy S R, 'Customer Profitability : As Critical as Product Profitability', *Management Accounting*, September 1990, pp 26–35

Kaplan R S, 'Measuring Manufacturing Performance : A New Challenge for Managerial Accounting Research', *The Accounting Review*, Vol 58, 1983 pp 20–4

Kaplan R S, 'One Cost System Isn't Enough', *Harvard Business Review*, January–February 1988, pp 61–66

Kaplan R S, 'The Four-Stage Model of Cost Systems Design', *Management Accounting*, February 1990, pp 22–25

Kaplan R S, 'In Defence of Activity-Based Cost Management', *Management Accounting*, November 1992, pp 58–63

Smith M, 'The Rise and Rise of the NFI', *Management Accounting* (UK), May 1990, pp 24–26

Smith M, *New Tools for Management Accountants*, Longman, Melbourne, 1994

Waldron D and Galloway D, 'Throughput Accounting: Ranking Products Profitably', *Management Accounting* (UK), December 1988, pp 34–5

CASE 10: WILLINGHAM FURNITURE LTD

This case highlights the problems that arise when a company lacks clear strategic goals or the management accounting control procedures to supply the information necessary to monitor or direct the progress of the business. It provides the opportunity to identify and correct major accounting deficiencies.

Willingham is a manufacturer of high quality lounge suites. It is run by its two directors, the husband and wife team of Barry and Margaret Noble. The company produces leather and fabric output in its Norwich factory and operates exclusively on a factory direct basis in East Anglia and through appointed agents and retailers in the South of England. They have no other outlets in East Anglia other than the factory showroom.

The company has been established for 10 years and recently moved to purpose-built accommodation adjacent to its original site to coincide with a rapid expansion into the South East and West European markets. While it does produce a range of standard lounge suites, its output is largely market-led with the great majority of suites produced in response to orders. With the exception of minimal showroom requirements, no suites are specifically produced for stock and three product lines account for nearly 90% of total production. The goal of avoiding mass production techniques has allowed the company to stay small, employing only eight full-time staff: John Higgins and Ken Szabo in the frameshop; Len Mladenovic in the cutting room; Joan Ristic in sewing; and Ron Jenkinson, Wayne Dobbins, Jill Bradtkee and Leanne Day in upholstery. Each of the staff works a 40 hour week and each of the processes functions independently, apart from the matching up of orders at the sewing and upholstering stages.

Figure C10.1 illustrates the sales and production flows. The employee mix and inflexibility of functions effectively governs Willingham's productive capacity. The maximum number of units of output for each process over a three week cycle is:

Framemaking 60 (120 hours × 2 employees @ 4 hours per suite)

Cutting 15 (120 hours × 1 employee @ 8 hours per suite)

Sewing 15 (120 hours × 1 employee @ 8 hours per suite)

Upholstery 34 (120 hours × 4 employees @ 14 hours per suite)

The directors are keen to expand their presence in the South East further and can accommodate the additional four to five production staff that this would require without significant capital expenditure outlays. Currently they are only operating at 70 per cent of maximum productive capacity.

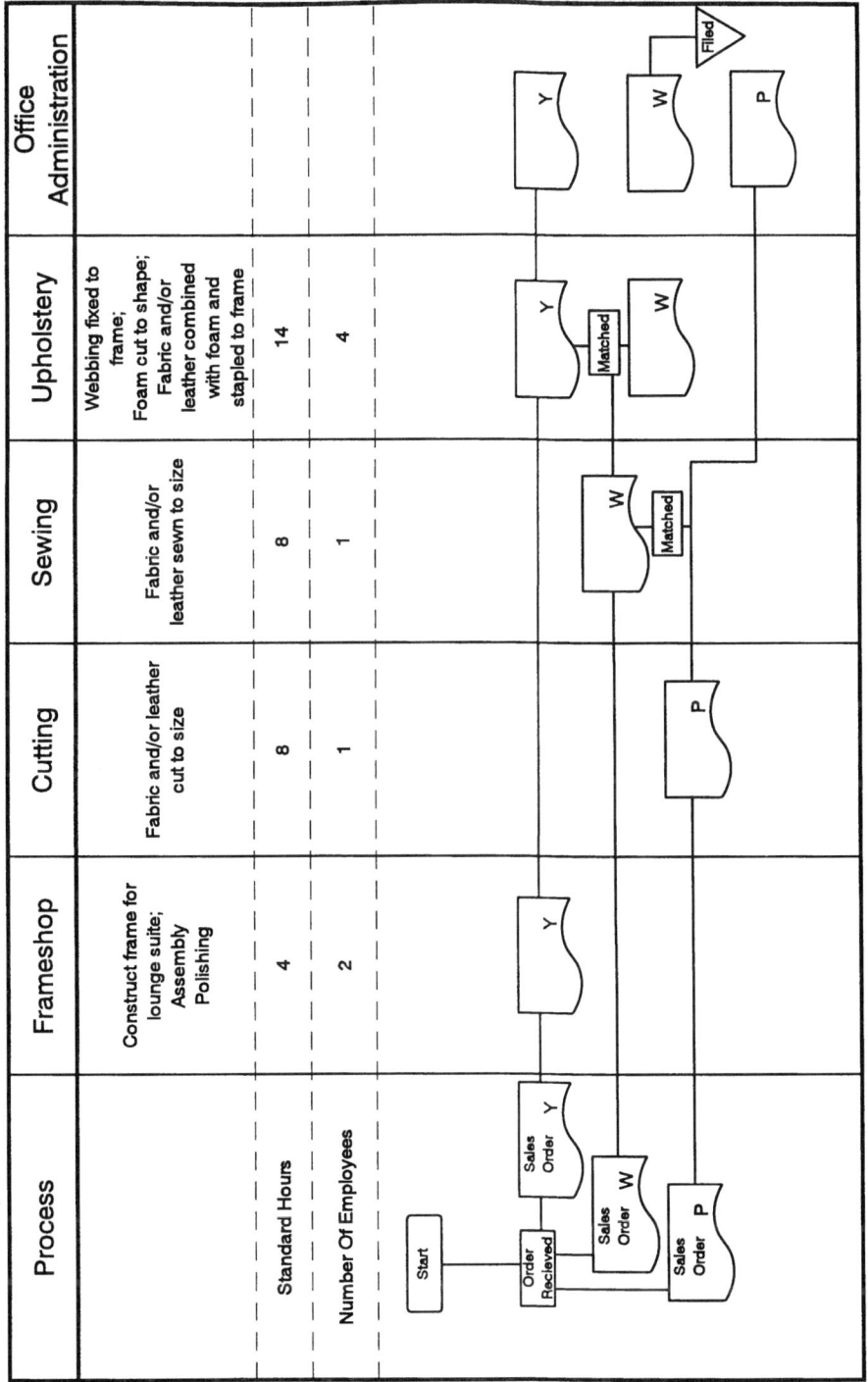

Figure C10.1: Sales and Production Flow at Willingham

Willingham has no formal stock control records or procedures. Orders for leather and fabric are placed in response to orders and availability of materials is generally good (about one week) with the exception of local materials (leadtime greater than four weeks). No economic order levels are set for materials and consumables and just-in-time manufacturing procedures have never been considered appropriate. Consequently stockouts, and consequent disruptions to the production process, have been known to occur because of minimal stocks of raw materials, and despite this work in progress, in the form of assembled frames and sewn materials, is very high and consistent with mass production manufacturing techniques. The standard suite produced comprises one two-seater settee and two armchairs. Production scheduling is on a three week cycle with local sales requirements completed in week 1, south east and European requirements in weeks 2 and 3. This schedule is consistent with the existing three week period between deliveries to south east and overseas customers, but imposes constraints which are contributing to the company's existing cash flow problems.

Full absorption costing is employed at present so that factory overhead (including an idle capacity allowance) and general overheads are incorporated. The hourly direct labour charge would thus be calculated:

Direct Labour	£ 5.40
Factory Overhead @ 45%	£15.00
General Overhead @ 125%	£12.00
	£32.40

Standard direct material costs, including a 10 per cent wastage allowance, are added to these direct labour costs when the product is initiated, but no subsequent comparison is made with actual costs.

The existing accounting system at Willingham classifies all consumables and electricity as cost of goods sold. This, together with absence of recognition of the closing values of work in process and finished goods, contributes to reported losses in the net profits of Figure C10.2.

The nature of the business, with a standard selling price in excess of £6000 per unit, dictates that the majority of sales are on credit. Bad debts are rare but most debts are converted into cash in a period ranging from 60 to 120 days. This long delay contributes to the cash flow problems of the company. South east retailers (responsible for 70 per cent of sales) are seen to be the major culprits, but the directors are wary of pressuring debtors for fear of losing business in a sensitive and competitive market. The directors acknowledge that the cash flow problem did not exist prior to the south east and overseas marketing ventures.

Concerned that the growth in sales is not being matched with corresponding profits, the directors have initiated an analysis of P + L and B/S ratios. These are detailed in Figure C10.3.

You are required to examine the strategic alternatives available to Willingham and to make recommendations which would ensure that the financial procedures and management controls in place are consistent with the goals of the company.

Product and Customer Profitability

£000	July–Sept	Oct–Dec	Jan–Mar	Apr–June	Year to Date
Sales	**200.0**	**260.0**	**170.0**	**180.0**	**810.0**
Purchases	126.0	149.0	85.0	98.0	448.0
Consumables	0.1	0.5	0.3	0.2	1.1
Packing & Freight	1.0	1.5	1.2	6.5	10.2
Wages	31.0	48.0	23.0	19.0	121.0
Electricity	1.9	1.0	0.5	1.3	4.7
Cost of Sales	**160.0**	**200.0**	**110.0**	**125.0**	**595.0**
Gross Profit	**40.0**	**60.0**	**60.0**	**55.0**	**215.0**
Advertising	7.0	22.0	16.0	25.0	70.0
Bank Charges & Interest	6.0	4.0	6.0	3.0	19.0
Depreciation	3.0	3.0	3.0	3.0	12.0
Directors' Salaries	5.0	11.0	11.0	12.0	39.0
Motor Vehicle Expenses	2.0	3.0	8.0	2.0	15.0
Rates and Taxes	3.0	2.0	-	-	5.0
Equipment Rental	0.3	0.3	0.3	0.4	1.3
Rent and Repairs	8.0	10.0	5.0	7.0	30.0
Telephone	0.7	0.8	0.8	0.9	3.2
Superannuation	3.0	3.0	3.0	3.0	12.0
Miscellaneous	1.0	1.9	0.9	1.7	5.5
Total Expenses	**39.0**	**61.0**	**54.0**	**58.0**	**212.0**
Net Profit	**1**	**(1)**	**6**	**(3)**	**3**

Figure C10.2: Quarterly Profit and Loss Statement (Year Ending 30/6/93)

Ratio	Definition	Willingham	Industry Average
1. Current Ratio	CA/CL	0.7	1.0
2. Quick Ratio	(CA-Inventories)/CL	0.3	0.5
3. Stock Turnover	Sales/Inventory	7.0	12.0
4. Debt Collection Period	$\frac{\text{Receivables}}{\text{Credit Sales}} \times 365$	60.0	40.0
5. Rate of Return	Net Profit/TA	1.5%	3.5%
6. Gross Profit Margin	Gross Profit/Sales	26%	25%
7. Debt Ratio	TL/TA	100%	60%

Figure C10.3: Ratio Analysis for Willingham Furniture

CASE 11: ESAU CREEK WINERY

This case provides a cost minimisation problem which may be solved through the application of graphical or computer-based linear programming methods. It recognises the importance of non-financial and non-quantitative restrictions on the implementation of cost effective solutions.

The Esau Creek Winery is situated at Lyndoch, some 55 km north-east of Adelaide, in South Australia's Barossa Valley. The region is a major centre for wine production and the Esau Creek Winery produces a range of table wines, sherries, port and brandy commercially.

Geoffrey Daniels has recently been appointed to head up the marketing team of the business and has determined to make an impact with a more competitive display of the company's product. He has specifically targeted pre-Christmas sales, which in the two previous years have failed to reach budgeted levels.

He has decided to produce a 'Christmas Special' assortment of red and white wines, to be marketed as a novelty surprise package through the retail trade from November 1994. The boxed set will contain an assortment of Esau Creek branded $10 reds and whites at a significant discount to customers. All of the bottles will be of their own characteristic shape, with whites being taller and slimmer than reds; each variety of red and white wine will carry its normal label with an added flash indicating that it is part of a 'special—not for separate resale' consignment.

Following the advice of consultants, Esau Creek intends that each boxed set should contain at least 32 bottles, but no more than three dozen. The box space available may vary between 1248 cm² and 1560 cm² depending on the design of the cardboard partitions necessary to prevent transit breakage. These partitions are of negligible weight compared to that of the bottles and their contents. Each boxed set must weigh at least 46.2 kg.

Each full bottle of red wine weighs 1100 gm and occupies a base area of 52 cm². Each full bottle of white wine weighs 1650 gm and occupies an area of 39 cm². The cost of production per bottle is £4.80 for red wine and £4 for white wine. The winery wishes to fill the boxed sets at minimum cost, while satisfying all of the above constraints.

You are required to determine the optimum combination of red and white wines and make recommendations as to how the 'Christmas Special' package should be filled.

CASE 12: SUBIACO TECHNOLOGY

This case investigates product mix alternatives and provides an opportunity for the use of linear programming methods to develop a decision strategy for product concentration and departmental rationalisation.

Subiaco Technology has expanded rapidly at its Cambridge site, largely through the electronic ingenuity and charismatic approach of its Managing Director, Ralph George. The company produces six products, each of which makes conflicting demands on the capacity of its three processing departments. The marketing of new products has so far owed less to economic considerations than to the determined development of novel and innovatory ideas. The resulting degree of diversification has caused some disquiet within the company in the light of intense competition over part of the product range. Figure C12.1 details the products currently produced. Three of these are electronic calculators. The calculators, now modified, provide the foundation on which a profitable business was originally built, but more recent movements have taken the company towards the television and computer terminal end of the market.

Model	Description	Material and Labour Costs (£ per item)	Selling Price (£ per item)	Contribution to Profits (£ per item)
BC23	Basic, limited function calculator	6.1	8.0	1.9
SC37	Scientific, multiple memory calculator	24.2	27.0	2.8
PC84	Programmable calculator	34.9	38.0	3.1
CT79	Computer Terminal	65.3	99.0	33.7
MTV7	Micro Television set	133.4	154.0	20.6
FSP6	Flat screen, portable colour television	235.3	325.0	89.7

Figure C12.1: Range of Products

Each of the products needs processing time in each of the company's three production departments:

(i) electronic circuitry
(ii) assembly
(iii) inspection and packaging

131

Space and stock control considerations, detailed in Figure C12.2, have now necessitated a more rational view of the product/department matrix.

Department	Product					
	BC23	SC37	PC84	CT79	MTV7	FSP6
Electronic circuitry	0.3	0.3	0.8	2.1	1.4	2.9
Assembly	0.6	0.9	0.9	0.6	0.4	3.5
Inspection and Packaging	0.3	0.4	0.2	1.3	0.3	2.1

Figure C12.2: Matrix of Hourly Usage within each Department per Item of Product

The current daily capacity of the departments, expressed in labour hours, is respectively 60 hours, 60 hours and 40 hours, but, if necessary, capacity could be expanded by up to 30 per cent in each department, with modest cost implications, through more overtime and increased part-time employment. Further expansion would require either out-working, extensive capital investment or a move to a larger site, almost inevitably out of town.

The marketing department of the company has been considering the likely effects of substantial price changes for their products, while also toying with the idea of tendering for a contract with the BBC to produce the CT79 computer terminal in conjunction with a new BBC2 television series on computing. Considerable reservations exist within the company regarding this latter project in view of the large scale of operations necessary (especially when comparable producers have already rejected the contract as being too large for them to handle). Figure C12.3 details the current level of sales together with estimates of the price elasticity of demand.

	Current Sales per day	Estimated Daily Sales with Price Change	
		−20%	+20%
BC23	35	45	0
SC27	21	27	0
PC84	8	50	2
CT79	4	5	3
MTV7	2	10	4
FSP6	7	12	4

Figure C12.3: Daily Sales and Sales Projections

You are required to make recommendations to the company regarding an optimum product mix, together with a strategy for future rationalisation. Your report should focus on the importance of product abandonment, price changes and departmental expansion to the future development of the company.

Product and Customer Profitability

CASE 13: FIBRO LTD

This case looks at the use of financial and non-financial indicators of performance in the monitoring of a production process. It highlights the deficiencies apparent in the use of some indicators and provides opportunities for the implementation of preferred alternatives.

Fibro Ltd manufactures and distributes fibre cement products for the building industry. The company produces corrugated sheeting for roofing and fencing, pipes and flat sheets. The business has been running for over 50 years from its Northampton base, and all of the products were originally asbestos fibre based. They are now all asbestos free and have incorporated the very latest cellulose fibre technology.

Although it supplies its products nationwide, the south east is Fibro's biggest market. The simplicity of the product and its resistance to weather damage make it extremely popular. The only competition is from the suppliers of substitute building products.

A highly automated continuous mass production operation combines five basic raw materials in the stated proportions:

- cellulose pulp fibre   (8%)
- cement   (40%)
- alumin   (7%)
- bentonite   (5%)
- silica   (40%)

The raw materials are combined to form a cellulose cement fibre which passes through one of three alternative processes to generate corrugated sheeting, flat sheeting or pipes. In each instance, several thin sheets are compressed to form a single strong sheet. Each machine has the facility to redirect trimming and spoiled sheets back into the manufacturing process to reduce the wastage rate. Figure C13.1 illustrates the production process.

Cellulose pulp fibre is extracted from pine chippings and supplied on a weekly basis. Cement is received on a continuous flow from the adjacent cement works on an hourly basis. Cessation of cement supplies would halt production within a day. Silica, alumina and bentonite are supplied on a fortnightly basis by local manufacturers. Figure C13.2 details raw material usage.

Despite the quasi-monopolistic position it has in the area, the decline in housing starts has hit the business hard, particularly in the flat board area, where substitute products have penetrated Fibro's market. Consequently the company is concerned to reassess its product costing strategies. Maintenance, distribution and selling costs are costed to particular products but warehousing, administration and vehicle costs are expensed. There is no allocation of manufacturing overhead to product costs and this may, therefore, not be reflected appropriately in price fixing.

133

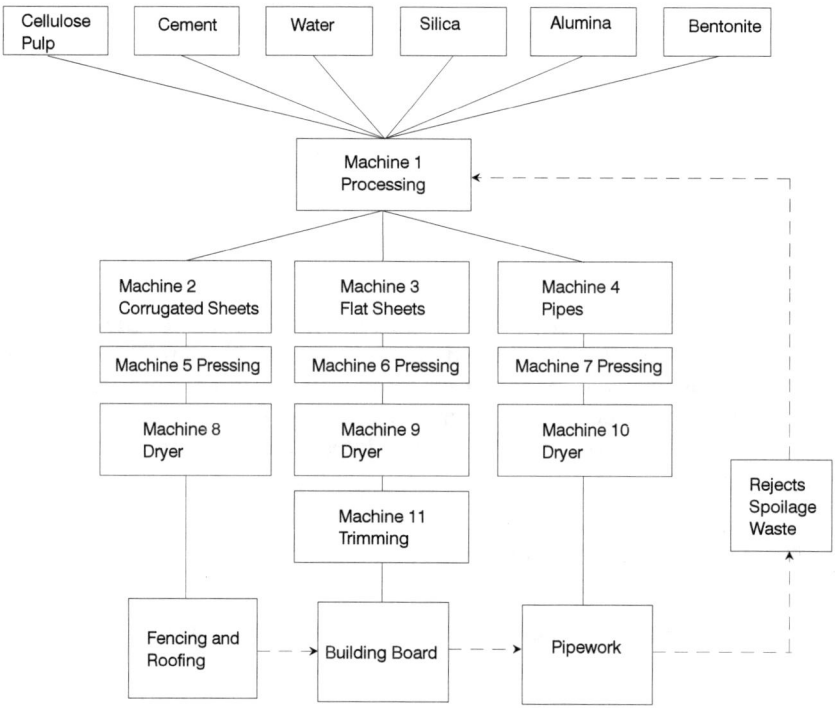

Figure C13.1: Fibro Production Process

The incorporation of the latest cellulose fibre technology has not been trouble free. Teething troubles have been experienced in ensuring that an environmentally acceptable asbestos free product is produced. Quality and consistency of product are thought to have suffered as a result.

Production performance is currently measured by a number of non-financial indicators:

- Standard Time (mins)   = No of metres produced/Standard production per hour
- Production Efficiency   = Standard Time/Total Time Taken
- Run Efficiency (per day)   = Total Time Taken/Schedule Time
- Processing Efficiency   = Production Efficiency * Run Efficiency
- Raw Material Usage   = Production (metres) * Actual weight per metre * % of Material
- Weight per Metre (kg)   = Weight of materials issued/ Production in metres

You are required to make recommendations on the use of performance indicators to meet Fibro's requirements. Your report should evaluate the product costings currently in use and the alternatives available.

| Raw Materials | Product | | | Total Usage (kg) | Raw Material Usage (%) | | Process Standards | Standard Cost Rate | Actual Value @ Standard Rate (£) |
	Corru-gated	Flat-board	Pipes		Actual	Standard			
Pulp	7000	3000	1500	11 500	9.2	8.0		1.05	12 075
Alumina	6000	1000	500	7500	6.0	7.0		0.25	1875
Cement	40 000	8000	4500	52 500	42.0	40.0		0.11	5775
Bentonite	2000	1000	500	3500	2.8	5.0		0.40	1400
Silica	37 000	9000	4000	50 000	40.0	40.0		0.02	1000
Total (KG)	92 000	22 000	11 000	125 000	100%	100%			22 125
Gross Metres	19 000	4000	2000	25 000			26 000		
Scrap (m)	350	150	100	600			0		
Net Metres	18 650	3850	1900	24 400			26 000		
Process Efficiency (m per hour) m	800	600	400	1800			2000		
Product Quality (weight per m) kg	4.93	5.71	5.79	5.12			5.60		

Figure C13.2: Material Usage by Product (per day)

CASE 14: DERRICK'S CONFECTIONERY

This case highlights the differences in the profitability possible when different customers are in receipt of substantially the same product. It provides the opportunity for developing a customer portfolio, along BCG matrix lines, as part of a customer profitability analysis.

Derrick's Confectionery is based in modern premises in Bristol, from where it manufactures and distributes 30 different ice cream product lines. The products are distributed by Derrick's own fleet of refrigerated trucks to six major wholesale distributors. Annual sales are currently around the £10 m level, distributed among the wholesalers as indicated in Figure C14.1. Derrick's controls about 35 per cent of the metropolitan market, but this shrinks to less than 10 per cent in outlying areas where there are many small competitors.

Customer	% Sales
Ardron's Wafers	19
Butler Ices	12
Cahill's Cones	25
Donleavy's Ices	9
England Wedges	14
Frankston Chocs	20
Others	1
	100%

Figure C14.1: Sales Distribution by Customer

Derrick's usually holds up to four weeks of stock in its central cold stores to meet the distribution requirements of its six major customers. The cold stores cost approximately £500 000 pa to run, but excess capacity can be hired out to other non-competing firms. This becomes especially important during the winter months when consumer demand is considerably reduced. Even during the summer months demand is highly temperature sensitive. Derrick's, therefore, bases its sales on a de-seasonalised forecast, related to increases in disposable real incomes, and hopes that stocks will be adequate to cope with extended periods of extreme high temperatures.

The raw materials — vegetable oil, butter, milk and sugar — are relatively inexpensive. They arrive at Derrick's by tanker and are stored on site. Ice cream is then manufactured in two major processes, mixing and forming, followed by packaging to meet the specific customer requirements.

Meeting these sometimes uniquely specific requirements of customers has been causing Derrick's management some serious headaches recently. They recognise the importance of a client-focused approach to marketing and distribution, but are beginning to feel that they are being exploited by some customers who are never satisfied with the level of service provided, however extensive it may be. The satisfaction of customer whims is beginning to cost big money, so Derrick's has determined to conduct a detailed analysis of the customers and their varying requirements. These have been abbreviated in Figure C14.2.

Ardron's Wafers are located within 1 km of Derrick's base and employ standard packaging and bar-code reading systems. **Ardron's** insist on only low discounts for volume and maintains large regular orders. Consequently their delivery requests and inventory holding requirements are highly predictable.

Butler Ices are located nearly 50 km north of Bristol and require packaging unique to them. Despite their remote location they insist on free deliveries and require large discounts for volume orders. Their internal inventory control procedures are not well developed, resulting in not uncommon requests for 'crisis' deliveries to deal with stock-outs.

Cahill's Cones have the reputation of always paying on time and requiring low discounts and commissions. Their inventory holding procedures are perhaps the best in the business and they have a JIT scheduling system which is entirely compatible with Derrick's own. Deliveries have no special fleet requirements for refrigerated vehicles.

Donleavy's Ices always pay late but demand all available discounts, even when they are not strictly applicable. They insist on daily deliveries, with the requirement of special deliveries should demand merit them. They have threatened to take their business elsewhere if all their inventory holding requirements are not met in full.

England Wedges rely on bulk orders which are shipped on an infrequent basis. They require rare visits from Derrick personnel and are prepared to collate sales credits and make monthly claims.

Frankston Chocs are not noted for the strength of their internal organisation. They require frequent calls which extend to assistance with administrative operations and help with the merchandising of stock and in-store dislplays. They initiate separate sales credits for each item of product returned and inevitably generate complex orders whose details are unclear, so that multiple queries follow almost every transaction.

Figure C14.2: Profiles for Derrick's Customer Base

You are required to conduct a customer profitability analysis and devise alternative strategies for the manner in which Derrick's might proceed.

CASE 15: PITCAIRN ELECTRONICS

This case highlights the deficiencies of traditional methods of product costing which employ single volume methods of overhead cost allocation. It provides the opportunity to apply, among others, activity-based costing (ABC) methods, in order to demonstrate differences in cost and price outcomes.

Pitcairn Electronics has been at the forefront of hi-tech products in Britain since the information technology explosion of the 1970s. From modest premises in the Chelmsford suburbs, founder and now Chief Executive, Rick Pitts has driven the company to a respected position among leaders in the market, with a reputation for meeting consumer needs. Rick's genius has always been in providing products in anticipation of the market and in bringing those products in ahead of competitors. Costing and pricing have always been much lower on his priorities because new, well-marketed products have always been successful.

The management at Pitcairn is now worried. The company's bottom line displays a disconcerting downturn for the second successive year — the first time this has happened in a 20 year history. This relatively poor performance is largely attributable to lack of sales revenue stemming from an inexplicable failure to win orders in competitive tenders. The Chief Executive feels that the pricing policies must be wrong and has called for a full investigation of current procedures in order to identify deficiencies. Pitcairn has always prided itself on staying at the cutting edge of new manufacturing technologies and has diversified to take advantage of new marketing opportunities. The company reckons itself to be the most efficient producer worldwide of its two traditional products, Alphanumeric (A) and Betaplus (B), electronic calculators whose sophistication almost places them in the category of mini-computers. Both are mature and proven products with the latter recently upgraded to accommodate a series of statistical functions. Pitcairn has recently marketed two further products, the Chameleon (C) screen-enhancer for lap-top computers and the Dromedary (D), a memory-conserving PC add-on. The success of the new products has surprised even the most optimistic members of management.

Although the new products have been successfully launched, it is the sales of the traditional products which are the greatest cause of concern. Pitcairn has failed to win orders that it fully expected to win, and worse still, has lost out to competitors that it views as inferior and less efficient. Inferior producers have been able to tender at more competitive prices, suggesting that there is something wrong with pricing procedures at Pitcairn. Each of the products proceeds through the same four-stage production process, though the time spent and resources consumed at each stage vary between products:

STAGE 1 — supply of raw material components;

STAGE 2 — set-up and run of production engineering;

STAGE 3 — vacuum packing of finished product;

STAGE 4 — distribution of product to wholesalers and retailers.

Product and Customer Profitability

Figure C15.1 shows the monthly cost information which is employed by Pitcairn in its current pricing procedures:

	Total				Total
	A	B	C	D	
Units of Output	30 000	20 000	8000	10 000	68 000
Resource Use per Unit					
Raw Materials	4	5	10	15	450 000
Labour Hours	1	2	1.25	1	90 000
Machine Hours	1	1	2.5	1	80 000
Production Costs Per Unit					
Raw Materials	£12	£15	£30	£45	£1 350 000
Direct Labour	£8	£16	£10	£8	£720 000
Overheads					
Machining (per hour)	£10	£10	£10	£10	£800 000
Engineering set-ups	3	7	20	10	£40 000
Component Receipts	20	40	240	100	£400 000
Orders Packaged	10	2	20	18	£300 000
Distribution Deliveries	10	10	25	20	£260 000

Figure C15.1: Product Cost Information

Prices are currently calculated with respect to unit costs computed on the basis of direct labour, direct material and a share of overhead costs. Overheads are allocated on the basis of direct labour hours (DLH) using an overhead rate of 1 800 000/ 90 000 = £20 per DLH. Figure C15.2 illustrates the calculation of selling prices for each of the products:

	Product			
	A	B	C	D
Direct Labour (£)	8.0	16.0	10.0	8.0
Direct Materials (£)	12.0	15.0	30.0	45.0
Allocated Overhead (£)	20.0	40.0	25.0	20.0
Total Cost (£)	40.0	71.0	65.0	73.0
Mark-up (50%) (£)	20	35.5	32.5	36.5
Selling Price (£)	60	106.5	97.5	109.5

Figure C15.2: Product Pricing

You are required to examine the current method of establishing product costs and prices and make recommendations for an improved system. Your report should include a consideration of the impact on prices of alternative cost bases and of alternative methods of allocating overhead costs to products.

Chapter 6

Project Appraisal

6.1 INTRODUCTION

Too often management accounting textbooks focus on the number-crunching aspects of project appraisal at the expense of all else. Frequently in practice the numbers side of things is peripheral at best, certainly of a lesser consequence than the strategic aspects of the investment decision. Just as with the activity based problems of Chapter 5, it is all too easy to focus on monetary issues to the exclusion of the non-financials. To overcome this misleading emphasis — one which is often mirrored in student treatment of case studies in this area — it is helpful to adopt a classification similar to that adopted for ABM.

A four-strand focus then emerges: Returns/Risks/Quality/Time. Let us consider project appraisal with respect to each strand in turn, and establish a case study scenario for analysis in each area:

6.2 RETURNS

The monetary focus moves beyond just costs to include revenues, so that projected profits and cash flows can both be estimated. The first problem then arises in determining how to evaluate the returns, especially when these occur as an income stream over a number of different time periods.

Consider, for example, an initial investment of £A (say, in a new machine) which generates cash flows of £B, C, D, E and F respectively, in successive periods over the next five years. In the simplest terms, as long as net proceeds are positive then the investment is beneficial to the organisation. This benefit might be quantified by either:

- accounting rate of return (%) = $\dfrac{(B + C + D + E + F - A)}{A} \times 100\%$

  (indicating the size of the returns compared to the initial outlay: the bigger the better)

- payback period (years) = when $\Sigma(B+C+D+E+F) > A$

  (indicating how long it takes for the cumulative returns to recover the initial investment: the shorter the better).

Project Appraisal

But both the accounting rate of return (%) and payback period ignore the timing differences associated with the receipt of cash flows. Since a pound today is worth more than a pound tomorrow (because it could be invested to earn interest) then adjustments need to be made before the income stream can be added.

This is accomplished through the use of **Discounted Cash Flows (DCF)**. Timing differences are eliminated by discounting all cash flows back to the same period prior to comparison.

i.e. where i = discount rate $\dfrac{\%}{100}$

The **Present Value (PV)** of the original stream:

$$PV = \frac{B}{(1+i)} + \frac{C}{(1+i)^2} + \frac{D}{(1+i)^3} + \frac{E}{(1+i)^4} + \frac{F}{(1+i)^5}$$

can be compared with original outlay £A

i.e. **Net Present Value (NPV)** = $PV - A$

If $NPV > \emptyset$ the project should be accepted because it adds value to the company but this outcome may be sensitive to the choice of discount rate.

In practice the choice may be arbitrary, but is usually dependent upon one or more of:

- Company Cost of Capital
- Cost of Borrowing
- Target Rate of Return
- Hurdle Rate for Project Acceptance

The problem is that these may all be different! Even so, DCF analysis represents a significant improvement over the accounting rate of return. The payback period calculation may similarly be adapted so that the analysis employs discounted rather than absolute cash flows.

An alternative method, the **Internal Rate of Return (IRR)**, avoids an arbitrary choice of discount factor.

IRR (%) is that rate of discount which equates outflows with discounted inflows.

$$A = \frac{B}{(1+r)} + \frac{C}{(1+r)^2} + \frac{D}{(1+r)^3} + \frac{E}{(1+r)^4} + \frac{F}{(1+r)^5}$$

We should choose projects with the highest 'r' values.

These values will usually coincide with the greatest NPV values but the incidence of negative cash flows in the income stream (e.g. from refurbishment or promotional activities) may generate multiple or nonsensical values of 'r'.

Although practitioners often prefer to work with percentage outcomes, like that from the IRR, the NPV approach is to be preferred as long as a reasonable compromise can be reached regarding the appropriate discount factor to be used, in conjunction with the conduct of a detailed sensitivity analysis.

The choice of appraisal method and rate of discount are just two of the problems with the analysis of investment projects. The estimation of the cash flows necessary even to conduct the analysis is itself fraught with danger and wide open to error and/or deliberate manipulation. *Case 17: Jarrahdale Minesite* provides a good example of the problems associated with the appraisal of alternative solutions to a single investment problem.

6.3 RISK

The focus on returns frequently causes the assessment of the risk attaching to a project to be neglected. Managerial decision making requires information on both risks and projected returns to be available. Risk assessment should, at the very least, incorporate an examination of the likelihood and outcomes of the best and worst scenarios. Ideally, it will include a probability distribution of all possible outcomes so that a realistic judgement can be made on the risk/return compromise. Where projected risk can be considered to be normally distributed the risk profile of the investment decision will resemble that of Figure 18.

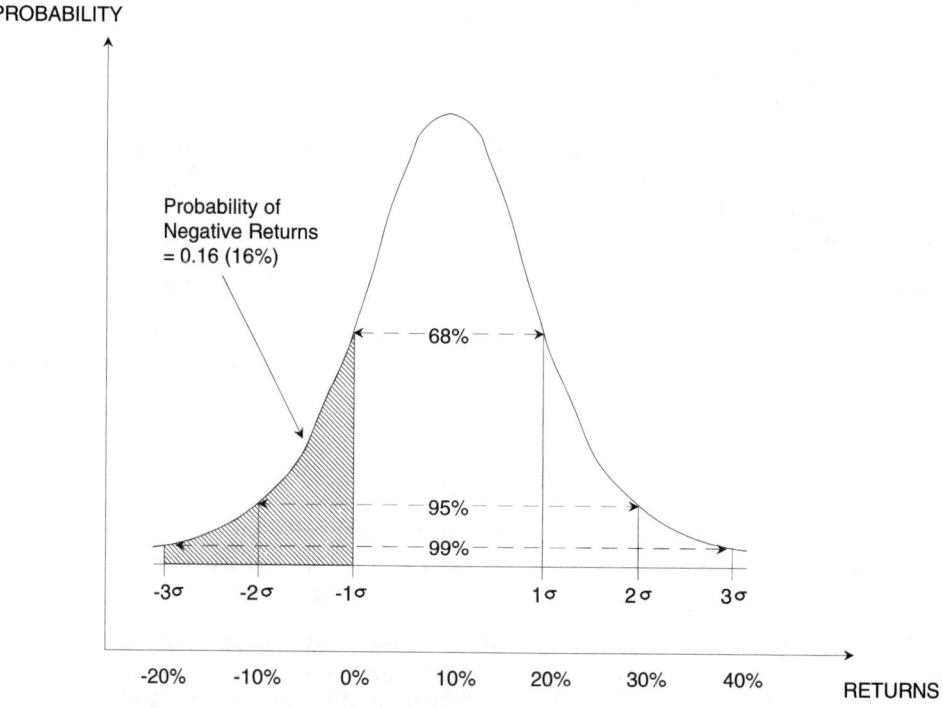

Figure 18: Probability Distribution of Projected Returns

Project Appraisal

It might be argued that cash flow projections are only estimates, so that the probabilities attaching to such estimates can only be figments of the imagination! But if we have evidence to suggest that one outcome is more likely than another then that is useful, and potentially significant, information that can be incorporated into the analysis with probability weightings of, say, 0.55 and 0.45 respectively. Probability estimates for alternative outcomes can be combined through decision trees to give an indication of the distribution of possibilities. *Minicase C: Cable Technology* illustrates their usefulness:

Cable Technology is heavily dependent on export markets and its sales revenues are highly susceptible to variations in economic factors, particularly exchange rates, interest rates and the rate of price inflation. It sources much of its raw material requirements overseas too, so that its import prices can vary wildly. It exercises a tight control over those costs under direct control, particularly labour costs. Forecasts of price and wage-cost inflation are an important part of Cable Technology's planning and budgeting process and it relies heavily on estimates from the Marketing Department.

Current estimates suggest that the rate of price inflation will lie between 6 per cent and 9 per cent over the next quarter, with 7 per cent the most likely figure, with a 40 per cent chance. There is a 30 per cent chance of it being 8 per cent, 20 per cent of it being 9 per cent and only 10 per cent of it being as low as 6 per cent. The rate of wage-cost inflation is reckoned to be 1 per cent or 1.5 per cent higher than the corresponding rate of price inflation. For the two lower rates of price inflation there is a 40 per cent chance of a 1 per cent difference, and a 60 per cent chance of a 1.5 per cent difference. For the two higher rates of price inflation there is thought to be a 70 per cent chance of a 1 per cent difference and only a 30 per cent chance of a 1.5 per cent difference. If the expected rate of wage cost inflation exceeds 8.5 per cent or the chances of a blow-out to a figure greater than 9.5 per cent exceed a 10 per cent chance, then Cable Technology institutes further short-term cost-cutting measures.

The rates of price and wage-cost inflation, together with their respective probabilities, can be represented in the form of a decision tree structure. The rates of wage-cost inflation are conditional on a pre-determined rate of price inflation, and the associated conditional probabilities measure the coincidence of two separate events. The joint probability of a particular rate of wage-inflation is, therefore, the product of two separate probabilities:

(i) that for a particular rate of price inflation, and
(ii) the subsequent conditional probability.

These are detailed in Figure 19.

The expected rate of price inflation is a weighted arithmetic mean:

$$(0.1) * 6 + (0.4) * 7 + (0.3) * 8 + (0.2) * 9 = 7.6\%$$

The expected rate of wage-cost inflation, using the joint probabilities as weights, is, similarly:

$$(0.04) * 7 + (0.06) * 7.5 + (0.16) * 8 + (0.24) * 8.5 + (0.21) * 9 +$$
$$(0.09) * 9.5 + (0.14) * 10 + (0.06) * 10.5 = 8.825\%$$

The latter figure marginally exceeds Cable Technology's target figure of 8.5 per cent. Reference to the distribution of rates of wage-cost inflation in the final column of Figure 19 indicates a 20 per cent chance (i.e. 0.14 + 0.06) of a rate greater or equal to 10 per cent. The likelihood of a rate in excess of 9.5 per cent is, therefore, well beyond Cable Technology's acceptable levels. Both of these outcomes will trigger increased cost-cutting activity.

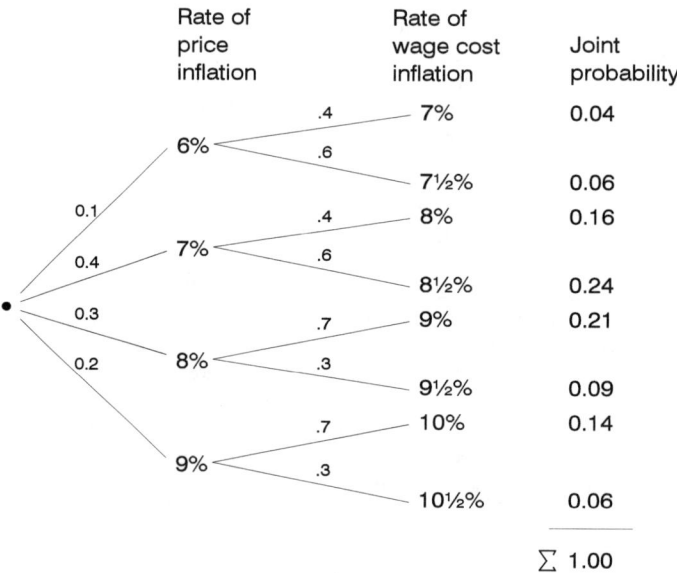

Figure 19: Decision Trees for Cable Technology

In practice decision tree structures can be much larger than those in Figure 19 — both longer (representing more separate outcomes identified) and wider (with additional dependent outcomes and more probabilities). In theory there is no limit to the number of conditional probabilities that might be considered jointly. When all outcomes, and their distribution, have been determined, a thorough spreadsheet-based sensitivity analysis might be conducted to evaluate the significance of any probability assumptions. Brewer *et al* (1993) discuss the use of 'fuzzy logic' which adds a new dimension to the spreadsheet-based appraisal of risk by incorporating uncertainty into each of the cells of the analysis. *Case 19: Boutique Fashions* provides an opportunity to construct and integrate a number of intricate decision trees in a scenario where the analysis of resultant probabilities allows a risk profile to be generated and more informed project viability recommendations to be made.

6.4 QUALITY

Any appraisal of the quality of investment decisions should address the way in which the decisions have been taken as well as their consequences. This would include the following stages:

- project generation: which projects are put forward for examination?
- cash flows: how and by whom are these estimated?
- analysis: what methods and assumptions are employed?
- selection: importance of financials/non-financials in project choice?
- authorisation: documentation of monitoring process for project implementation?
- evaluation: do the project outcomes match/exceed expectations?

A post-audit investigation can potentially have a significant impact on the manner in which future appraisals are conducted. If it is viewed as a learning experience, seeking improvement opportunities, rather than as a witch-hunt of those who have made errors, then real bottom line benefits are achievable.

Problems with implementing post-audit schemes range across the whole gamut of which? where? how? and by whom? Big companies may be able to audit internally, others may need to employ consultants. Either way, the continued cooperation of those individuals involved in implementing the project is essential. Any breach of confidence or finger-pointing will reduce the levels of active cooperation and may destroy the learning opportunities. The post-audit could extend over:

- all projects currently underperforming;
- all projects implemented (underperforming or not);
- all projects considered (implemented or not);
- a sample of any of the above.

The dangers of choosing to look only at underperforming projects is that of bias: some projects performing to expectations might actually be doing much better, because of changed circumstances or unrealistically low expectations. Valuable improvement opportunities might be lost as a consequence. Conversely, the assessment of all projects might be extremely expensive and stretch resources — especially where the same managerial team is evaluating both future and existing projects. The 'one-off' project with no learning opportunities is frequently foisted upon the audit team as an excuse for non-investigation, but the process of evaluation is still one which can yield real benefits from examination.

The time period for the detailed analysis will likely be industry, or even company, specific: one-year may be too soon for all the projected benefits to be evaluated, or on the other hand too late to do anything of a corrective nature.

A clear examination of the validity of assumptions made is essential. Project analysts can be incredibly devious by:

- estimating cost savings just sufficient to ensure that the project clears the company hurdle rate;

- creating a buffer of cost-savings for use in future, more doubtful projects; or

- using non-financial arguments like 'health and safety' when a desired project is clearly uneconomical in financial terms.

Case 18: Alumina Refineries provides an example of a post-audit investigation where improvement opportunities are apparent and the underlying motives of the protagonists can also be speculated upon.

6.5 TIME

The lead-time to project implementation is frequently one of the variables to which project outcomes are most sensitive. We need to estimate both the likelihood of delays (as part of our risk management strategy) and their financial impact (as part of our analysis of the sensitivity of returns). There may be some scope for varying the order in which the project is completed or the amount of resources each component consumes. Either way, we need to know the alternatives available and be aware of their costs and benefits, as part of our detailed analysis. Trend diagrams, Gantt charts, Network and Critical Path Analysis are all useful techniques to assist choices concerning timing and associated costs. *Case 16 : The Sandy Bay Development* provides an example where such techniques may be applied to reduce the risks attached to a project, while quantifying the extent of the increased involvement.

The most common form of individual scheduling problem, for both batch and process production flows, is job shop scheduling (JSS). This is characterised by the ordering and allocation of multiple jobs (n) to alternative machines (m). There are a very large number of alternative schedules even for a relatively small number of jobs to be processed (e.g. the scheduling of only five jobs on three machines produces $(5!)^3$ or 1.7 million alternatives).

In practice technological restrictions, and the existence of specified processing routes, will reduce the number of alternatives. Jobs may be sequentially ordered (with all jobs subject to the same procedures in the same sequence), sequentially broken-ordered (so that certain jobs miss out certain stages) or randomly assigned (non-sequential and non-ordered). Even so, the feasible set of alternatives is still usually too large for complete enumeration, and results in the adoption of heuristics to provide satisfactory solutions. These short cut rules generate alternative schedules which may be judged on their achievement of particular targets, e.g.:

(i)   minimum time to complete the entire current job schedule (makespan time);
(ii) minimum number of jobs in progress;
(iii) minimum waiting time for jobs in the queue;
(iv) minimum lateness of completion (i.e., delivery date minus due date).

Project Appraisal

Scheduling problems can be represented graphically or through networks, similar to those used in project evaluation. Calculations of expected completion time are complicated both by the variability in job processing times and the interdependence of jobs and machines. Unless both jobs in process and machine are free simultaneously then a delay will result because one is waiting for the other. This is characterised by either machine idle time or job queuing. These complications are identical to those associated with earliest start/latest finish time for sequential projects. Although heuristic rules are rarely developed from scientific principles, they are generally better than intuition and may provide optimum solutions in specific circumstances. A number of commonly employed rules exist for the ordering of jobs:

(i)   first-come first-served (FCFS);
(ii)   shortest-operating-time (for entire job) first (SOT);
(iii) shortest-operating-time (for first processing operation) first (SPT);
(iv)   longest-operating-time (for first operation) first (LOT);
(v)   critical ratio method (work content ÷ time remaining available) lowest (C/T).

Simulation-based research has shown that adoption of the SOT rule will, on average, help achieve the minimisation targets specified above. But it may have some socially unacceptable disadvantages, in that some jobs may remain in the queue for a very long time! A truncated SOT rule may therefore be necessary in practice, so that normal priorities can be overridden to bring a job to the front of the queue if it has been in the system longer than a specified time. This could be accomplished less arbitrarily by using C/T as a priority index in conjunction with the normal SOT rule. This would allow higher priority to attach to a job as its due date approaches, but complicates the single rule method.

Minicase D: Donovan Furnishings illustrates the problems.

Donovan Furnishings is processing an order for three different styles of chair, designated Jobs 1, 2 and 3 respectively. Each of the jobs passes through the same operations in identical order, but each makes different requirements of the resource.

Job 1 requires five hours in cutting, six hours in machining and three hours in staining and polishing. Job 2 requires four hours in cutting, three hours in machining and four hours in staining and polishing. Job 3 requires six hours in cutting, three hours in machining and another three hours in staining and polishing. The minimum time to process each job separately, independent of the requirements of the others, is therefore 14 hours, 11 hours and 12 hours respectively.

Donovan's target time for the completion of all three jobs is 16 hours, but it wishes to minimise total throughput time while at the same time ensuring that machine idle time, job waiting time and job delivery times are as low as possible. They are investigating alternative job schedules.

The Gantt chart detailed in Figure 20 shows how resources are consumed and jobs completed relative to the horizontal time scale. It provides a means of facilitating job scheduling, but one which might be improved upon with a matrix approach. The latter shows waiting time, resource slack and the completion times for each separate operation more clearly. Figure 21 shows the outcome of adopting the FCFS (first-come first-served) scheduling rule, processing the jobs 1, 2 and 3 in that order.

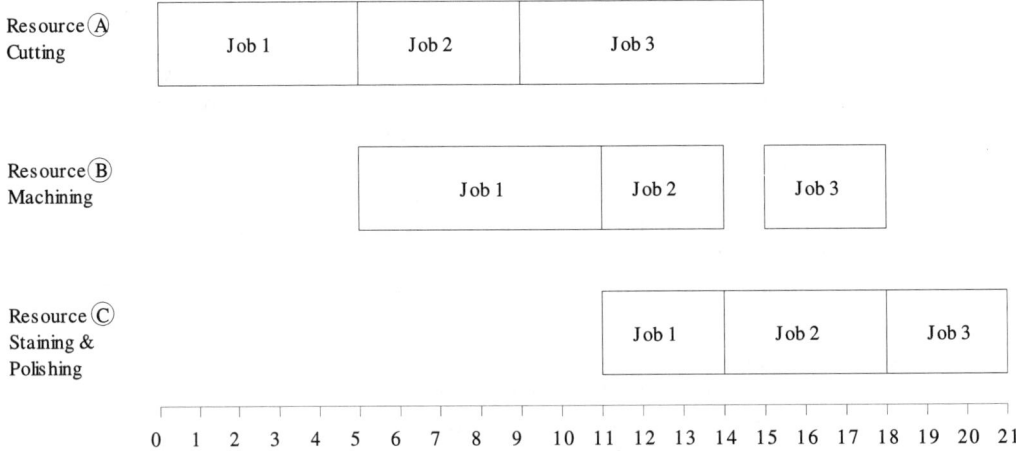

Figure 20: Gantt Chart

Figure 21 (see page 149) shows all jobs to be completed within 21 hours using the FCFS (i.e. 1-2-3) rule, but with the incurrence of both machine idle time and job queuing time. Job 2 must wait for two hours for the availability of Resource B (machining), and spare capacity of one hour exists in machining while it waits for Job 3 to clear cutting. Both Jobs 2 and 3 fail to meet the target time of 16 hours, Job 2 is two hours late and Job 3 is five hours late (i.e. 3.5 hours per job late on average).

Several more heuristics might be employed to schedule these jobs, with the following results:

The SOT rule (shortest overall processing time scheduled first), i.e. Jobs 2, 3, 1 results in:

- a total processing time of 24 hours;
- waiting time of 0 hours;
- idle time of 7 hours (5 in B and 2 in C);
- only Job 2 failing to meet the delivery target, but it is 8 hours late.

The SPT rule processes the Jobs 2,1,3 and results in:

- a total processing time of 21 hours;
- waiting time of 0 hours;
- idle time of 6 hours (2 in B and 4 in C);
- both Job 1 and Job 3 failing to meet delivery target, being 2 hours and 5 hours late respectively.

None of the other alternatives, 1-3-2, 3-1-2 or 3-2-1 results in a total through-put time of less than 21 hours. In choosing between FCFS and the widely used SPT scheduling, Donovan must rank their requirements for minimising job queuing time or machine utilisation. Similar matrix based approaches can be employed in the analysis of larger projects and capital expenditures. Network techniques represent the jobs by nodes (O) and designate the schedule sequence with arrows for an 'activity on node' approach, or vice versa for an 'activity on arrow' approach like critical path analysis (CPA) or the programme evaluation review technique (PERT).

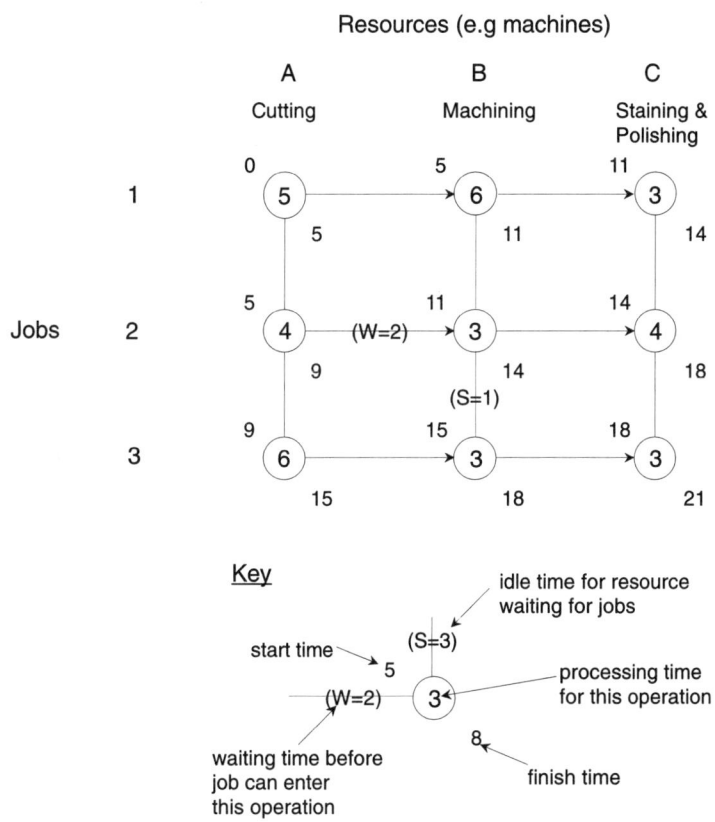

Figure 21: FCFS Matrix for Job Schedule

Whichever method is employed they all recognise the same basic features:

- the time taken to complete the operation;
- the earliest time at which the operation may start;
- the latest time at which the operation may finish;
- the interdependence and sequencing of operations.

In practice all of these are variables because:

- time to complete will follow a distribution with a mean and standard deviation. The degree of acceptable variation will be critical to the progress of the project;

- time to complete may be reduced by 'crashing' the activity i.e. employing additional resources (at a cost) to advance the status of the project;

- the degree of interdependence might be influenced by additional equipment and/or job flexibility to reduce bottlenecks.

REFERENCES

Brewer P C, Gatian A W and Reeve J M, 'Managing Uncertainty', *Management Accounting* (US), October 1993, pp 39–45

Lockyer K G, *Production Control in Practice*, Pitman, London, 1975

Lockyer K G, *An Introduction to Critical Path Analysis*, Pitman, London, 1977

Neale W and Holmes D, 'Post-Completion Audits: The Costs and Benefits', *Management Accounting* (UK), March 1988, pp 27–30

Pike R, 'The Capital Budgeting Revolution', *Management Accounting* (UK), October 1988, pp 28–30

Smith M and Stephens D, 'Cash Flow Evaluation: Beware the Hidden Pitfalls', *Accounting Forum*, March 1991, pp 33–50

Project Appraisal

CASE 16: THE SANDY BAY DEVELOPMENT

This case provides the opportunity to demonstrate the usefulness of network analysis in relieving bottlenecks and reducing levels of uncertainty in complex projects with interdependent events.

Improved road access to the secluded beaches of North West Wales has provided new tourism opportunities — and environmental dilemmas — in the Sandy Bay area. Up to now most tourists have stayed in a beach-side caravan and camping area which has a limited number of static chalets with basic amenities. The local council has repeatedly voiced concern over the environmental impact of such a development on the shore line — waterborne pollution would endanger the beaches, and therefore tourism.

The council has therefore determined to build a new development, nestling behind adjacent sand dunes, and to eliminate the possibility of future pollution (particularly sewage seepage) with the construction of a hard-core base. The existing development will eventually be phased out and the site rehabilitated, but this process will not start until completion dates have been firmly established on the new development and siteworks have commenced. The council planning authority has accepted final plans from Angelsey Contractors, completed the formalities for rezoning the required parcel of land and identified 10 distinct activities which need to be completed before the new development can commence trading:

A. Site clearance and levelling.
B. Surveying and drainage.
C. Channels for pipework and foundations.
D. Transportation of equipment and raw materials to the site.
E. Marketing planning and demand targeting.
F. Promotional activities for the new complex.
G. Assembly of prefabricated buildings.
H. Human resource planning based on local conditions.
I. Recruitment and staffing of the new complex.
J. Final inspection prior to handover.

The relationship between these activities and their relative ordering can be represented by Figure C16.1.The council has set a target time for completion of 20 weeks and a budget of £800 000. It will exact a penalty from the contractors of £20 000 a week for overruns. Anything greater than a four-week overrun will not be tolerated, since this will throw bookings into total disarray and threaten the credibility and future viability of the site. The contractors will receive an 'early finish' bonus of £25 000 a week for completion within the 20 week target.

The expected completion time and cost, together with the estimated variance for each of the activities, is detailed in Figure C16.2. Also shown is the time that the contractors might save on each activity by 'crashing' (i.e. using overtime and shift working) together with the additional cost of such endeavours.

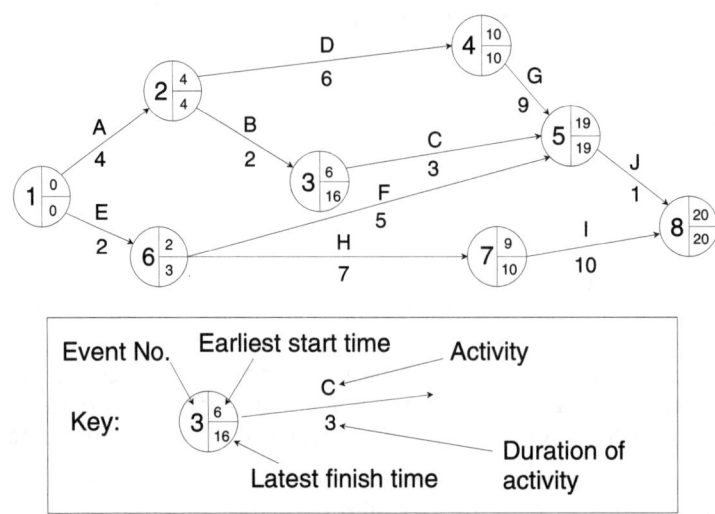

Figure C16.1: Network of Activities in Sandy Bay Development

Activity	Expected Time (Weeks)		Expected Cost (£000)	Crash Time	
	Normal	Variance		Weeks	Extra Cost (£000)
A	4	1	50	3	20
B	2	1	30	2	0
C	3	1	40	2	20
D	6	2	90	4	25
E	2	1	20	1	20
F	5	1	120	4	10
G	9	5	200	7	25
H	7	8	70	5	30
I	10	16	140	7	40
J	1	1	40	1	0
			£800 000		£180 000

Figure C16.2: Target Costs and Completion

You are required to examine the alternative approaches that the contractors might take in reaching a compromise between cost of contract and time to completion and to recommend an optimum strategy.

CASE 17: JARRAHDALE MINESITE

This case provides the opportunity to conduct a project evaluation which requires a choice between a number of stated alternatives. Discounted Cash Flow (DCF) methods are central to the analysis, but strategic factors and non-financials also form a critical part of the appraisal.

Front end loaders (FELs) are used in two locations at Jarrahdale's minesite in Western Australia. They are employed in the process of transporting bauxite ore to the adjacent alumina refinery. Bauxite is loaded onto conveyor systems destined for storage in the Bauxite Sheds and for loading the railway carriers at the Loading Station. The Loading Station is serviced by two Caterpillar FELs and the Bauxite Sheds by three Komatsu FELs. Although there is some interchange between sites of the five machines in the fleet, the Caterpillars are not popular because they are old, slow and lack manoeuvrability.

The two Caterpillar loaders are both in excess of 25 years old and are beyond their economic service life. They are both over double the age of any other unit in the fleet. The availability of these two machines is now 16 per cent lower than that of the more recently purchased machines, and the additional maintenance costs associated with this increased downtime are further affected by the increasing difficulty of obtaining parts for machines of this age.

The company is more than happy with the Komatsu loaders but now that the Caterpillars are due for major overhaul and refit to improve their reliability, a number of alternative actions are being considered. These are summarised in Figure C17.1:

Option	Action	Capital Expenditure
1	Do nothing	$0
2	Overhaul one Caterpillar	$0
3	Overhaul both Caterpillars	$0
4	Replace one Caterpillar with <u>one</u> new FEL	$500 000
5	Replace <u>both</u> Caterpillars with <u>one</u> new FEL	$500 000
6	Replace <u>both</u> Caterpillars with a hired FEL	$0

Figure C17.1: Alternative Scenarios for Caterpillar Front End Loaders

A decision to purchase new FEL equipment could be justified on one or more of several grounds:

- the existing fleet is unable to maintain production because of declining availability and increased downtime associated with ageing;

- capital costs of new machines can be offset against the reduced maintenance costs compared to the old machines;

- the new machines are more flexible and manoeuvrable and so are capable of greater productivity than the existing machines;

- the new machines are significantly safer to operate than the old machines;

- the running costs, other than maintenance, are significantly lower for the new machines and can be used to offset the capital costs.

Safety is considered paramount, so where safety is an issue no studies of future economic viability are considered necessary. Where safety aspects are not in question then the maintenance of present and future anticipated production levels assumes top priority. Considerations of alternative equipment purchases therefore centre around the first of the above grounds, with the Mitsubishi WA60 unit currently being touted as the most economic replacement option.

The new Mitsubishi loader will involve capital expenditure of $500 000 in total: $400 000 for the basic unit, $74 000 for spare parts and $26 000 for the tyres. Warranty procedures mean that maintenance costs for the Mitsubishi can be ignored for five years. The alternatives must be considered in detail to determine whether such expenditure is justified. Operating costs, other than maintenance, are not expected to differ significantly from those under the current arrangements.

OPTION 1

Do nothing. Continue to operate the plant in its existing state, with three Komatsus and two Caterpillars.

There is no capital expenditure required and this option can be used to evaluate the effective savings/costs of the other options. Adoption of this option has a number of disadvantages:

- A hired machine may have to be employed from time to time to cover the breakdown of the existing units and to meet production demands.

- The lack of availability of parts for the Caterpillar front end loaders (FELs) will increase the amount of downtime experienced and may result in lost production.

- The fleet will become unreliable and require more maintenance.

- The reduced manoeuvrability of the Caterpillars in comparison to the Komatsus will result in continued lower productivity and will negatively impact on staff morale.

Project Appraisal

OPTION 2

Overhaul one of the Caterpillars to improve its reliability and availability. Retain both Caterpillars in the present fleet arrangements. As with the previous option there is no capital outlay required, but additional expenditure on the overhaul will result.

This option has similar disadvantages to Option 1, but a higher level of availability for the overhauled Caterpillar would be obtained.

OPTION 3

Overhaul both Caterpillars to improve their reliability and availability. Retain both Caterpillars in the present fleet arrangements. As with the previous options there is no capital outlay but additional expenditure on overhauls would result.

This option has similar disadvantages to the previous options, but a higher level of availability for the overhauled Caterpillars would be obtained.

OPTION 4

Replace one Caterpillar FEL with a new Mitsubishi WA60 FEL. The replacement option requires a capital expenditure of $500 000. It is estimated that $35 000 could be recovered by the sale of a Caterpillar.

The advantages of this option are:

- The capacity of the FEL fleet would be significantly increased.
- The availability of the FEL fleet would be increased.
- The maintenance requirements of the FEL fleet would be reduced.
- A reduction in total operating cash flows would result.
- FEL mobility would improve and result in higher levels of staff morale.

OPTION 5

Replace both Caterpillars with a new Mitsubishi WA60 FEL. This option requires a capital expenditure of $500 000. It is estimated that $70 000 could be recovered from the sale of both Caterpillars.

This option would provide similar advantages to Option 4 including:

- Reduced inventory of spare parts as they would not be needed for the Caterpillars.
- A reduced maintenance expenditure requirement for the front end loader fleet.

OPTION 6

Retire both Caterpillars and operate with an additional hired Komatsu. Salvage of $70 000 could be realised from this option and no capital expenditure would be required. This option would have similar advantages to Option 5.

PRODUCTION REQUIREMENTS

The planned production rate for the upcoming year of operations is 4500 tonnes of alumina per day. An estimated 10 484 operating hours for FELs would be needed to fulfil these requirements. They are projected using the same ratio of operating hours per tonne of bauxite handled as recorded in the last complete year of operation. No allowance has been made for any possible improvement in the effectiveness of FEL operation.

FEL Type	Unit	1991	1992	1993
Caterpillar	1	790	750	430
	2	550	1160	1170
Komatsu	1	750	1870	1970
	2	3900	3400	3300
	3	2600	4030	2950
Total Fleet Hours		8590	11210	9820
Bauxite Sheds		7250	9300	8220
Loading Station		1340	1910	1600

Figure C17.2: FEL Operating Hours

Figure C17.2 shows operating hours for the machines over the last three years. The most recent annual rates suggest a requirement of:

Bauxite Sheds	8220 h	(i.e. 3 * 2740 hours per Komatsu machine)
Loading Station	1600 h	(i.e. 2 * 800 hours per Caterpillar machine)

FEL Type	Unit	Availability (%)			Utilisation (%)		
		1991	1992	1993	1991	1992	1993
Caterpillar	1	84	91	71	12	10	8
	2	74	88	89	9	16	16
Komatsu	1	74	90	92	13	26	27
	2	84	84	87	58	51	47
	3	97	92	88	34	55	42

Figure C17.3: Percentage Availability/Utilisation of FELs

The number of FELs required to meet this demand is dependent upon plant availability and utilisation, together with a downtime allowance for standby or maintenance. Figure C17.3 displays the availability/utilisation data. To allow for service and breakdowns, we might expect actual production availability to be some

5 or 10 per cent below these figures. Availability (%) incorporates the impact of major maintenance works and service breakdowns. Utilisation (%) is calculated as:

$$\frac{\text{Total Operating Hours}}{\text{Total Available Hours}}$$

The figures reflect the lack of popularity of the Caterpillar units and highlight the point made by management: fewer than five operating units are required. The appropriate combination of FELs must allow the organisation to meet its required daily throughput while providing sufficient operating margin to cover the risk of a multiple FEL failure. Figure C17.4 (see page 158) details operating hours for each of the six options under consideration at alternative production levels (tonnes per day). For simplicity this diagram assumes arbitrary availability and utilisation levels of 75 per cent and 45 per cent respectively.

MAINTENANCE COSTS

Historical data for maintenance costs and costs per hour for the five units in the fleet are available for the last five years, and shows considerable variation. Maintenance work carried out in one year, particularly major overhauls, is associated with reduced maintenance costs in succeeding years. Advantage might be taken of reduced unit operations to plan major maintenance works to coincide. Figure C17.5 shows the maintenance data.

Maintenance costs per operating hour reflect the burden of the older equipment, and the predicted costs of future maintenance appear to be age dependent for all units, though the relationship is far from perfect. The decision to purchase new plant rather than maintain the old plant might be justified on the basis of the resultant maintenance cost savings. The company uses a 15 per cent rate of discount for its appraisal of investment projects and a 27 per cent reducing balance rate of depreciation (the maximum permitted by the Australian Tax Office).

You are required to evaluate the alternatives available and advise the company which option best satisfies its requirements. Your report should include a detailed sensitivity analysis together with a discussion of assumptions and limitations.

FEL Type	Unit	In Service Year	Age (Years)	Maintenance Costs ($000)				
				1989	1990	1991	1992	1993
Caterpillar	1	1967	>25	69.5	57.9	18.8	31.2	18.4
	2	1967	>25	46.4	61.6	11.2	81.0	36.4
Caterpillar Fleet				115.9	119.5	30.0	112.2	54.8
Komatsu	1	1982	11	72.6	35.6	67.2	80.8	87.5
	2	1986	7	64.3	68.3	12.8	86.3	88.7
	3	1989	4	3.7	46.0	45.5	62.8	48.1
Komatsu Fleet				140.6	149.9	125.5	229.9	224.3
Total Fleet				256.5	269.4	155.5	342.1	279.1

Figure C17.5: Maintenance Costs for FEL Fleet

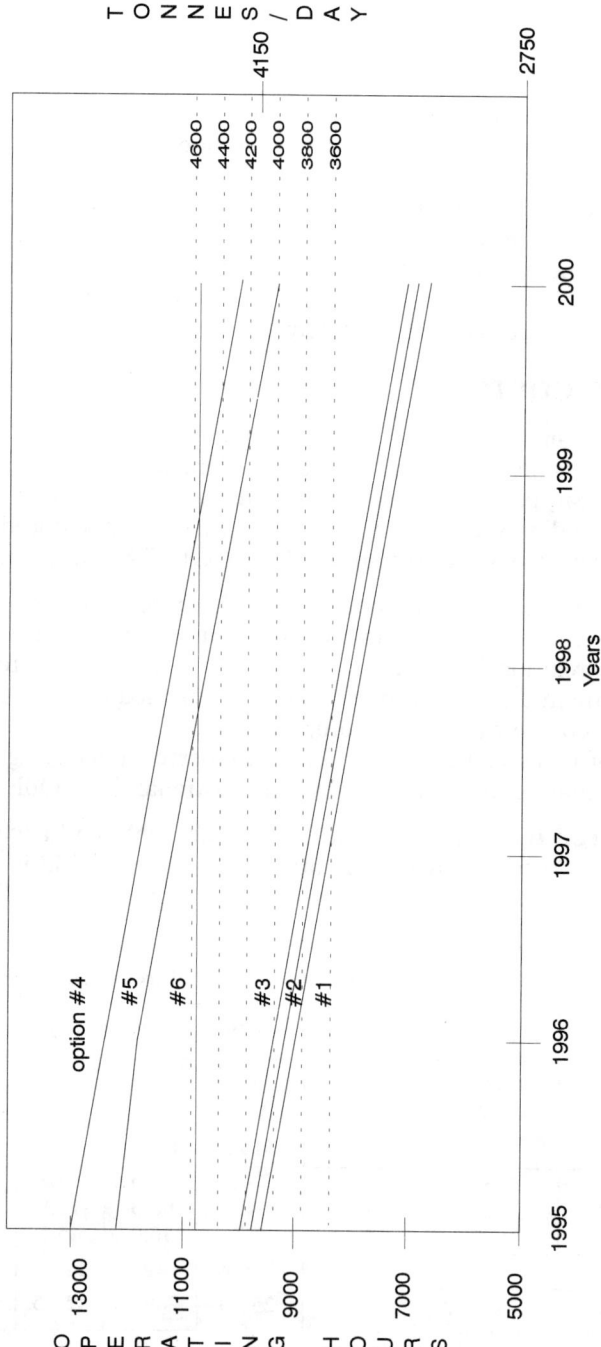

Figure C17.4: Projected FEL Management

CASE 18: ALUMINA REFINERIES

This case is concerned with the appraisal of an investment project using Discounted Cash Flow (DCF) procedures. Details of the project evaluation are supplied, sufficient to allow a post-audit of the procedure followed in its evaluation and approval.

The Engineering department at Alumina Refineries has spent £200 000 on purchasing the following mobile equipment:

1. A Grove low profile mobile crane at £140 000.
2. A Longreach mobile aerial platform at £60 000.

This equipment replaces the existing Steelweld crane and mobile work platform, both nearly 25 years old. The existing equipment has accumulated high maintenance costs over the last five years and parts are increasingly difficult to obtain, being outdated models and requiring specific manufacture in most instances.

The replacement equipment comprises the latest models available. They are more capable and can provide a service which reduces or removes costly work practices and reduces the need for equipment hire.

ECONOMIC JUSTIFICATION

Alumina Refineries currently operates a 40 feet [12.2 m] high reach aerial work platform and a Steelweld crane. The work platform is used in various locations as maintenance access to valves, piping and structures, while the crane is used extensively by maintenance personnel, particularly shift maintenance, in buildings where access is tight and confined. Both units are essential for maintenance departments to carry out day-to-day activities that require aerial access or lifting capabilities in confined areas.

MOBILE AERIAL WORK PLATFORM

The physical dimensions of the platform are too large to operate in confined areas. This then requires the erection of scaffolds to gain access to equipment such as valves, pumps and piping structures. Scaffolding takes on average in excess of three days to erect and dismantle when an appropriate aerial work platform would take less than a day. Sometimes a similar and smaller machine is hired to perform such duties. The slow travelling speed (0.5 km/h) of the existing platform is a disadvantage and causes its non-return to the central cranes parking area. This then ties up personnel time in trying to locate the machine for use in other areas.

STEELWELD CRANE

The existing Steelweld is considered to be an asset to maintenance users as it is the only crane on site that can be used in confined areas and the rod mills, due to its low profile height and slewable jib. This crane does not have an operator's cab

159

and would not normally be allowed for use by the appropriate safety and licensing authorities for crane and lifting operations. If the cab were installed, then the effect on the crane's profile would mean that it could not be used in any of the confined areas for which it is currently uniquely suitable. This would drastically limit the maintenance department's effectiveness.

This crane is not easy to maintain as virtually all parts have to be manufactured and downtime can be considerable. This type of crane is obsolete and vendor technical expertise is virtually non-existent. Maintenance costs are detailed in Figure C18.1. Overhaul is not recommended on either machine since the same parts difficulties would still be encountered.

Unit	Year in Service	Salvage Value	O/Haul Cost	1984	1985	1986	1987	1988	1989 to Aug 1989
Mobile Work Platform	1970	10 000	Not Recomd	4976	1091	14902	8831	6255	1274
Steelweld Crane (Fleet Average)	1970	10 000	Not Recomd	1266	2030	2095	4368	6218	838

Figure C18.1: Maintenance Costs (£)

PROPOSAL

It is recommended to replace both machines with the following:
1. The Grove low profile mobile crane at £140 000
2. The Longreach mobile aerial work platform at £60 000

These replacement machines would enhance maintenance effectiveness by providing the same maintenance service plus additional duties not provided by the older machines. The Grove cranes are already used extensively at sister refineries and have been very reliable, accumulating low maintenance costs. The load range and extendable boom would also allow the use of this crane in areas normally serviced by the existing Steelweld crane as well as reducing hire requirements.

Another advantage is the carry decks which will eliminate the use of a dogman to accompany the crane. It is proposed to install a forklift and work platform accessories to provide additional capabilities for maintenance.

The aerial lift mobile work platform will be utilised in confined areas of low height and width accessways and can reach up and over obstructing pipework and structures. These capabilities will eliminate the need to build scaffolds to reach valves and piping to carry out maintenance work. It is estimated that the erection and dismantling of scaffolds could cause in excess of two to three days' downtime of precipitator tanks.

Project Appraisal

BENEFITS

The replacement of this equipment will generate the cost savings and profit improvements detailed in Figure C18.2 by reducing the need for scaffolding and increasing production opportunities due to the earlier return of out of circuit equipment to production.

Savings/ Profits	Yr 1	Yr 2	Yr 3	Yr 4	Yr 5
Labour Savings	50 000	50 000	50 000	50 000	50 000
Scaffold Inventory	10 000	10 000	10 000	10 000	10 000
Increased Production	54 000	54 000	54 000	54 000	54 000
Maintenance Reduction	6 000	8 000	12 000	16 ,000	18 000
Hire Reductions	6400	6400	6400	6400	6400
Total	126 400	128 400	132 400	136 400	138 400

Figure C18.2: Cost Savings and Increased Profits (£)

Evaluation of this project leads to the following conclusions:

NPV at 13%   =   £342 000
IRR   =   54.3%
Payback (discounted)   =   1.8 years

Depreciation is charged half-yearly on a reducing balance basis. Details of the project appraisal are shown in Figure C18.3.

You are required to conduct a post-audit of this project and to make recommendations for the improvement of the procedure adopted. Your report should include a detailed sensitivity analysis and any assumptions necessary to allow the two components of the project to be appraised separately.

	Base	Y1		Y2		Y3		Y4		Y5	
		Y1H1	Y1H2	Y2H1	Y2H2	Y3H1	Y3H2	Y4H1	Y4H2	Y5H1	Y5H2
Investment & Depreciation											
Investment	200.0										
Depreciation		18.0	18.0	14.8	14.8	12.1	12.1	9.9	9.9	8.1	8.1
Depreciated Value	200.0	182.0	164.0	149.2	134.5	122.4	110.3	100.3	90.4	82.3	74.1
Working Capital	0.0										
Salvage	0.0	20.0									
Cash Flow from Operations											
Cash from Ops		63.2	63.2	64.2	64.2	66.2	66.2	68.2	68.2	69.2	69.2
plus salvage	0.0	20.0	0.0	0.0	0.0	0.0	0.0	0.0	0.0	0.0	0.0
less depreciatn	0.0	18.0	18.0	14.8	14.8	12.1	12.1	9.9	9.9	8.1	8.1
Taxable income	0.0	65.2	45.2	49.4	49.4	54.1	54.1	58.3	58.3	61.1	61.1
less tax paid				43.1		38.6		42.2		45.5	
After Tax Cash from Ops	0.0	65.2	45.2	6.4	49.4	15.5	54.1	16.1	58.3	15.6	61.1
less working capital	0.0	0.0	0.0	0.0	0.0	0.0	0.0	0.0	0.0	0.0	0.0
less investment	200.0	0.0	0.0	0.0	0.0	0.0	0.0	0.0	0.0	0.0	0.0
plus depreciatn	0.0	18.0	18.0	14.8	14.8	12.1	12.1	9.9	9.9	8.1	8.1
Net Cash Flow	-200.0	83.2	63.2	21.1	64.2	27.6	66.2	26.0	68.2	23.7	69.2
Accum Net Cash Flow	-200.0	-116.8	-53.6	-32.5	31.7	59.4	125.6	151.6	219.8	243.5	312.7
Discounted Cash Flow											
Discount Factor %	13.0										
Net Present Value	-200.0	-121.9	-66.2	-48.7	1.3	21.4	66.8	83.5	124.7	138.2	175.1
Benefit Cost Ratio	0.0	0.4	0.7	0.8	1.0	1.1	1.3	1.4	1.6	1.7	1.9
IRR		0.0	0.0	0.0	13.6	22.2	35.3	38.7	44.8	46.2	49.3
Discounted Factor			0	1	2	3	4	5	6	7	8
NPV			757.0	710.3	666.9	626.4	588.7	553.5	520.7	490.0	461.3

Figure 18.3a: 10 Year Appraisal for Mobile Crane and Aerial Work Platform — Years 1–5

Project Appraisal

	Base	Y6		Y7		Y8		Y9		Y10	
		Y6H1	Y6H2	Y7H1	Y7H2	Y8H1	Y8H2	Y9H1	Y9H2	Y10H1	Y10H2
Investment & Depreciation											
Investment	200.0										
Depreciation		6.7	6.7	5.5	5.5	4.5	4.5	3.7	3.7	3.0	3.0
Depreciated Value	200.0	67.5	60.8	55.3	49.9	45.4	40.9	37.2	33.5	30.5	27.5
Working Capital	0.0										
Salvage	20.0										
Cash Flow from Operations											
Cash from Ops		69.2	69.2	69.2	69.2	69.2	69.2	69.2	69.2	69.2	69.2
plus salvage	0.0	0.0	0.0	0.0	0.0	0.0	0.0	0.0	0.0	0.0	0.0
less depreciatn	0.0	6.7	6.7	5.5	5.5	4.5	4.5	3.7	3.7	3.0	3.0
Taxable income	0.0	62.5	62.5	63.7	63.7	64.7	64.7	65.5	65.5	66.2	66.2
less tax paid		47.6		48.8		49.7		50.5		51.1	
After Tax Cash from Ops	0.0	14.9	62.5	15.0	63.7	15.0	64.7	15.0	65.5	15.1	66.2
less working capital	0.0	0.0	0.0	0.0	0.0	0.0	0.0	0.0	0.0	0.0	0.0
less investment	200.0	0.0	0.0	0.0	0.0	0.0	0.0	0.0	0.0	0.0	0.0
plus depreciatn	0.0	6.7	6.7	5.5	5.5	4.5	4.5	3.7	3.7	3.0	3.0
Net Cash Flow	-200.0	21.6	69.2	20.4	69.2	19.5	69.2	18.7	69.2	18.1	69.2
Accum Net Cash Flow	-200.0	334.3	403.5	423.9	493.1	512.6	581.8	600.5	669.7	687.8	757.0
Discounted Cash Flow											
Discount Factor %	13.0										
Net Present Value	-200.0	185.9	218.4	227.4	256.0	263.6	288.9	295.3	317.6	323.0	342.7
Benefit Cost Ratio	0.0	1.9	2.1	2.1	2.3	2.3	2.4	2.5	2.6	2.6	2.7
IRR		50.0	51.6	52.0	52.9	53.1	53.6	53.7	54.0	54.1	54.3
Discounted Factor		9	10	11	12	13	14	15	16	17	18
NPV		434.5	409.3	385.7	363.5	342.7	323.1	304.6	287.2	270.8	255.4

Figure 18.3b: 10 Year Appraisal for Mobile Crane and Aerial Work Platform — Years 6–10

CASE 19: BOUTIQUE FASHIONS

This case is concerned with the potential risks and returns attaching to an investment opportunity. It combines probabilistic estimates of risk, via decision trees, with traditional spreadsheet-based project evaluation, to allow the development of a distribution of returns and an appreciation of risk profile.

Boutique Fashions is a national retail chain considering an increase in its number of outlets by moving into the Meadowhall Shopping Centre in Sheffield. It has been attracted by the success of other similar stores in the Centre and is now carrying out a full project appraisal. Its market research team has made the following estimates relating to sales, profits and the economy to aid the decision making process:

COSTS

(a) A ten year lease on suitable premises is available with an annual rental of £0.5 m payable annually in advance and fixed at this level for the entire period.

(b) Staffing costs are thought to vary directly with the volume of goods sold (measured by the value of sales turnover) and to increase in line with the rate of wage inflation. Real wage costs have been estimated at 7 per cent of turnover, before any adjustment for wage inflation.

(c) Inventory holding costs are estimated to be 15% of the annual value of inventory. Turnover has been estimated to lie in the range of 14 to 18 times the value of inventory, so that values of 14, 15, 16, 17 and 18 can be thought of as equally likely multiples.

(d) Start-up costs, including the fitting out and furnishing of the store, recruitment, equipment installation and initial inventory requirements, amount to £5 m payable at the beginning of the project.

(e) Maintenance costs incurred in all but the first year are expected to be more or less constant in real terms at £0.4 m and to be independent of sales volume, though increasing in line with the rate of price inflation.

SALES

The number of customers entering the store each week is largely outside the control of management, but marketing surveys have provided estimates of the number of people likely to visit the Centre development when fully operational. The turnover of the store is expected to be between 6 and 8 per cent of the total number of shoppers visiting the centre.

In the first year the average weekly number of visitors to the shopping centre has been estimated to be either 50 000, 100 000, 150 000 or 200 000, all equally likely.

Project Appraisal

In the case of the two lower estimates, there is a 20 per cent chance of 6 per cent entering the store, 40 per cent of 7 per cent and 40 per cent of 8 per cent entering the store. For the two higher estimates, the respective probabilities have been estimated as 20 per cent of 6 per cent entering the store, 50 per cent of 7 per cent and 30 per cent of 8 per cent entering the store. The average purchase size per customer has been estimated as being between £20 and £60 in the first year of trading — with a 20 per cent chance of it being £20, a 30 per cent chance of it being £30, a 40 per cent chance of it being £40 and a 10 per cent chance of it being £60.

The growth in the number of customers at the centre is expected to be compound at 10 per cent per annum for three years after the initial period, then slowing down to a compound rate of 4 per cent per annum.

Returns

Boutique's management has a policy of employing a 25 per cent markup on all product lines, so that cost of sales can be considered to be four-fifths of the value of sales turnover. Management expects to be able to maintain this profit margin in the foreseeable future. Shrinkage (i.e. pilferage, damaged goods) is not expected to exceed a level of 1 per cent per annum.

Boutique would normally expect projects of this kind to satisfy an 18 per cent internal rate of return hurdle.

Economy

(a) The annual rate of price inflation over the life of the project has been estimated at 6 per cent, with a 10 per cent chance, at 7 per cent with a 40 per cent chance, at 8 per cent with a 30 per cent chance and at 9 per cent with a 20 per cent chance.

(b) Wage-cost inflation is thought to be directly related to the rate of price inflation, so that if price inflation is running at 7 per cent or below, wage inflation has a 50 per cent chance of being 1 per cent lower, a 30 per cent chance of being 1.5 per cent lower and a 20 per cent chance of being 2 per cent lower.

If price inflation is higher than 7 per cent, wage inflation has a 50 per cent chance of being 1 per cent lower, a 30 per cent chance of being 2 per cent lower and a 20 per cent chance of being 3 per cent lower.

(c) Tax on profits is payable one year in arrears and the rate of taxation level can be considered to be fixed over the duration of the project. Depreciation for tax purposes can be charged on start-up costs and maintenance costs in the year in which these costs are incurred.

(d) Cash shortfalls in the project can currently be financed by the company at a cost of capital of 12 per cent per annum.

You are required to evaluate this project and make appropriate recommendations to Boutique's management as to its viability. Your analysis should include an examination of the likely risks and returns together with a detailed sensitivity analysis.

Chapter 7

Total Quality Management

7.1 INTRODUCTION

As recently as 30 years ago Japanese products were frequently noted in the West for their shoddiness and unreliability. The transformation in the reputation of Japanese goods in the 1990s — led by their electronics and motor sectors — has much to do with the readiness of the Japanese to accept and apply the latest management principles. This flexibility results largely from the restructuring of unions and institutions following World War II, which allowed the changes necessary to incorporate Just-in-Time (JIT), value added management (VAM) and total quality management (TQM) to be made. The initial forays into South East Asia during the 1950s of W Edwards Deming, the celebrated US guru of quality management, meant that his ideas were incorporated at a time when inflexibility of attitudes and union resistance to change prevented them from being adopted in his home country. Deming, Juran and Crosby have since led the international popularisation of TQM as a process of continuous improvement.

TQM seeks to increase customer satisfaction by finding the factors that limit current performance. The practice of TQM, so far mainly in manufacturing environments, has produced tangible improvements in efficiency and profitability as a result of many small improvements. The TQM approach highlights the need for a customer-oriented approach, including the elimination of some traditional practices.

On the shop floor quality concepts have been based around the involvement of employees and 'the next person on the assembly line is my customer' approach. The application of quality concepts to service areas requires a similar approach, necessitating a focus on customer requirements. In a manufacturing environment the 'cost of quality' might be viewed as the sum of the costs associated with scrap, reworks, warranty claims and inspection expenses. In a service environment, the same costs are those associated with procedures which produce inaccurate, error-prone or untimely services provided to 'customers'. Problem solving in a management accounting environment requires a precise definition of the problem, an awareness of inhibiting constraints, a willingness to accept the existence of alternatives, and avoidance of a closed mind attitude focusing on a single most obvious solution.

Total Quality Management

A number of essential requirements emerge, which may be described as the six Cs of TQM:

- **Commitment**. If a TQM culture is to be developed, so that quality improvement becomes a normal part of everyone's job, a clear commitment from the top must be provided. Without this all else fails. It is not sufficient to delegate 'quality' issues to a single person since this will not provide an environment for changing attitudes and breaking down the barriers to quality improvement. Such expectations must be made clear, together with the support and training necessary to their achievement.

- **Culture**. Training lies at the centre of effecting a change in culture and attitudes. Management accountants too often associate 'creativity' with 'creative accounting' and associated negative perceptions. This must be changed to encourage individual contributions and to make 'quality' a normal part of everyone's job.

- **Continuous Improvement**. Recognition that TQM is a 'process' not a 'program' necessitates that we are committed in the long term to the never-ending search for ways to do the job better. There will always be room for improvements, however small.

- **Cooperation**. The application of Total Employee Involvement (TEI) principles is paramount. The on-the-job experience of all employees must be fully utilised and their involvement and cooperation sought in the development of improvement strategies and associated performance measures.

- **Customer Focus**. The needs of the customer are the major driving thrust; not just the external customer (in receipt of the final product or service) but also the internal customer (colleagues who receive and supply goods, services or information). Perfect service with zero defects is all that is acceptable at either internal or external levels. Too frequently, in practice, TQM implementations focus entirely on the external customer to the exclusion of internal relationships: they will not survive the short-term unless they foster the mutual respect necessary to preserve morale and employee participation.

- **Control**. Documentation, procedures and awareness of current best practice are essential if TQM implementations are to function appropriately. The need for control mechanisms is frequently overlooked in practice, in the euphoria of improved customer service and employee empowerment. Unless procedures are in place improvements cannot be monitored and measured nor deficiencies corrected.

The quality improvement process should be a vehicle for positive and constructive movement within an organisation but we must also be aware of the destructive potential of the process. Failure to observe the fundamental principles of quality improvement may destroy motivation irrecoverably.

Some authors, notably Carlzon (1987) and Albrecht (1985, 1988) have criticised the direction that TQM implementations have tended to take in practice, in particular:

167

- the focus on documentation of process and ill-measurable outcomes;

- the emphasis on quality assurance rather than improvement; and

- an internal focus which is at odds with the alleged customer orientation.

Carlzon has revived the customer focus with an emphasis on total employee involvement (TEI) culminating in the empowerment of the 'front-line' of customer service troops. The main features of his empowerment thrust have been:

- loyalty to the vision of the company through the pursuit of tough, visible goals;

- recognition of satisfied customers and motivated employees as the true assets of a company;

- delegation of decision making to the point of responsibility by eliminating hierarchical tiers of authority to allow direct and speedy response to customer needs;

- decentralisation of management to make best use of the creative energy of the workforce.

Albrecht suggests that TQM may not be appropriate for service based industries, because the standards based approach of 'industry best practice' ignores the culture of organisations. He recommends a move towards TQS (total quality service), which is more customer oriented and creates an environment to promote enthusiasm and commitment. Albrecht suggests that poor service is associated with sloppy procedures, errors, inaccuracies and oversights, and poor coordination, all of which represent improvement opportunities which can be achieved through tighter controls.

7.2 IMPLEMENTING TQM

A systematic quality improvement process like the **PRAISE** system of Figure 22 restricts the adoption of sub-optimum quick-fix solutions and increases the awareness of participants of the barriers to change. We should avoid jumping to conclusions and seeking quick-fix solutions without examining the options and the consequences of our actions. Problems rarely exist in isolation and the chain of dependent events must be examined. Understanding of the root problem, not merely its symptoms, requires a clarity of thought too often lacking. A team approach is much to be preferred in the generation and evaluation of ideas. A structured group decision making process for assigning rank priorities and reaching consensus provides an environment conducive to the development of creative suggestions. Management tools and techniques like brainstorming, lateral thinking, synectics, fishbone diagrams and force fields are all useful in this respect.

Awareness of the usefulness of TQM is not difficult to achieve, but the ability to implement it can be a problem. Inertia associated with behavioural issues, individual motivation and group dynamics provides a barrier. Little attention has so far been paid to the practical problems of overcoming the inertia of organisations and the reluctance of some individuals to adopt the new tools of management accounting.

Stage 1	Problem identification	• Areas of customer dissatisfaction • Absence of competitive advantage • Complacency regarding present arrangements
Stage 2	Ranking	• Prioritise problems/opportunities by: perceived importance and ease of measurement and solution
Stage 3	Analysis	• Ask *why*, to identify possible causes • Keep asking *why*, to move beyond the symptoms and to avoid jumping to premature conclusions • Ask *what*, to consider potential implications • Ask *how* much, to quantify cause and effect
Stage 4	Innovation	• Use creative thinking to generate potential solutions • Implement these solutions by identifying: barriers to implementation enablers available people whose cooperation is sought
Stage 5	Solution	• Implement the preferred solution • Take appropriate action to bring about the required changes • Reinforce with training and documentation back-up
Stage 6	Evaluation	• Monitor the effectiveness of actions • Establish and interpret performance indicators to track progress towards objectives • Identify the potential for further improvements and a return to Stage 1 in the process

Figure 22: The PRAISE System of Quality Improvement

An analysis of group dynamics identifies four major features essential to effective operation. Smith (1992) refers to them as the four Ps of quality improvement:

- **People**. Some individuals are not suitable to the participatory process. Where these individuals are given the responsibility for driving the group then progress will be slow or negligible.

- **Process**. An inflexible process will have a de-motivating effect on group activity. It is essential to adopt a practical approach to problem solving and to regard any formal process as a system designed to prevent participants from jumping to conclusions.

- **Problem**. The least successful groups will be those approaching problems that are too big to provide meaningful solutions within a finite time period. A 'bite-sized chunk' approach of tackling solvable problems with a direct economic impact is preferred.

- **Preparation**. Training in the workings of quality improvement processes alone is inadequate. Additional courses devoted to creative thinking and statistical processes are necessary to give participants greater appreciation of the diversity of the process. Training should be practical, avoiding unnecessary abstractions and keeping management jargon to a minimum. It may even be necessary to replace the TQM acronym itself with one based on a 'quality improvement process'. This training should be extended to include employees at the plant supervisory level who are involved at the data input stage.

A suitable guide for the choice of project and implementation of process is provided by the following:

- **A bite-sized chunk approach**. It is tempting to seek a large cherry to pluck but big improvement opportunities are inevitably complex and require extensive interdepartmental cooperation. The choice of a relatively small problem in the first instance provides a greater guarantee of success. It is fruitless to identify 'communications' or 'low morale' as problems; problems must be framed much more specifically.

- **A solvable problem**. It should not be a trivial problem, but one with potential impact and a clear improvement opportunity. Measurable progress towards implementation should be accomplished within at most three months in order to maintain the motivation of participants and advertise the success of the improvement process itself.

- **Recognition of those involved**. The successful projects and team members should receive appropriate recognition throughout the enterprise. Prominent individuals should be rewarded for their efforts for personal recognition and to encourage others. Such rewards are usually non-monetary prizes.

Smith (1994) describes the conduct of a TQM implementation in the accounting function of a large Australian manufacturer. It is instructive to identify the different stages of the process employed, as detailed in Figure 23. The first four stages of this procedure represent an internal analysis without direct reference to the customer base. The perceptions of the accounting team are used to prioritise customers and services and to identify strengths and weaknesses in the accounting function. A benchmarking procedure (see Chapter 4) is conducted at Stage 5 to identify industry best practice and to highlight deficiencies relative to other process manufacturers which offer clear improvement opportunities.

The outcomes from the first five stages provide the groundwork for an in depth customer survey at Stage 6, from which multiple improvement opportunities emerge, varying from the trivial to the critical. At Stage 7 these problems/opportunities are prioritised and the top ranking issues assigned to teams for in depth consideration. These then form the base material at Stage 8 for the conduct of the team-based quality improvement process following the six steps of the PRAISE mechanism, detailed in Figure 22. A structured procedure ensures that the teams develop and explore alternative solutions without jumping to conclusions, so that they are confident they have 'got it right the first time' when they reach the implementation stage. Fully documented solutions, with training implications explored, are then instituted and carefully monitored against appropriate performance measures. Successes are trumpeted through in-house journals; any failures are redirected to the change teams responsible for further consideration.

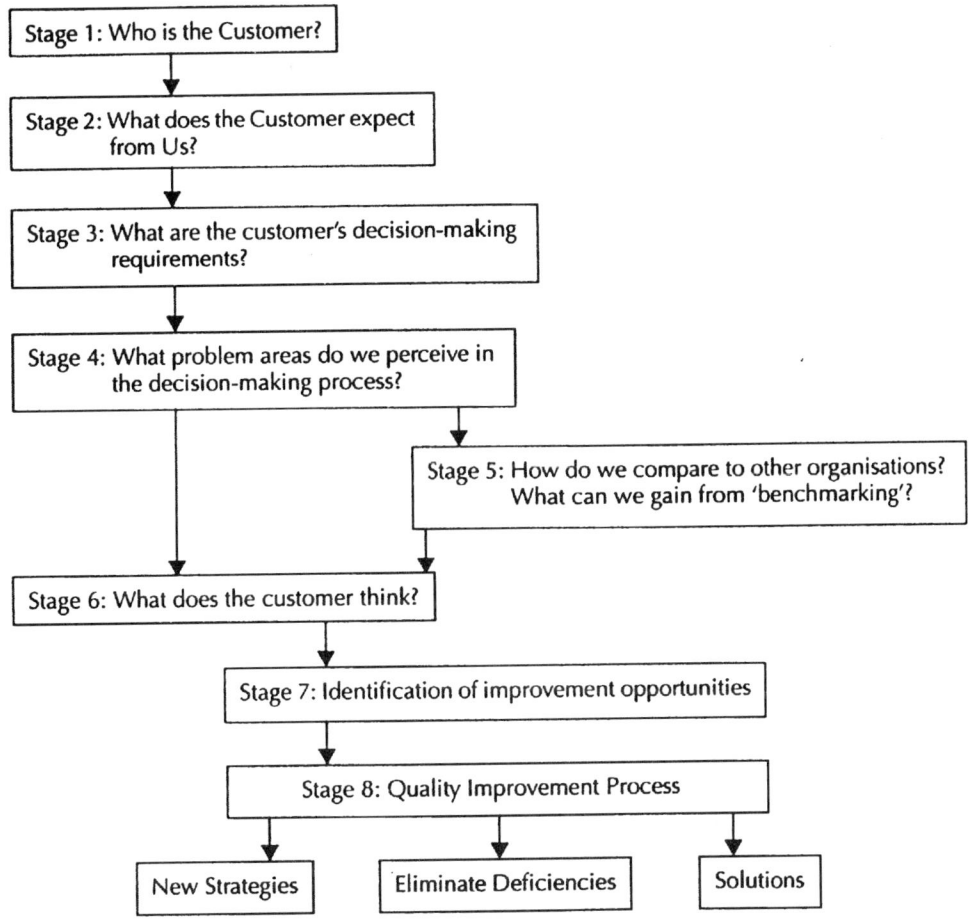

Figure 23: Process for Reviewing the Management Accounting Function

The success of the improvement process is firmly grounded in the principles of TQM, TEI and process measurement. Practical implementations would be expected to include:

- a clear exposition of the benefits of any project;

- involvement of all customers and contributors;

- the elimination of non-relevant data;

- an understanding of the needs of the whole process;

- the employment of graphic and pictorial techniques to achieve understanding;

- the establishment of clear performance specifications and targets;

- the use of errors for learning and to prompt continuous improvement; and

- the use of statistics to tell people how well they are doing.

The following cases demonstrate the usefulness of the TQM process in two diverse environments:

- a large process-based manufacturing company in *Case 20: Blackburn Chemicals*, and

- a small service-based company in *Case 21: Spick 'N' Span Dry Cleaners*.

REFERENCES

Albrecht K, *At America's Service: How Corporations can Revolutionise the Way they treat their Customers*, Dow Jones-Irwin, Homewood, Illinois, 1988

Albrecht K and Zemke R, *Service America!: Doing Business in the New Economy*, Dow Jones-Irwin, Homewood, Illinois, 1985

Carlzon J, *Moments of Truth: New Strategies for Today's Customer Driven Economy*, Ballinger Publishing, Cambridge, Mass, 1987

Crosby P B, *Quality is Free*, McGraw Hill, New York, 1979

Crosby P B, *Quality Without Tears: The Art of Hassle-free Management*, New American Library, New York, 1985

Deming W E, *Out of the Crisis: Quality, Productivity and Competitive Position*, CUP, Cambridge, 1986

Garvin D A, 'Competing on the Eight Dimensions of Quality', *Harvard Business Review*, November–December 1987, pp 101–109

Juran J, *Juran on Leadership for Quality: An Executive Handbook*, Free Press, New York, 1989

Mills R, 'Making TQM work in Practice', *Accountancy*, May 1987, pp 118–119

Smith M, 'Management Accounting for Total Quality Management', *Management Accounting* (UK), June 1990, pp 44–46

Smith M, 'Overcoming Total Quality Paralysis', *Charter*, August 1992, pp 44–45

Smith M, 'Improving Management Accounting Reporting Practices: A Total Quality Management Approach (Part I)', *Journal of Cost Management*, Vol 7 No 4, Winter 1994, pp 50–57

Smith M, 'Improving Management Accounting Reporting Practices: A Total Quality Management Approach (Part II)', *Journal of Cost Management*, Vol 8 No 1, Spring 1994, pp 47–56

Woods M D, 'How we changed our Accounting', *Management Accounting*, February 1989, pp 42–45

CASE 20: BLACKBURN CHEMICALS

This case provides a scenario for the conduct of a process which aims to highlight improvement opportunities and use a systematic procedure in the development of alternative solutions. The syndicate exercises employed might easily be adapted to alternative scenarios in both manufacturing and non-manufacturing environments.

Blackburn Chemicals is based in Manchester's major industrial zone at Trafford Park and specialises in the production of acetone, phenol and phenolic resins. The management accounting team at Blackburn Chemicals, led by Chief Accountant Ross Nicholls, is concerned about the effectiveness and efficiency of the service they provide within the organisation. Ross has recently attended a TQM seminar and is determined to apply this philosophy to the accountants under his control. He has identified three key areas of concern which he intends to address:

1. The establishment of customer requirements.

2. The identification of deficiencies and missed opportunities in the current service provision.

3. The suitability of corporate performance indicators and their congruence with strategic objectives.

Morale is low among the accounting team members because of doubts about the usefulness of the job they do. In particular there is a general feeling that:

- Few people read the accounting information distributed in reports.

- Those that do read the reports, don't understand them.

- The content of the reports is not targeted appropriately nor tailored to the requirements of users.

- The timing of hard copy reports makes them useless for decision making purposes.

- The lack of credible, timely information forces the divisions to establish their own ad hoc data collection and analysis teams.

- The lack of a clear executive statement on strategy makes it impossible for management to pursue coherent congruent goals.

- The emphasis on upwards reporting leaves foremen and supervisors in the dark regarding objectives, achievements and expectations.

In order to manage the current situation, Ross Nicholls has initiated a formal review procedure which will incorporate a systematic quality improvement process. His intention is to restore the enthusiasm of the accounting team through constructive direction.

Ross has determined to adopt a team approach using a number of syndicate exercises to generate priorities and critical issues in the provision of decision support information. He wants to encourage creativity and individual contributions to the team effort and has organised seminars on management tools (e.g. brain-storming, lateral thinking) to aid group learning. However, he is fully aware that choices will need to be made and is prepared to use multi-voting techniques as a democratic procedure if consensus cannot be reached. Voting will also help to eliminate 'way-out' suggestions which do not have widespread support and the pet plans of senior management, which they might otherwise attempt to force through.

The first syndicate exercise is designed to develop a customer focus by empha-sising that the customer is not just the final recipient of the product but anyone in the organisation in receipt of your contribution. Ross wishes to change current attitudes by instituting a 'next person in the production line is my customer' mentality:

SYNDICATE EXERCISE 1: CUSTOMER ANALYSIS

1. Identify the major customer groups in receipt of the contribution *you* make to this organisation.

2. Identify customer expectations of the service to be received.

3. What are the customer's requirements? Are they being satisfied?

The focus on customers and their requirements yields a number of potential improvement opportunities. The temptation is to jump to quick-fix solutions without a detailed analysis of benefits and consequences. Ross wants to avoid this and does so with a second exercise, a SWOT analysis designed to widen the focus of attention and seek answers to some fundamental questions, particularly 'what goals are we trying to achieve?' and 'what strategy do we adopt to achieve them?'

SYNDICATE EXERCISE 2: SWOT ANALYSIS

1. Identify what you perceive to be the:

    Strengths
    Weaknesses
    Opportunities
    Threats

    of this organisation.

2. Specify the *strategies* that would need to be undertaken for outcomes to be consistent with Corporate Goals.

These initial stages help to clarify the service provided, the customers and the context of the company as a whole. As a next step Ross institutes a 'benchmark-ing' operation seeking the cooperation of five similarly sized process industry based companies in the area. The benchmarking survey demonstrates a great diversity of accounting systems and procedures — representing the heights and depths of current practice. Blackburn is able to gain considerable encouragement from recognition of the inadequacies of the systems operated by other manufacturers. The TQM philosophy is not well advanced in any of the companies, highlighting the great potential for improved efficiency.

The absence of integrated centralised database systems was widespread. Only one company integrated costs-budgeting-payroll-supply-accounts payable, while incorporating variance analysis. At the other extreme three companies relied heavily on unlinked manual procedures, without any integrated on-line information system. The inflexibility of systems frequently necessitated the downloading of information (manually) onto PC in order to generate useful reports. The extent of the reliance on manual systems, diary form, handwritten logs or card based, was surprising for the 1990s, as was the absence of PCs and therefore manual generation of reports, including hand-drawn graphs and diagrams. Many systems comprised a ramshackle assortment of hardware and software (mainframe/network/stand-alone PC/homegrown/bought-in) often not fully compatible or failing to interface, and necessitating an alarming degree of keying and re-keying of data.

Non-Financial Indicators (NFI) were in common use in the measurement of process performance, but only two companies combined such measures with financial indicators in a single report. The NFI was much more of a problem in service areas where a diversity of approaches was apparent in both scope and definition.

Measures based on inter-site or inter-departmental comparisons were universally absent, even where the potential for such meaningful measurements was apparent. The overriding impression was one of management accountants as number-crunchers, too busy collecting and disseminating information to spend the time to analyse and interpret its key features in a way meaningful to the user.

The benchmarking procedure encourages an outward-looking attitude and allows the Blackburn accounting team to approach their own problems in a more informed manner. The third syndicate exercise highlights existing improvement opportunities:

SYNDICATE EXERCISE 3: IMPROVEMENT OPPORTUNITIES

1. Identify instances in your organisation where improvements might be made in the areas of:

   (a) waste elimination;
   (b) quality of product or service;
   (c) inter-employee communications.

2. Prioritise your improvement opportunities on the basis of:

   (a) achievability;
   (b) economic impact.

Ross is fully aware that up to now deliberations have been confined to the accounting team, producing what might be a biased view of events. The next stage is to find out exactly what the 'customer' thinks of the service provided by conducting a customer survey. Interviews are conducted to determine the degree of customer satisfaction with the services provided by the Management Accounting team:

(a) to highlight opportunities for improvements to the service;

(b) to conduct a 'needs analysis' of potential customers.

Customer opinions, together with the findings of the benchmarking procedure and Syndicate Exercise 3, allow the development of a number of priority improvement opportunities which have the greatest potential pay-off. The accounting group ranks all of these opportunities and selects the top five for in depth consideration in sub-groups of the accounting team. Ross institutes the PRAISE six step quality improvement process (detailed earlier in this chapter) as a systematic way of developing solutions for implementation.

Ross analyses feedback from the sub-groups regarding their rate of progress, the difficulties experienced and the generation of further and related problems. Concerns with performance measurements and the use of non-financial indicators highlight the need for a fourth syndicate session:

SYNDICATE EXERCISE 4: PERFORMANCE APPRAISAL

1. Identify current financial and non-financial measures used to assess the performance of the organisation.

2. Discuss their suitability in a number of respects, for example:
   (a) accuracy/reliability of measurement;
   (b) appropriate indicators of process performance;
   (c) achievement consistent with strategic goals.

3. Formulate new non-financial indicators which more accurately reflect the needs of the organisation.

Recognition of the factors critical to determining a successful process highlight the need for a fifth syndicate exercise, see opposite page.

The complete procedure suggests solutions to priority problems, together with an awareness of the inherent difficulties of implementation. Once solutions are in place, Ross monitors the situation carefully for further improvements, and to measure the extent of the improvements achieved. If improvements are less than expected he has more questions to ask and further exercises in mind.

You are required to apply the Quality Improvement Process detailed above to Blackburn Chemicals (or to another company with which you are more familiar). Your report should include a detailed plan of action for the implementation of solutions to potential and/or actual problems.

SYNDICATE EXERCISE 5: BARRIERS AND ENABLERS

1. Formulate strategies for the achievement of those improvement opportunities designated as priorities.

2. Identify those negative aspects of the organisation providing potential *barriers* to the implementation of a successful strategy.

3. Identify those positive features in the organisation acting as *enablers* in achieving a successful implementation.

CASE 21: SPICK'N'SPAN DRY CLEANERS

This case provides an opportunity for the application of the latest management accounting developments to a non-manufacturing environment. A problematic small business scenario highlights improvement opportunities which might involve the employment of TQM, TEI and VAM methodologies.

David Kelly has spent 10 years building a successful chain of eight dry-cleaning outlets in Birmingham, situated in the shopping centres dotted around the West Midlands metropolitan area. He feels that the 1990s is a time for consolidation and has abandoned ideas of expanding the chain to concentrate on improving the profitability of his existing outlets. Each shop has a full-time manager and three part-time employees. The word 'manager' is something of a misnomer, since David effectively manages the whole operation, with very little delegated decision making. There is very little communication between the shops, virtually all information and direction being provided by David in his daily shuttle between them.

David monitors the competition carefully. He regularly takes pieces of his dry-cleaning to his rivals for service, one first thing in the morning and another last thing in the evening. The difference in the numbered dockets allows him to estimate weekly revenue and to make comparisons with his own takings. His survey findings show Spick'N'Span to be the number two outlet in each of the locations, with no single competitor consistently occupying the number one position. The chain is doing well, with each of the outlets separately profitable, but David is anxious to occupy the number one slot in at least half of his eight locations. A number of alternative ideas have been trialed in his 'Blue Riband' shops in the Solihull and Sutton Coldfield centres, with a view to implementation across the whole chain if successful:

1. close control on raw material usage in order to reduce the use of solvents while maintaining cleaning quality;

2. implementation of a computer system to track items, costs and give immediate feedback on daily progress;

3. staff training to target 'lost' customers by encouraging knock-on sales;

4. repackaging of the existing product to provide a deluxe service, at an increased margin, to existing customers.

Staff reaction to the trials has not been favourable. Staff members feel they are not trusted because of the close monitoring imposed. The implementation of a computer system without consultation or training has further advanced their perception of being watched constantly. The introduction of formal staff training sessions is associated with a feeling that they are not doing their jobs properly and need to be re-instructed, apparently in the basics of providing customer service. David is disillusioned by the lack of success of his attempts to implement improvements. He needs help.

You are required to make recommendations for actions which will improve the performance of the Spick'N'Span chain and devise a strategy for their implementation.

Chapter 8

Management Science

8.1 INTRODUCTION

Earlier chapters have covered the use of a number of analytical techniques for the examination of product and customer profitability, product mix and project viability. We have so far ignored decision support mechanisms based on prediction models, but this omission is corrected here with the provision of six major case study scenarios, each with the data available to allow the application of sophisticated management science methods to support analysis and recommendations.

The methods described here are best classified according to the nature of the data available:

- **quantitative** — i.e. numerical (financial or non-financial), continuous (e.g. 0.35) or categorical (e.g. a 0, 1 dummy);

- **qualitative** — i.e. non-numerical (e.g. good/bad, high/low), descriptive (e.g. colour, build), or narrative. Dummy variables may frequently be used to 'quantify' what would otherwise be qualitative variables.

For both data types different forecasting methods might be employed depending on whether the data is:

- **time series data** — where trend data is available for several variables across a number of successive time periods. Time series data will attempt to forecast values for future time periods;

- **cross-section data** — where data is collected at a single point of time for several variables across a number of different cases. Cross-section data will attempt to forecast values for new cases outside the sample under consideration.

The methods available for different purposes might be categorised as shown in the table. The 'best' method will depend upon the circumstances in which the forecasting is taking place, in particular:

- the purpose of the forecast,
- the relevance and availability of historical data,
- the desired degree of accuracy,

- the time period to be forecast,
- the costs of achievement, and
- the time available.

Conflicts are inevitable in this list of requirements, e.g. the desired degree of accuracy may be incompatible with both the time available and the financial resources provided to conduct a survey. Compromises must be made.

This chapter focuses on the use of decision making heuristics, to illustrate qualitative methods, and three quantitative methods: time series analysis, regression analysis and discriminant analysis.

	Time Series	**Cross-Section**
Quantitative	Systematic variation in historical data (e.g. moving averages, exponential smoothing, Box-Jenkins methods, time series analysis, regression analysis)	Causal methods specifying explicit explanatory relationships (e.g. leading indicators, regression analysis, discriminant analysis)
Qualitative	Opinions, Heuristics, Judgments, Attitudes (e.g. Delphi Method, market research)	

8.2 DECISION-MAKING MODELS

The cognitive processes used by decision makers to deal with the available information and overcome information overload will have implications for the optimum management accounting information system. Human information processing may be characterised by two styles.

- **analytic** — involving a systematic approach to the decision task and often embracing the use of mathematical models to analyse the information; and

- **heuristic** — involving apparently intuitive decision making based on the application of simple (and sometimes simplistic) rules in the processing of information.

In practice, such heuristics may resemble trial and error, but are often 'rules of thumb' or standard operating procedures based on a wealth of knowledge and experience. For example, Thorngate (1980) provides examples of optimum decisions using decision making heuristics and Ashton (1976) demonstrates the robust nature of simple linear models used to approximate complex multivariate situations. The use of heuristic models to simplify job scheduling problems has already been described in Chapter 6.

However, there is the danger that biased decision outcomes may result because inefficient information strategies have been adopted and/or the heuristics employed to overcome information overload are statistically inaccurate. Five particular areas of concern may be identified where heuristics can potentially cause bias:

- **Availability** — undue emphasis is given to recent or imaginable cases, e.g. recent instances of equipment failure may be accorded inappropriate seriousness because equipment histories and the probability distribution of breakdowns have not been examined.

- **Representativeness** — decisions are made on flimsy evidence which ignores prior probabilities. In practice hard numerical data giving the likely distribution of outcomes may be ignored, especially if 'softer' qualitative or narrative information is supplied simultaneously. Kahnemann and Tversky (1972) suggest that such narratives may be accorded a greatly inflated level of importance compared to their information content, a suggestion borne out by empirical evidence.

- **Integration** — inconsistent simplification methods might be adopted to combine information from different sources. For accounting information, this may coincide with the choice of inappropriate cues, inappropriate cue weightings, inappropriate mathematical relationships in the formation of multivariate models, or the erroneous amalgamation of time series and cross-section estimates.

- **Concreteness** — decisions are made using only explicitly stated information, ignoring that which may be assumed or derived indirectly. Inadequate investigations may, therefore, yield biased outcomes.

- **Anchoring and adjustment** — overconfidence in these initial estimates exists, which provides an 'anchor' to further adjustments made when additional information becomes available. Irrelevant information may form the basis of the initial 'anchor' so that subsequent adjustments result in hopelessly biased estimates.

The implication is that an heuristic approach, especially where conflicting messages are being conveyed by the available information sources, may result in biased outcomes.

Rather than limiting simplifying procedures to instances of 'information overload', some form of decision models may have to be introduced because of a lack of available data. Simulation or 'Monte Carlo' methods make it possible to 'create' hypothetical observations where no actual observations exist. In project planning and in predicting outcomes there may be no real observations, only estimates of values and relationships. This information is far from perfect but is certainly better than nothing. It may be very representative of future outcomes and can be used to generate realistic future scenarios based on many fictitious observations where:

- each of the outcomes satisfies known or assumed relationships between the variables, and

- each of the outcomes is representative for that variable.

The simulation approach necessitates the use of a computer model and multiple iterations (at least 100) to cope with the quantity of data, but the approach is essentially a simple one. Alternative approaches are possible depending on the assumptions made.

Consider again *Minicase C: Cable Technology* from Chapter 6 where the simulation method might be used to predict the likely rate of wage-cost inflation in a particular period. Economic estimates reveal that the rate of price inflation will be 6 per cent (with a probability of 0.1), or 7 per cent (with a probability of 0.4), or 8 per cent (with a probability of 0.3) or 9 per cent (with a probability of 0.2).

The simplest method of simulating observations involves making no assumptions about the actual distribution of the price inflation variable. The probabilities provided are accepted as fact, and no possibilities outside the 6 to 9 per cent range are considered. Random numbers from a two digit range 00 to 99 are assigned to the variable values in accordance with the stated probability.

e.g. price inflation of 6 per cent has a 0.1 (i.e. one in ten) probability. Ten of the 100 random numbers are, therefore, allocated to this possibility (i.e. 00 to 09).

The complete allocation would be:

Price Inflation (%)	Probability	Random No Range
6	0.1	00–09
7	0.4	10–49
8	0.3	50–79
9	0.2	80–99

The appropriate random number range is simple to derive and corresponds exactly with the probabilities provided. Thus the generation of a random number equal to 23, say, from tables or from a Lottery-like random number generator would select inflation = 7% as the corresponding value. This value can then be treated as a representative observation in any further analysis. Given a rate of price inflation of 7 per cent, the corresponding rate of wage inflation will be either 8 or 8.5 per cent. A second random number generation allows this selection to be made in accord with the respective probabilities of 0.4 and 0.6:

Price Inflation (%)	Wage Cost Inflation (%)	Random No Range
7	8	00–39
	8.5	40–99

Successive random numbers of, say, 23 and 31, would therefore select a price inflation of 7 per cent and a wage cost inflation of 8 per cent. If price inflation is not a relevant variable for further analysis and forecasting we could go straight to wage-cost inflation by directing attention to the right-hand column of Figure 19

Rate of Wage Cost Inflation (%)	Probability	Random No Range
7	0.04	00–03
7.5	0.06	04–09
8	0.16	10–25
8.5	0.24	26–49
9	0.21	50–70
9.5	0.09	71–79
10	0.14	80–93
10.5	0.06	94–99

(page 144). A random number range in accord with the stated conditional probabilities allows the selection of a single rate:

A single random number of, say, 67 would then select a 9 per cent rate of wage-cost inflation.

Alternatively we might assume that the rate of price inflation is actually distributed normally, with our estimates representing sample observations from a normal population. Then we can use the calculated sample mean and standard deviation to smooth out the discontinuities of the estimated pattern and provide a normal distribution with the following ranges of values and associated probabilities:

Inflation (%) (X)	Probability (P)	(P.X)	(X–X̄)	(P.X̄)²
6	0.1	0.6	–1.6	0.0256
7	0.4	2.8	–0.6	0.1440
8	0.3	2.4	0.4	0.0480
9	0.2	1.8	1.4	0.3920
		7.6		0.6096

Mean $(\bar{X}) = \Sigma PX = 7.6\%$

Standard Deviation $(S) = \sqrt{P(X - \bar{X})^2} = \sqrt{0.6096} = 0.78076\ \%$

Where the Normal Distribution ordinate $Z = \dfrac{X - \bar{X}}{S}$ distribution of values, and associated normal probabilities can be established by calculating $Z = \dfrac{X - 7.6}{0.78076}$ for different class boundaries. These are detailed in Figure 24.

Mid Point	Class Boundaries	Z Ordinate	Normal Curve Area	Z Probability	Random Number Range
	5.25	−3.01	0.49869		
5.5				0.01	00
	5.75	−2.37	0.49111		
6				0.03	01–03
	6.25	−1.73	0.45818		
6.5				0.10	04–13
	6.75	−1.09	0.36214		
7				0.19	14–32
	7.25	−0.45	0.17364		
7.5				0.25	33–57
	7.75	0.19	0.7535		
8				0.22	58–79
	8.25	0.83	0.29673		
8.5				0.13	80–92
	8.75	1.47	0.42922		
9				0.05	93–97
	9.25	2.11	0.48257		
9.5				0.02	98–99
	9.75	2.75	0.49702		
			Sum 1.00		

Figure 24: Normal Distribution Simulation

The Normal Curve area is derived from tables of the Normal distribution, and the difference in these values provides the probability of an observation occurring between the respective class boundaries. This probability establishes the range of random numbers to be selected from the two digit random number range of 00 to 99.

Thus the probability of an observation in the range 7.75 to 8.25 is 0.22, equivalent to 22 of the 100 random numbers, i.e. numbers 58 to 79 inclusive.

If any of these random numbers is chosen in the simulation it will generate a value of 8 per cent for Price Inflation. Other random numbers will generate different values, directly in accordance with their relative probability. Similar distributions, and corresponding sets of random numbers for each variable in any analysis allow all combinations to be considered and a distribution of overall outcomes produced. This method might therefore also be applied to the rate of wage-cost inflation by using the data of Figure 19 as the basis for the construction of the normal distribution.

The remaining sections of this chapter focus on analytic approaches to problem solving using mathematical models for forecasting.

8.3 TIME SERIES ANALYSIS

Figure 25 illustrates the basis of classical time series decomposition analysis. A relationship $Y = f(T, C, S, R)$ is hypothesised, such that the variable to be forecast (Y) is subject to the influence of a time trend (T), the trade cycle (C), seasonal factors (S) and random fluctuation (R).

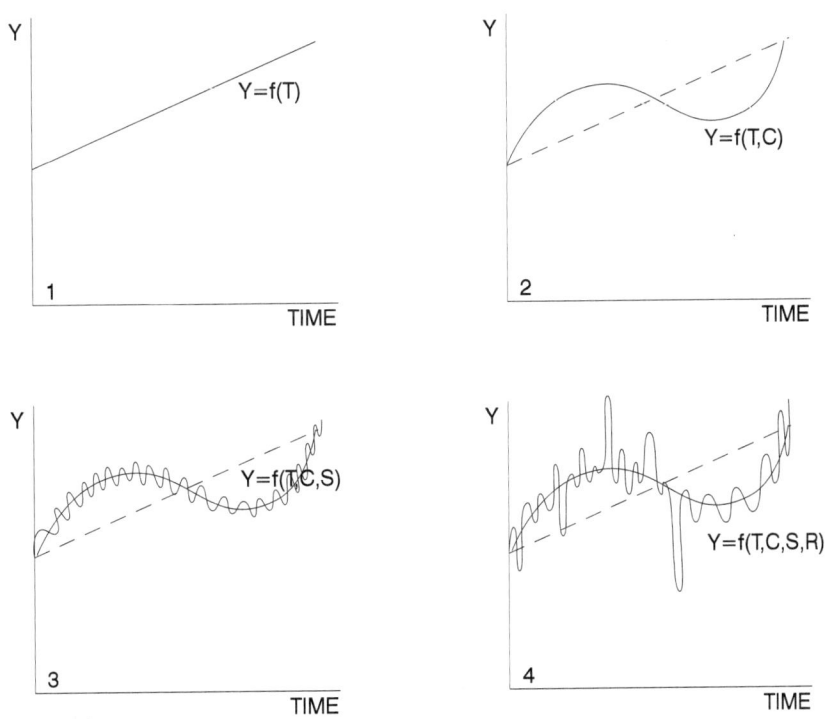

Figure 25: Classical Time Series Decomposition

The observed data is that displayed in the fourth quadrant (bottom right) of Figure 25. We wish to project this series in order to forecast values of Y in future time periods. Because of the irregular nature of the series this is difficult by eye, so we attempt to break up the series into its component parts so that each can be

Strategic Management Accounting

projected separately and the separate forecasts combined to give an integrated prediction. We therefore need to specify carefully the different components:

T the directional trend of the series for Y over time, which may be upwards, downwards or static. The trend line may be linear or curves, either of which may be modelled with regression type methods;

C the business cycle, imposing short-term periods of boom and slump onto the long-term trend. A curved pattern is likely, possibly extending over a period of many years. In practical terms it may be very difficult to isolate the 'cycle' and we may have to be satisfied with estimating a composite of 'trend and cycle' together, despite the errors so introduced;

S seasonal fluctuations do not necessarily correspond with seasons of the year; they are concerned with any systematic variation occurring within the time period under consideration. They would include quarterly variations within the year, monthly variations within the quarter, weekly variations within the month, daily variations within the week and hourly variations within the day. All are seasons as long as they are associated with a systematic variation within the time period *whatever the time period.*

The italicised phrase provides the clue to the elimination, and then isolation, of seasonal factors. If identical variation is attributable to Monday in any week, then Monday in Week 1 is equated with Monday in Week 2 for averaging purposes. Seasonal variation (+ and −) will cancel out completely when the week is totalled, and a moving average over successive weeks allows it to be eliminated from the series completely. This is clarified in *Minicase E: Exploration Holdings* later using quarterly data.

R random fluctuations are by definition unpredictable. Over time we must expect positive and negative variations to cancel out. Summation of a series (provided that it is long enough) will eliminate random variation totally.

Tight definitions allow simple arithmetic processes to be used to model the time series. This sequence is illustrated in Figure 25:

- summation of the series eliminates R and moves us from quadrant 4 to quadrant 3;

- moving averages eliminate S and move us from quadrant 3 to quadrant 2. Subtraction of the remainder from the original series allows S to be isolated for each time period;

- fitting a straight line trend allows T to be identified in quadrant 1 so that the C pattern can be isolated in quadrant 2. Alternatively a curvilinear fit can be used to model T and C together.

However, before we proceed to fit the model and make predictions we must expand the simple functional relationship $Y = f(T, C, S, R)$ into something more specific. Most commonly this would be either:

$Y = T+C+S+R$ the simple additive model, or
$Y = T^{\star}C^{\star}S^{\star}R$ the simple multiplicative model

186

The former is the easiest to fit and works well as long as the trend (T) is not too pronounced. When T is moving steeply (up or down) it will tend to blanket out all other fluctuations, so that a multiplicative model measuring the other factors relative to trend is to be preferred.

In practice there are infinite numbers of possible models, with various weightings and combinations. More sophisticated models can be introduced which weight the data items (i.e. giving greater emphasis to more recent time periods) as well as the components.

Consider the simple example in *Minicase E : Exploration Holdings*.

Quarterly sales data is provided for Exploration Holdings over a period of six years, 1988–1993 inclusive. We want to predict future sales for the next four quarters of 1994, using simple additive and simple multiplicative models:

		Sales (£000)			Sales (£000)
1988	Q1	6	1991	Q1	62
	Q2	8		Q2	24
	Q3	10		Q3	58
	Q4	16		Q4	96
1989	Q1	30	1992	Q1	70
	Q2	16		Q2	24
	Q3	18		Q3	90
	Q4	16		Q4	176
1990	Q1	38	1993	Q1	94
	Q2	16		Q2	32
	Q3	50		Q3	98
	Q4	96		Q4	176

PROCEDURE ADOPTED

1. Graph the data points to detect trends and extreme observations. A steep trend may highlight the need for a multiplicative model.

2. Order the data vertically as in Column 1 of Figure 26, ideally on a spreadsheet. Since most of the arithmetic procedures are cell-relative they are ideal for spreadsheet purposes.

3. Conduct a four period moving sum (MS) as in Column 2, i.e. add (Q1+Q2+Q3+Q4) for 1988, then drop Q1 for 1988 and include Q1 for 1989. Continue down the series so that each successive item contains a combination of each of the four quarters. This manoeuvre will eliminate seasonal fluctuations completely and random fluctuations approximately.

187

	1	2	3	4	5	6	7	8	9	10	11
		4-Period					Additive Model		Multiplicative Model		
	Y	MS	MA	CMA	T	(S+R)	(S)	(C)	(SxR)	(S)	(C)
Quarters	(£000)				Trend	Y-CMA	Seasonal	CMA-(T)	Y/CMA	Seasonal	CMA/T
1988 I	6				-4		+7			1.25	
II	8				1		-35			0.46	
III	10	40	10	13	6	-3	-3	7	0.77	0.92	2.11
IV	16	64	16	17	11	-1	+31	6	0.94	1.37	1.53
1989 I	30	72	18	19	16	11	+7	3	1.58	1.25	1.18
II	16	80	20	20	21	-4	-35	-1	0.80	0.46	0.95
III	18	80	20	21	26	-3	-3	-5	0.86	0.92	0.81
IV	16	88	22	22	31	-6	+31	-9	0.73	1.37	0.71
1990 I	38	88	22	26	36	12	+7	-10	1.46	1.25	0.72
II	16	120	30	40	41	-24	-35	-1	0.40	0.46	0.98
III	50	200	50	53	46	-3	-3	7	0.94	0.92	1.16
IV	96	224	56	57	51	39	+31	6	1.68	1.37	1.12
1991 I	62	232	58	59	56	3	+7	3	1.05	1.25	1.06
II	24	240	60	60	61	-36	-35	-1	0.40	0.46	0.99
III	58	240	60	61	66	-3	-3	-5	0.95	0.92	0.93
IV	96	248	62	62	71	34	+31	-9	1.55	1.37	0.88
1992 I	70	248	62	66	76	4	+7	-10	1.06	1.25	0.87
II	24	280	70	80	81	-56	-35	-1	0.30	0.46	0.99
III	90	360	90	93	86	-3	-3	7	0.97	0.92	1.08
IV	176	384	96	97	91	79	+31	6	1.81	1.37	1.07
1993 I	94	392	98	99	96	-5	+7	3	0.95	1.25	1.03
II	32	400	100	100	101	-68	-35	-1	0.32	0.46	0.99
III	98	400	100		106		-3			0.92	
IV	176				111		+31			1.37	

Figure 26: Time Series Analysis for Exploration Holdings

4. Divide the 'sums' by 4 so they are of the same order of size as the original series to give the moving average (MA) of Column 3. Centre the values by averaging successive pairs. We then have centred moving averages (CMAs) in Column 4 of the same time period as the initial data points.

$$CMA = f(T, C) \quad \text{i.e.} \quad \begin{aligned} CMA &= T{+}C \quad \text{for additive model} \\ CMA &= T{*}C \quad \text{for multiplicative model} \end{aligned}$$

The centring will cause us to lose data items at both ends of the series.

5. Isolate the seasonal variation (S):

$$S = Y - (T{+}C) \qquad = Y - CMA \qquad \text{for additive model (in Column 6)}$$

$$S = \frac{Y}{(T{+}C)} \qquad = \frac{Y}{CMA} \qquad \text{for multiplicative model (in Column 9)}$$

The seasonal values must be the same for a particular quarter whenever that quarter occurs. The fact the values of Column 6 in Figure 26 do not so correspond reflects the presence of some unremoved random variation. Further averaging across seasons, will remove it:

Standard Variation (Additive Model)

	Q1	Q2	Q3	Q4		
1988			−3	−1		
1989	11	−4	−3	−6		
1990	12	−24	−3	39		
1991	3	−36	−3	34		
1992	4	−56	−3	79		
1993	−5	−68				
Sum:	25	−188	−15	145		
Mean:	5	−37.6	−3	29	Total:	−6.6
Adjusted(S):	**7**	**−35**	**−3**	**31**	**Total:**	**0**

Spreading the error (−6.6) across each of the seasons and rounding to whole numbers gives single seasonal figures detailed in Column 7 for every quarter. However, the extent of the variation (particularly in the second and fourth quarters) gives us an early clue that the simple additive model is likely to be unsuitable, and that a multiplicative model might be preferred.

6. The trend component (T) can be identified by fitting a single-variable linear regression equation $T = a + bt$, where T comprises the CMA values computed above, and 't' is the corresponding time periods between $t = 3$ and $t = 22$ (i.e. third quarter of 1988 to second quarter of 1993). The trend line, $T = -8.7 + 5t$ results, and the trend values of Column 5 can be calculated for each quarter.

7. Since the trend component can now be identified for each time period, then so can the cyclical component (C);

$$C = CMA - T \qquad \text{for the simple additive model in Column 8, and}$$

$$C = \frac{CMA}{T} \qquad \text{for the simple multiplicative model in Column 11.}$$

The cycle values so computed for time periods 3 through to 22 can be graphed to determine if a pattern emerges which may realistically be projected. If not we may have to ignore the cyclical component completely or make an adjustment to trend for simple and multiplicative models, respectively, for its absolute size impact on the regression intercept. Figures 27 and 28, for additive and multiplicative models respectively, represent relatively regular cycle projections.

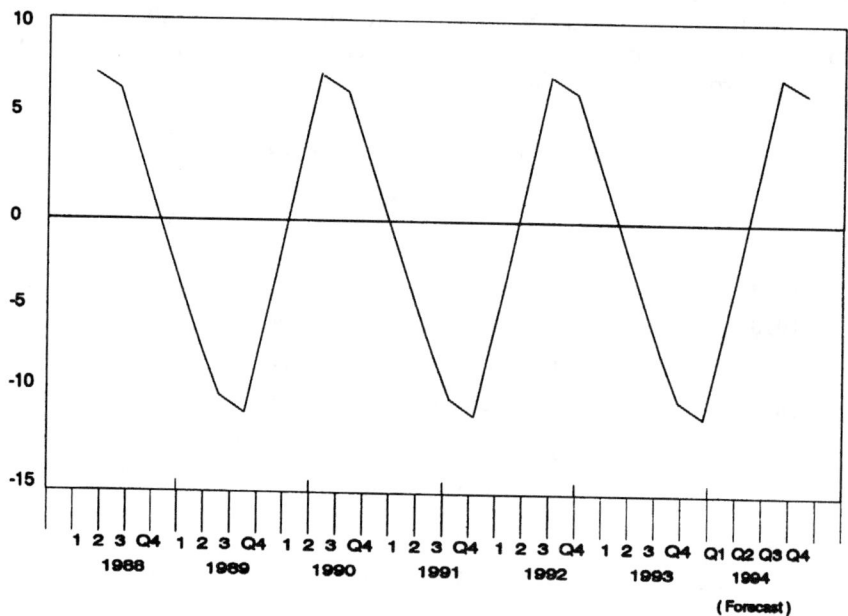

Figure 27: Cyclical Component (Additive Model)

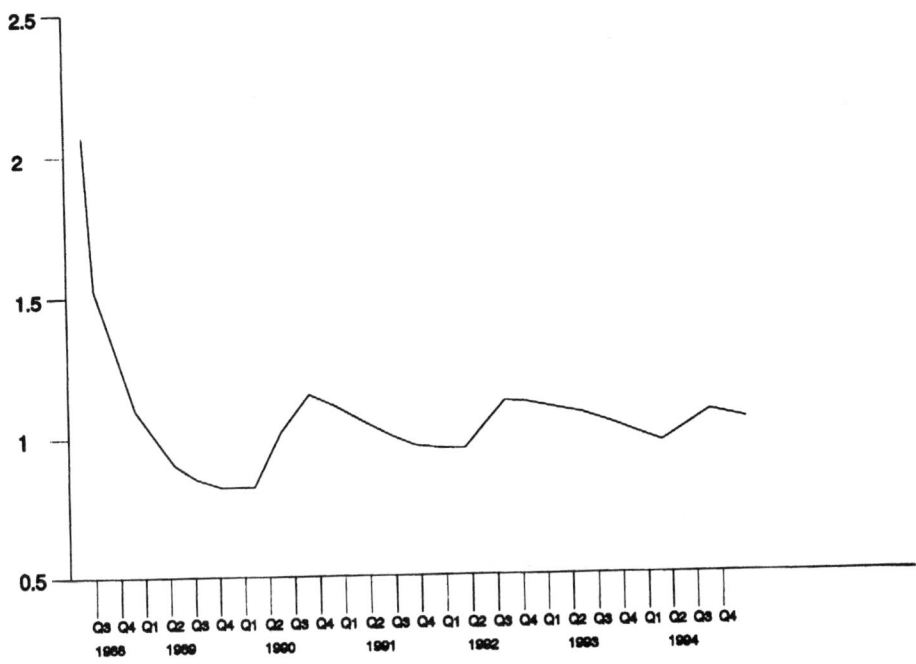

Figure 28: Cyclical Component (Multiplicative Model)

8. Combine the three predictable components in order to make predictions for the required time periods. We want to make forecasts for 1994 (i.e. periods $t = 25$ to $t = 28$) initially on the basis of $Y = T + S + C$, i.e.:

1994	Q1	Q2	Q3	Q4
time period (t)	25	26	27	28
T ($-8.7+5t$)	116.3	121.3	126.3	131.3
S	7	−35	−3	31
C (from Figure 26)	−10	−1	9	8
Forecast Y (£000)	113	85	132	170

Our earlier fears about the suitability of the simple additive model in this case are justified; our fourth quarter forecast for 1994, at £170 000, is below our 1993 actual (£176 000) despite our perception of an upward trend. This result and the extensive variation in the additive seasonal calculation table suggest that we must prefer a multiplicative model.

We therefore return to Stage 5 of our procedure to recompute the seasonal factors for the multiplicative model:

191

	Q1	Q2	Q3	Q4		
1988			0.77	0.94		
1989	1.58	0.80	0.86	0.73		
1990	1.46	0.40	0.94	1.68		
1991	1.05	0.40	0.95	1.55		
1992	1.06	0.30	0.97	1.81		
1993	0.95	0.32				
Sum:	6.10	2.22	4.49	6.71		
Mean:	1.22	0.44	0.90	1.34	Total:	3.90
Adjusted(S):	**1.25**	**0.46**	**0.92**	**1.37**	**Total**	**4.00**

The required sum equals one for a multiplicative model, so that seasonal variation cancels out over the year, requiring relatively minor adjustments to the calculated averages. The absence of wide variations at this stage is reassuring and allows revised seasonal factors to be detailed in Column 10 for each quarter.

Step 7 dictates a revisit of the cyclical component calculated using $C = CMA/T$ from Column 11 of Figure 26 and graphed in Figure 28.

Revised forecasts can then be computed on the basis of $Y = T*S*C$

1994	Q1	Q2	Q3	Q4
T	116.30	121.30	126.30	131.30
S	1.25	0.46	0.92	1.37
C	0.92	0.99	1.06	1.04
Forecast Y (£000)	**132.00**	**55.00**	**123.00**	**187.00**

This is apparently a more appropriate set of forecasts for 1994 than those provided by the additive model. However, only time will tell how well either of these simple models predicts in practice.

The additive and multiplicative models so far considered treat all items of data as of equal value, however outdated they might be, and weights all the forecasting variables equally. A number of alternative time series forecasting methods exist which attempt to relax one or both of these constraints. Their added complexity makes computer-based analysis essential.

Exponential smoothing uses a 'smoothing constant' at the moving average stage to place more emphasis on the most recent data items. Each smoothed data point is equal to the previous smoothed data point, plus a fraction of the difference between that and the actual data point. The calculations of successive values are linked so that they form an exponential series. Thus,

$$D_t = D_{t-1} + \alpha(Y_t - D_{t-1})$$

where

Y_t is the actual data point, for time period t

D_t, D_{t-1} are smoothed data points

i.e. for $\alpha = 0.2$

$$
\begin{aligned}
D_t &= D_{t-1} + (0.2)\ Y_t - (0.2)\ D_{t-1} \\
&= (0.2)\ Y_t + (0.8)\ D_{t-1}
\end{aligned}
$$

a relationship which will smooth out 80 per cent of the random errors in the data points Y_t. The value of α is chosen arbitrarily in the first place and modified in the light of the outcomes.

Similar smoothing methods can be used for trend and seasonal factors, each employing separate arbitrary smoothing constants, in order to build up a composite forecasting model. Thus a trend (T_t) is calculated from,

$$T_t = (1 - \beta)\ T_{t-1} + \beta\ (D_t - D_{t-1})$$

where β = the trend smoothing constant.

A seasonal factor (S_t) is calculated from,

$$S_t = (1 - \gamma)\ S_{t-p} + \gamma$$

where γ = the seasonal smoothing constant, and
p = length of the season in time periods

Forecasts are again based on trend (T) and seasonal (S) components, but have the advantage of not requiring large quantities of historical data. But they are sensitive to the choice of arbitrary smoothing constant and may require fine tuning.

Fortunately a detailed knowledge of these algorithms is not usually necessary since most statistical software (e.g. SPSS-X) accommodates them within sophisticated time series forecasting models. For example, the **Box–Jenkins** procedure provides the opportunity for data transformation in the fitting and forecasting of time series using an iterative procedure requiring multiple computer runs in which the sensitivity of smoothing constants can easily be monitored.

Case 27: Balmain Breweries provides a case scenario where alternative time series forecasting methods may be applied in the context of an inventory control model.

8.4 REGRESSION ANALYSIS

Whereas time series analysis can provide us with trend projections for a key variable, in practice this may not be enough. If we wish to influence future values, through appropriate management action, we need to know which variables impact on the values assumed by the key variable. In essence we wish to establish:

- degrees of association between variables (correlation) and

- causal relationships between variables (regression), in order to develop

- an *explanatory* relationship which allows us to show *why* a key variable is changing, not just *how*.

Consider the data below for maintenance expenditure (Y) in £000 and volume of output (X) for ten pairs of observations

Volume of Output (m tons)	Maintenance Expenditure (£000)
X	Y
15	180
11	140
20	230
17	190
12	160
25	300
22	270
9	110
19	240
30	320

A scatter diagram with Y on the vertical axis and X on the horizontal would reveal a close linear relationship between the two variables, but not a perfect one. We might speculate on the existence of a linear relationship of the form $Y = a + bX$, where the extent of the maintenance requirement is largely attributable to the throughput. To specify the values of the parameters 'a' and 'b' we need to fit a straight line to the points — effectively average out their position and establish the average to which they regress.

The Ordinary Least Squares (OLS) solution to this problem measures the deviation of points away from a fitted line, either vertically or horizontally, and ensures that the optimum fit is such that the sum of the squares of these distances, over all the points, is as small as possible.

Figure 29 illustrates the situation in fitting a line to only four points. The line is designated $\hat{Y} = \hat{a} + \hat{b}X$, with the 'hats' (^) added to signify that we are dealing with estimates based on a sample of observations. The line is fitted with reference to the vertical distances $(Y - \hat{Y}_i)$ of the points from the line, where $e_i = (Y - \hat{Y}_i)$ signifies the 'error' involved in fitting.

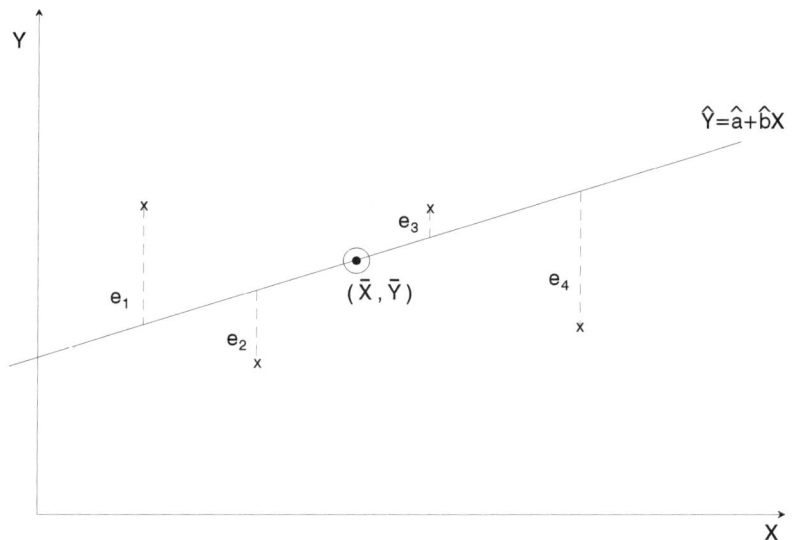

Figure 29: Ordinary Least Squares (OLS) Regression Fit

The OLS regression line is fitted to satisfy simultaneously two conditions:

(i) $\Sigma e_i = \phi$

Positive and negative deviations must exactly balance, and

(ii) Σe_i^2 is a minimum.

The sum of the squares of the vertical deviations from the line is as small as possible.

The specification of the 'a' and 'b' parameters to minimise Σe^2 can be derived using differential calculus such that:

$$\hat{b} = \frac{\Sigma XY - n\overline{XY}}{\Sigma X^2 \neq nX^2}$$

for n pairs of observations, and

$$\hat{a} = \overline{Y} - \hat{b}\overline{X}$$

The goodness of fit of this line can be measured by $\hat{r}$, the linear correlation coefficient, where

$$\hat{r} = \frac{\Sigma XY - n\overline{XY}}{\sqrt{(\Sigma X^2 - n\overline{X}^2)(\Sigma Y^2 - n\overline{Y}^2)}}$$

Fortunately, most spreadsheet software will calculate regression and correlation coefficients, as well as providing a graphic plot of the extent of the linearity, without the user needing recourse to the above formulae!

$r = \phi$ where no linear relationship exists,

  $= +1$ where a perfect positive relationship exists,

  $= -1$ where a perfect inverse relationship exists.

For practical purposes r lies between $+1$ and -1, and r^2 (the coefficient of determination) lies between 0 and 1. If $r = 0.8$ say, then $r^2 = 0.64$ for the relationship $\hat{Y} = \hat{a} + \hat{b}X$, and this signifies that 64 per cent of the observed changes in the Y variable are explained by the changes in the X variable.

For the above data these formulae give a regression line
$Y = 26.62 + (10.41)\ X$
$r = 0.984$
$r^2 = 0.968$

i.e. almost 97 per cent of the changes in maintenance expenditure are explainable in terms of the changes taking place in the volume of output.

The strength of the fit of the relationship allows us to be confident about predicting maintenance expenditures within the relevant range for which we have outputs (i.e. 9m tonnes to 30m tonnes). We must still be wary of making predictions outside this range. Even so, we must take care in the interpretation of both correlation and regression coefficients:

- If $\hat{r} = 0$ it does not necessarily mean that no relationship exists only that no meaningful *linear* relationship exists.

    For example, a circular relationship between X and Y would generate a linear correlation coefficient, $r = 0$. But a perfect non-linear relationship would be in existence.

- If $\hat{r} \neq 0$ it does not necessarily mean that a significant linear relationship exists. Two totally unrelated variables will inevitably yield a small, but non-zero, correlation coefficient by chance. Statistical tests of significance will demonstrate whether or not such values are small enough to constitute non-zero sample estimates from a zero population.

As a rule of thumb for sample sizes in excess of thirty, if the ratio

$$\frac{\text{Sample Estimate}}{\text{Standard error of the estimate } (se)} > 2$$

then the sample estimate is statistically significant (i.e. it is too big to be a chance estimate of a non-existent relationship).

In practice, if

$$\frac{\hat{b}}{se_{\hat{b}}} > 2$$

or

$$\left(\frac{\hat{b}}{se_{\hat{b}}}\right)^2 > 4$$

and

$$\frac{\hat{r}}{se_{\hat{r}}} > 2$$

or

$$\left(\frac{\hat{r}}{se_{\hat{r}}}\right)^2 > 4$$

then we have significant relationships.

These critical values (2 for the t-test and 4 for the F-test) will each vary depending on the size of sample (n) used, and the number of parameters (k) which the data has been used to estimate. As ($n-k$) gets smaller the critical values of the t-test and F-test will increase. In our example we have only two parameters ('a' and 'b') so $k = 2$, while $n = 10$, so ($n-k$) = 8. The tabulated values at a 5 per cent level of significance are $t_8 = 2.306$ and $F_8 = 5.318$.

We must, however, beware of jumping to conclusions. Consider the following sample of maintenance/volume data from a further seven observations:

Output Volume (m tonnes)	Maintenance Expenditure (£000)
X	Y
2	12
3	27
5	75
7	147
8	192
9	243
11	363

We might suspect that a relationship of the form $Y = a + bX$ exists, but that it might differ from that fitted earlier because the X values are almost entirely outside the previous relevant range. Fitting this relationship gives us $Y = -93 + 38X$ rounding to whole numbers; $r = 0.98$ and $r^2 = 0.96$. Ninety six per cent of changes in Y are explained by the changes in X; apparently evidence of an excellent regression fit. However, a simple check reveals the contrary.

One of the assumptions implicit in the fitting of ordinary least squares regression lines is that the error terms (the extent to which each of the points varies from the fitted line) should be random. No discernible pattern should exist for the $e = (Y - \hat{Y})$ terms.

The facts of this case are somewhat different:

X	Y	$\hat{Y} = -93 + 38X$	$e = (Y - \hat{Y})$
2	12	−17	29
3	27	21	6
5	75	97	−22
7	147	173	−26
8	192	211	−19
9	243	249	−6
11	363	325	38
			$\Sigma e = 0$

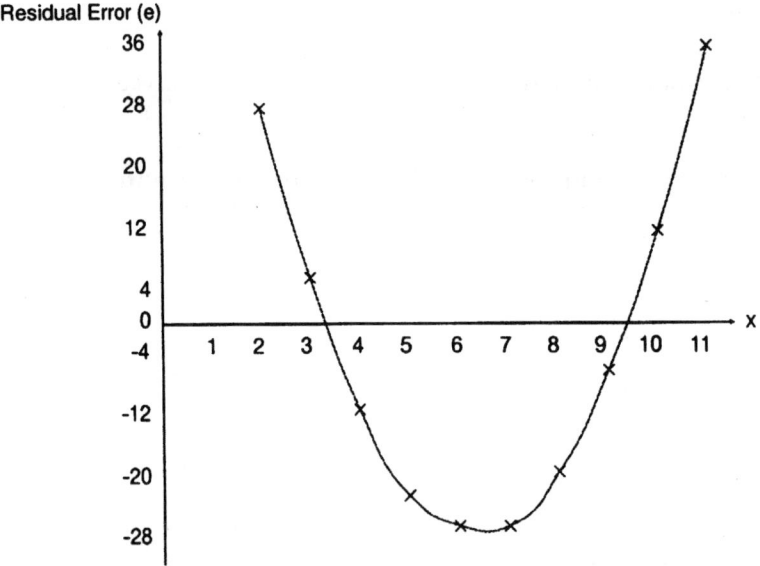

Figure 30: Evidence of Misspecification

The regression line is fitted such that $\Sigma e = 0$ and Σe^2 is at a minimum, but examination of Figure 30 shows that the graph of 'e' against 'X' is far from random.

The curved relationship is evidence of a serious error. The original equation has been mis-specified. The linear assumption made is totally inappropriate, despite the r^2 of 0.96. Closer examination of the data reveals that we are actually dealing with the perfect non-linear relationship $Y = 3X^2$.

Although the curve and straight line are close to each other within the relevant range, they diverge significantly outside it, so that any predictions would be seriously in error. In this case the mis-specification of the original equation should have been readily apparent from an initial scatter diagram of the data. In practice, sample datasets will rarely, if ever, be so perfectly formulated that the scatter diagram totally dispels fears of mis-specification. In such circumstances, in the absence of firm evidence of a curved relationship, we would fit a linear one (i.e. $Y = a + bX$ for one variable, $Y = a + bX_1 + cX_2$ ... for multivariate), confirm the statistical significance of the slope parameters and then confirm the validity of the ordinary least squares (OLS) assumptions.

OLS regression methods attempt to estimate the *actual* relationship $Y_i = a + bX_i + \mu_i$ with an estimated relationship $\hat{Y}_i = \hat{a} + \hat{b}X_i + e_i$ based on a finite sample size of n observations. The error term μ_i in the relationship is estimated by the residual of the equation e_i.

OLS fits make a number of assumptions, the violation of which can result in unreliable equations:

1. μ is a random variable;
2. the mean value of μ is zero;
3. the variance of μ is constant;
4. the variable μ is normally distributed;
5. the random terms from different observations (μ_t, μ_{t-1}) are independent;
6. μ_i is independent of the explanatory variables;
7. the explanatory variables are measured without error;
8. the explanatory variables are not perfectly linearly correlated;
9. any variable aggregation has been carried out appropriately;
10. the identified relationship has a unique mathematical relationship;
11. the relationship has been correctly specified.

For analysis the assumptions fall conveniently into two groups. The first six assumptions (nos 1 to 6) concern the error term μ_i, as estimated by the residual term e_i. The last six assumptions (nos 6 to 11) concern the behaviour of the explanatory variables. Several of the assumptions may be difficult to test, especially when only limited data is available. In practice, the verification of assumptions 2, 3, 5, 6 and 8 is the most critical.

Assumption 2 suggests that $\mu = 0$ and assumption 6 that $^r\mu.x_i = 0$. If either is violated then parameter estimates will be both biased and inconsistent, i.e. OLS will generate wrong answers, which will not be improved upon by seeking a larger sample size. In practice, we will fit the regression to ensure that $e_i = 0$ so that we need only observe $^re^2.x_i$ to verify assumption 6.

Assumption 3 suggests that σ^2_μ is constant, verified in practice by observing any variance in the estimate $\Sigma e^2/n-k$ around a fitted regression equation embracing the estimation of k parameters. If this assumption is not satisfied then heteroscedasticity exists and formulae for parameter estimates, and associated significance tests, will be inappropriate. Assumption 5 suggests that $^r e_t.e_{t-1} = 0$ and applies only to time series data. If not satisfied, autocorrelation exists, resulting in incorrect estimates of both parameter values and their variances. Most critically of all, assumption 8 suggests that $^r x_1.x_2 = 0$. If this is seriously violated then multicollinearity exists, which may again result in parameter estimates which are both biased and inconsistent.

After fitting a regression equation we must, therefore, conduct at least three tests of the violation of ordinary least squares assumptions, all of which may provide evidence of the mis-specification of the OLS equation:

*   monitor the size of correlation coefficient between X variables.

*   confirm the explanatory variables (X_i) are independent of the residuals (e_i) and the absence of heteroscedasticity by ensuring that the correlation coefficient $^r e^2.x_i$ is not statistically significant for any explanatory variable. Graphically this may be apparent from a wedge-shaped X-Y scatter indicative of a size relationship so that e_i increases as X_i increases.

*   for the time series data ensure that $^r e_t.e_{t-1}$ is not statistically significant, or alternatively that tabular values of the Durbin–Watson d-statistic are within acceptable bounds. Graphically, plots of e_t against e_{t-1} in successive time periods should be random but may reveal a positive relationship (through clearly increasing or decreasing trends) or a negative relationship (through a sawtooth pattern). Both are indicative of key variables omitted from the regression equation.

The regression procedure, statistical testing of parameters and tests for violation of OLS assumptions are best considered in the context of an example. Consider *Minicase F: Ferrous Castings* (facing).

The correlation coefficient matrix for the four variables shows:

	Y	X_1	X_2
Y (M.O)	1.000		
X_1 (D.M)	0.889	1.000	
X_2 (D.L)	0.824	0.952	1.000
X_3 (I.M)	0.411	0.356	0.418

Ferrous Castings is conducting an activity analysis and has decided to use regression analysis as a means of identifying the causal factors affecting the cost function for manufacturing overhead. The manufacturing overhead application rate is currently based on direct labour hours, but the latest figures suggest that direct labour comprises only 15 per cent of total costs, compared to 50 per cent for direct materials, 5 per cent for indirect materials and 30 per cent for overheads. Ferrous Castings therefore intends to model the relationship between manufacturing overhead (Y) and three explanatory variables, direct materials (X_1), direct labour (X_2) and indirect materials (X_3), in the expectation that they will be able to improve on an application rate based on X_2 alone. Despite the dearth of recent available data, Ferrous Castings has managed to collect time series data for the previous 15 months, as follows, to form the basis of the analysis:

	Manufacturing Overhead (Y)	Direct Materials (X_1)	Direct Labour (X_2)	Indirect Materials (X_3)
	(£000)	(£000)	(£000)	(£000)
Jan 1993	269	357	19.4	31.8
Feb 1993	281	427	20.2	31.7
Mar 1993	267	356	19.4	31.9
Apr 1993	277	308	16.1	32.6
May 1993	269	286	14.9	29.6
Jun 1993	265	326	17.9	32.0
Jul 1993	268	323	15.1	33.0
Aug 1993	278	288	14.4	33.5
Sept 1993	258	280	14.8	29.5
Oct 1993	247	228	15.0	33.0
Nov 1993	295	445	23.0	33.7
Dec 1993	291	394	20.5	34.0
Jan 1994	310	443	22.7	34.2
Feb 1994	314	468	24.2	34.2
Mar 1994	314	454	22.2	30.8

Several features emerge from the correlation coefficient matrix:

- all the associations between Y and X_1, X_2, X_3 are positive. We would not expect to find any negative slope coefficients in computed regression equations, unless there are problems;

- manufacturing overhead is closely related to both direct materials and direct labour hours;

- the intercorrelations between the explanatory variables are all statistically significant and potentially problematical. That between X_1 and X_2 at 0.952 is so high as to make problems of multicollinearity inevitable between these two variables.

Separate regressions of Y on X_i reveal:

(i) $Y = 193.39 + 0.242\ X_1$ $R^2 = 0.790$
     $(se = 0.035)$
     $t = 6.99$

(ii) $Y = 188.25 + 4.93\ X_2$ $R^2 = 0.679$
      $(se = 0.939)$
      $t = 5.25$

(iii) $Y = 101.14 + 5.53\ X_3$ $R^2 = 0.169$
       $(se = 3.40)$
       $t = 1.63$

The equations provide evidence of strong positive relationships between Y and X_1 and X_2, significant at the one per cent level, but of a statistically insignificant relationship between Y and X_3.

A multiple regression of Y on X_1, X_2 and X_3 reveals:

(iv) $Y = 143.86 + 0.318\ X_1 - 2.06\ X_2 + 1.88\ X_3$ $R^2 = 0.811$
      $(se = 0.118)(se = 2.66)\ (se = 1.96)$
      $t = 2.70\quad t = -0.78\quad t = 0.96$

The addition of the two variables X_2, X_3 to the univariate relationship with X_1 has increased the R^2 value, but by only two per cent. R^2 increases from 0.79 to 0.81, but the X_1 coefficient is the only one exhibiting a statistically significant relationship. Worse, the coefficient of the X_2 variable is now negative, a change from +4.93 (in the univariate model) to -2.06 (in the multivariate model). This is clear evidence of the existence of multicollinearity in the multivariate relationship, questioning the presence there of the X_2 variable (direct labour hours).

Computation of the alternative two-variable equations clarifies the picture:

(v) $Y = 197.63 + 0.301\ X_1 - 1.36\ X_2$ $R^2 = 0.795$
     $(se = 0.116)\ (se = 2.54)$
     $t = 1.11\quad t = -0.228$

(vi) $Y = 149.90 + 0.231\ X_1 + 1.46\ X_3$ $R^2 = 0.800$
      $(se = 0.038)\ (se = 1.86)$
      $t = 6.16\quad t = 0.79$

(vii) $Y = 156.68 + 4.73\ X_2 + 1.09\ X_3$ $R^2 = 0.684$
       $(se = 1.07)\ (se = 2.40)$
       $t = 4.43\quad t = 0.46$

Equation (v) indicates the impossibility of an equation including both X_1 and X_2 as explanatory variables. The consequences of multicollinearity are:

- a negative coefficient for the X_2 variable,

- a statistically insignificant coefficient for the X_1 variable, and

- an increase in R^2 of only one half of one percent compared to the univariate equation in X_1.

Equation (vi) is more promising in that all coefficients are appropriately positive, but the R^2 increase (only 1%) and the reduced significance of the X_3 variable suggest that multicollinearity may still be playing a part.

Interference in equation (vii) between variables X_2 and X_3 is much less marked than in equation (v), but the overall R^2 represents only a marginal increase over that for X_2 alone. The message from the regression calculations appears to favour a univariate equation — equation (i) in Direct Materials — as the best explanation of Manufacturing Overhead.

Further problems are still possible in that the error term of the fitted equation may not be behaving randomly, a requirement of our use of Ordinary Least Squares regression methods. The size of the error term (e_t) can be computed by subtracting the value of the predicted manufacturing overhead (i.e. $\hat{Y} = 193.39 + 0.242X_1$) from the *actual* manufacturing overhead (Y).

i.e. $e_t = Y - \hat{Y}$

To test for the existence of heteroscedasticity and autocorrelation we also need to compute e_t^2 (the square of the error term) and e_{t-1} (the error term in the previous time period) as follows:

MO Y	DM X_1	$\hat{Y}$	$Y - \hat{Y}$ e_t	e_t^2	e_{t-1}
269	357	279.7	−10.75	115.5	
281	427	296.7	−15.68	245.9	−10.75
267	356	279.5	−12.51	156.4	−15.68
277	308	267.9	9.10	82.9	−12.51
269	286	262.6	6.43	41.3	9.10
265	326	272.2	−7.25	52.6	6.43
268	323	271.5	−3.52	12.4	−7.25
278	288	263.1	14.94	223.3	−3.52
258	280	261.1	−3.12	9.7	14.94
247	228	248.5	−1.54	2.4	−3.12
295	445	301.0	−6.04	36.4	−1.54
291	394	288.7	2.30	5.3	−6.03
310	443	300.6	9.45	89.3	2.30
314	468	306.6	7.40	54.8	9.45
314	454	303.2	10.79	116.4	7.40

The regression line has been fitted so that $\Sigma e_t = 0$ and so that Σe_t^2 is a minimum at a sum of 1244.56.

The correlation coefficient between e_t^2 and the direct materials explanatory variable (X_1), $r e^2_t . x_1 = 0.218$, not statistically significant at the five per cent level and providing reassurance as to the absence of heteroscedasticity.

The correlation coefficient between e_t and e_{t-1}, $r_{e_t \cdot e_{t-1}} = 0.329$, is again not statistically significant at the five per cent level and indicates the absence of autocorrelation in the residuals. Many statistical packages will automatically compute the Durbin–Watson d-statistic as a test for autocorrelation:

$$d = \frac{\Sigma(e_t - e_{t-1})^2}{\Sigma e_t^2} = \frac{1535.79}{1244.56} = 1.23$$

This value lies between the tabulated bounds of the d-statistic, registering an inconclusive result, partly attributable to the very small sample size under consideration. In this instance, and many in practice, autocorrelation and heteroscedasticity are much less serious problems than multicollinearity. It is easy to miss evidence of multicollinearity, because in practice changes of a large magnitude may not occur. The strength of the inter-relationship may be destructive but may not, for example, cause sign changes. It is therefore vitally important that we monitor the inclusion of new variables into an equation. This is especially true for those students who only look at the final stages of the output and who assign divine characteristics to computer printout!

We seek to improve on the explanatory power of the equation (R^2) while at the same time ensuring:

• coefficients remain statistically significant;

• coefficients and standard errors remain relatively stable;

• signs of coefficients remain intuitively correct.

For Ferrous Castings we should immediately recognise any negative sign for X_2 as nonsense, as we know there is a positive relationship and the correlation coefficient matrix has already given $r = 0.824$. We should dismiss results to the contrary and not be lulled into a 'the computer knows best' attitude.

It should be apparent by now that regression analysis is more difficult than it often seems in traditional management accounting textbooks. This chapter necessarily simplifies some of the concepts for ease of understanding, but increases the awareness of the pitfalls which may arise. In fitting a regression equation we need answers to three basic questions:

• Which variables?

• What variable weightings?

• What mathematical form of relationship?

In seeking appropriate answers to these questions it is advisable to adopt a systematic three stage approach:

1. DESCRIPTIVE BACKGROUND

A number of helpful procedures can be conducted which facilitate data reduction and give a 'feel' for the data and of the inter-relationships between the variables.

- **Mean and Standard Deviation**. Computation of the mean and standard deviation for each variable and the (mean ±2 standard deviations) range gives an indication of the existence of extreme values. This procedure is imperfect, because it implicitly, and erroneously, assumes the variables to be normally distributed, but nevertheless it can highlight data inaccuracies which should be re-investigated. It also identifies case outliers which might be eliminated from the study because they differ so significantly from the rest of the sample.

- **Scattergrams**. A scatter diagram of all combinations of the dependent variable with each potential explanatory variable in a two-dimensional plot will reveal:

  - the existence of any clear non-linear relationships,
  - the strength of any linear relationships, and
  - the relative position of any outlier observations.

  In practice, non-linear relationships are rarely, if ever, apparent; but, the risk of otherwise missing them is too great. The precise strength of relationships is better read from the correlation coefficient matrix.

- **Correlation Coefficient Matrix**. This is, arguably, the single most useful piece of preliminary information. It serves three vital functions:

  - establishes the direction of any relationship, which should be intuitively correct and which must correspond with the sign of this variable in any regression equation;
  - suggests those variables likely to be useful explanatory variables, because they are highly correlated with the dependent variable;
  - highlights potential multicollinearity problems by quantifying the strength of association between competing explanatory variables.

2. SPECIFICATION OF THE EQUATION

Unless there is convincing evidence to the contrary we begin by fitting a linear relationship of the form

$$Y = a + bX_1 + cX_2 + dX_3 + \ldots$$

for all cases in the dataset remaining after stage 1.

A forward or backward stepwise regression procedure can be employed for the purpose (e.g. SPSS-X), with additional variables appearing in the equation as long as:

- they add to the explanatory power of the equation, and

- they are individually statistically significant.

The resultant equation should have:

- the highest possible explanatory power (using the adjusted R^2 feature to filter out useless variables making a negligible contribution);

- a combination of variables for which appropriate tests ensure that all variables in the set are statistically significant;

- non-violation of the assumptions implicit in the use of ordinary least squares regression.

3. INTERPRETATION OF SOLUTION

The final equation may be a statistical optimum but:

- it may be impossible to implement its implicit recommendations (e.g. increase the value of those variables having a positive impact on the dependent variable);

- a cost–benefit analysis may reveal that it is not financially viable to contemplate the changes envisaged.

Case 22: Redfern Mutual Assurance, *Case 23: Charity Shops* and *Case 24: Countrywide Stores* provide real scenarios in which to apply regression techniques for forecasting purposes. In each case the actual data collected has been doctored so that some key issues emerge more clearly, but the resulting recommendations should be those actually put to the companies by the investigating consultants.

8.5 DISCRIMINANT ANALYSIS

The use of ordinary least squares regression methods in the previous section requires a dependent variable which can be measured continuously. However, there will be occasions where the variable which we want to explain and predict is not of a continuous nature. It may be categorical of the form high/medium/low, good/bad, or success/failure. These can be quantified by assigning dummy variables of the (1,2,3) or (0,1) variety to reflect the alternative states, but in each case these are the only values that the dependent variable can take. Changes in the value of the explanatory variable cannot change the continuous value, only its classification into one or other of the categories. In such circumstances we cannot use simple regression methods, but seek an alternative. Linear discriminant analysis (LDA) can be used when:

- the groups being identified are clearly separate;

- the explanatory variables are close to being normally distributed, or can be transformed to be so. This ensures 'univariate normality' where the stricter requirement of 'multivariate normality' is more difficult to test for in practice;

- there is no multicollinearity between the explanatory variables.

We seek to construct an equation of the form:

$$Z = a + bX_1 + cX_2 + dX_3 + \ldots$$

such that the resulting value of Z allows the categorisation of cases. Effectively we are generating the equation of a line (or lines) which can be positioned to divide the cases into the required groups. If we return to our simple linear model of Section 4.2,

$$\frac{PBT}{TA} + \frac{QA}{CL} - \frac{TL}{TA}$$

then the construction of a three-variable discriminant model using these financial ratios might be visualised relative to the space in a rectangular room where axes are constructed in the corner of the room: the profit ratio stretches vertically towards the ceiling, and liquidity and debt axes at right angles along the skirting boards. The company cases under consideration appear as points in space, representing three-ratio combinations, and discriminant analysis would try to position a plane in this space such that all the failed companies were on one side of this plane and all the healthy ones on the other. The equation of the optimum plane, even if it were impossible to classify all company cases correctly on either side, would be given by:

$$Z = a + b^\star \frac{PBT}{TA} + c^\star \frac{QA}{CL} - d^\star \frac{TL}{TA}$$

where b, c and d are the weightings attached to each of the ratios;

a is a constant term whose value determines the cut-off between failed and non-failed groups, and

Z is the value of the composite function, such that

$Z > 0$ corresponds with a state of financial health and

$Z < 0$ corresponds with a state of financial distress, in that the company has a financial profile similar to that of a previously failed company.

Discriminant analysis minimises the number of misclassifications and determines the corresponding optimum variable weightings. Consider an example of the application of the discriminant technique to financial ratio data: *Minicase G : Gresham State Bank.*

The Gresham State Bank has become concerned about its loan portfolio and, in particular, the extent of bad debts arising from the failure of a number of its corporate clients. It has determined to do something about it, and called in a firm of consultants to construct a prediction model, which will identify well in advance those companies which are likely to fail. To assist the consultants, Gresham has abstracted profit and loss account and balance sheet data for 20 of its client companies in the manufacturing sector—six of these companies have failed in the last two years, but the remaining 14 are trading profitably. These companies provide clear sets of 'fails' and 'non-fails' which can be classified as (0,1) respectively. The dataset is detailed in Figure 31.

The consultants advise of their intention to construct a three-variable model of the form:

$$Z = a + b * (\text{Profit}) + c * (\text{Gearing}) + d * (\text{Liquidity})$$

which will classify the 20 known cases with 100% accuracy, i.e. six failed: 14 non-failed, without mis-classification. They will use a cut-off of $Z = 0$ to distinguish the company groups, with negative values corresponding with failed companies and positive values corresponding with healthy companies. The model so constructed will then be used to screen future loan applications, the intention being to pay particularly close attention to those cases which have the financial profile of previous failures.

The data of Figure 31 allows the construction of numerous financial ratio variables, detailed in Figure 32. The consultants select eight possible ratios for consideration:

three profit ratios, three gearing ratios and two liquidity ratios. The final selection of the ratios to appear in the prediction equation will be made with the assistance of the SPSS-X linear discriminant analysis software.:

Case	Status	PBT	CA	CL	FA	INV	INT	LTL	Sales	SHF
						£(000)				
1	0	-293	3140	3660	1610	2130	127	20	12220	930
2	0	-560	28470	17240	6210	22300	1350	6500	51100	10800
3	0	-2890	9170	11070	10500	2000	1300	4610	27660	4020
4	0	80	12040	8730	4230	7210	1500	3160	26110	4200
5	0	1590	14970	17750	2420	7770	1620	4480	24010	8370
6	0	550	10800	12000	20380	3900	1200	4700	24750	14570
7	1	1288	5340	2330	1500	1440	213	0	10890	4840
8	1	2060	13080	6860	6700	6970	350	2380	29870	10350
9	1	3070	16020	10540	8870	4130	100	1360	52760	14160
10	1	2520	8600	4570	5590	3330	450	70	23190	9130
11	1	1213	9670	5590	4760	4350	140	60	18240	8700
12	1	108	1890	660	770	1400	8	0	5590	1950
13	1	340	5860	2800	5150	2830	100	1960	7640	5750
14	1	1120	7060	4080	3150	2190	120	10	12530	5960
15	1	8110	80200	42740	29400	46000	4380	20240	144170	26900
16	1	320	4200	1340	2380	1140	0	0	6400	5100
17	1	2230	15900	10090	10030	7340	600	1810	38200	15600
18	1	390	3990	1190	1600	990	90	0	4980	4500
19	1	1400	13210	8720	6270	6120	123	10	32210	10180
20	1	840	10840	5150	3150	5470	85	1000	22810	7570

Where   Status = 0 for a Failed Company
Status = 1 for a Healthy Company
(£000's)
PBT = Profit before Tax
CA = Current Assets
CL = Current Liabilities
FA = Tangible Fixed Assets
INV = Inventory
INT = Interest payable
LTL = Long Term Loans
Sales = Sales turnover
SHF = Shareholders Funds

Figure 31: Dataset for Gresham State Bank

Case	Profitability			Gearing			Liquidity	
	Prof1	Prof2	Prof3	Gear1	Gear2	Gear3	Ratio	Acid
1	-0.0240	-0.0349	-0.0801	0.7747	0.7705	0.0215	0.8579	0.2760
2	-0.0110	0.0228	-0.0325	0.6845	0.4971	0.6019	1.6514	0.3579
3	-0.1045	-0.0808	-0.2611	0.7972	0.5628	1.1468	0.8284	0.6477
4	0.0031	0.0971	0.0092	0.7308	0.5366	0.7524	1.3792	0.5533
5	0.0662	0.1846	0.0896	1.2783	1.0207	0.5352	0.8434	0.4056
6	0.0222	0.0561	0.0458	0.5356	0.3849	0.3226	0.9000	0.5750
7	0.1183	0.2194	0.5528	0.3406	0.3406	0.0000	2.2918	1.6738
8	0.0690	0.1218	0.3003	0.4671	0.3468	0.2300	1.9067	0.8907
9	0.0582	0.1274	0.2913	0.4781	0.4235	0.0960	1.5199	1.1281
10	0.1087	0.2093	0.5514	0.3270	0.3221	0.0077	1.8818	1.1532
11	0.0665	0.0938	0.2170	0.3915	0.3874	0.0069	1.7299	0.9517
12	0.0193	0.0436	0.1636	0.2481	0.2481	0.0000	2.8636	0.7424
13	0.0445	0.0400	0.1214	0.4323	0.2543	0.3409	2.0929	1.0821
14	0.0894	0.1214	0.2745	0.4006	0.3996	0.0017	1.7304	1.1936
15	0.0563	0.1140	0.1898	0.5746	0.3900	0.7524	1.8765	0.8002
16	0.0500	0.0486	0.2388	0.2036	0.2036	0.0000	3.1343	2.2836
17	0.0584	0.1091	0.2210	0.4589	0.3891	0.1160	1.5758	0.8484
18	0.0783	0.0859	0.3277	0.2129	0.2129	0.000	3.3529	2.5210
19	0.0435	0.0782	0.1606	0.4482	0.4476	0.0010	1.5149	0.8131
20	0.0368	0.0661	0.1631	0.4396	0.3681	0.1321	2.1049	1.0427

Figure 32: Financial Ratios for Gresham Z-model

The ratios under consideration have all been suggested by previous studies in this area, and are:

$$\text{Prof1} = \frac{PBT}{S} = \frac{\text{Profit before Tax}}{\text{Sales Turnover}} \quad (\text{profit margin})$$

$$\text{Prof2} = \frac{PBIT}{TA} = \frac{\text{Profit before Interest and Tax}}{\text{Total Tangible Assets}} = \frac{PBT + INT}{CA + FA}$$

$$\text{Prof3} = \frac{PBT}{CL} = \frac{\text{Profit before Tax}}{\text{Current Liabilities}}$$

$$\text{Gear1} = \frac{TL}{TA} = \frac{\text{Total Liabilities}}{\text{Total Assets}} = \frac{CL + LTL}{CA + FA}$$

$$\text{Gear2} = \frac{CL}{TA} = \frac{\text{Current Liabilities}}{\text{Total Assets}} = \frac{CL}{CA + FA}$$

$$\text{Gear3} = \frac{LTL}{SH} = \frac{\text{Long Term Liabilities}}{\text{Shareholders Funds}} \quad \text{(debt/equity ratio)}$$

$$\text{Ratio} = \frac{CA}{CL} = \frac{\text{Current Assets}}{\text{Current Liabilities}} \quad \text{(current ratio)}$$

$$\text{Acid} = \frac{QA}{CL} = \frac{\text{Current Assets} - \text{Inventory}}{\text{Current Liabilities}} = \frac{CA-INV}{CL} \quad \text{(acid test ratio)}$$

An initial run of the discriminant software with all potential explanatory variables, using the (0,1) STATUS variable as the basis for classification, where STATUS = 1 is healthy and STATUS = 0 is failed, generates the following univariate statistics:

Variable	F	Significance
Prof1	15.22	0.0010
Prof2	3.78	0.0676
Prof3	23.06	0.0001
Gear1	27.39	0.0001
Gear2	18.55	0.0004
Gear3	11.39	0.0034
Ratio	15.49	0.0010
Acid	10.52	0.0045

High values of the F-statistic identify the most prominent variables as Gear1, Prof3, Gear2, etc. Selecting the most prominent representative of each financial grouping initially gives Prof3 (profits), Gear1 (gearing), Ratio (liquidity). An initial discriminant run with these three variables allows only two of them to enter the equation: Gear1 and Prof3. Together these are sufficient for all of the company cases to be classified correctly. After adjusting the constant term to provide a zero cut-off between groups and rounding the coefficients, we produce the equation:

$$Z = 2.0 + 5.0 * \text{Prof3} - 4.5 * \text{Gear1}$$

This equation generates negative scores for all the failed cases (cases 1 to 6) and positive scores for all non-failed cases (cases 7 to 20) and satisfies our initial requirements. No liquidity variable appears in the equation, and this may be attributable to the small number of failed cases available for modelling. If further failures occur in the future then the model may be modified to include them, meanwhile the existing model may be used to monitor the performance of other companies that are trading at present. The exhibition of a negative score does not necessarily foreshadow bankruptcy, but gives an indication of financial distress, in that the company has the profile of a previously failed company. The negative score therefore provides early warning, in that future failures will almost certainly come from this distressed group, members of which require close attention.

Whereas traditional univariate balance sheet ratios like those for liquidity may give an adequate indication of vulnerability to current and short-term fluctuations, longer term predictions require a better indication of cash flows. In the absence of publicly available information relating to internal cash budgets, this must come via projections of cash generating abilities from the published accounts.

Beaver (1966) uses cash flow = (net profit + depreciation) as a dynamic measure, employing the ratio

$$\frac{\text{cash flow}}{\text{total debt}}$$

as a univariate measure predicting business failure.

Sorter and Benston (1960) suggest a number of other liquidity measures which treat liquidity as funds flow dependent rather than assets-liabilities based. Chief among these are the:

$$\text{Defensive Interval} = \frac{\text{Defensive Assets}}{\text{Projected Daily Expenditure}} \text{ and}$$

$$\text{No Credit Interval} = \frac{\text{Defensive Assets} - \text{Actual Liabilities}}{\text{Projected Daily Expenditure}}$$

These interval measures reflect assumptions about the firm's changing environment and indicate the period it might survive by financing its operations from its own resources when its revenues are cut off. These measures are appealing, readily understood and arguably underused. However, all such measures are univariate approaches to identifying impending insolvency. Despite their usefulness, significant improvements in predictive ability are made available by reference to multivariate approaches.

Simnett and Trotman (1992) identify three key reasons for non-use of financial distress models in practice:

- lack of formal training of most practitioners;
- criticism of the statistical assumptions underlying the models;
- failure to include non-financial variables widely accepted as useful discriminators.

More research is necessary to address the third of these issues but it is possible to demonstrate the usefulness of such models in the appraisal of financial performance, while recognising the limitations to their implementation.

The **Altman (1968)** study for listed US manufacturing companies provides a benchmark against which all other multivariate studies can be measured. The Altman model is a linear combination of five variables, and records a 95 per cent classification accuracy of failed/non-failed companies:

$$Z = (1.2)X_1 + (1.4)X_2 + (3.3)X_3 + (0.6)X_4 + (1.0)X_5$$

where X_1 = (current assets – current liabilities)/total assets
               X_2 = retained earnings/total assets
               X_3 = earnings before interest and tax/total assets
               $X_4 = \dfrac{\text{market value of preferred and common equity}}{\text{book value of total liabilities}}$
               X_5 = sales/total assets

and a Z-score below 1.8 corresponds with a company considered to be a 'prime candidate for bankruptcy'. The lower the Z-score the higher the perceived probability of failure.

In the UK the **Taffler (1982)** model is the most widely exposed failure prediction model and the one which has been subject to the most extensive testing. Of the 92 companies used in its construction only one was mis-classified, and that — Rolls Royce in 1969 — was a questionable failure in view of the circumstances of its voluntary liquidation. Since the model's inception in 1977 only one listed public company has failed without triggering the model — Polly Peck 1992 — and that under circumstances associated with executive fraud and false accounting. Despite its classification accuracy, Taffler argues that this is less important than predictive ability, in that the usefulness of any model can only be gauged by the efficiency of its operation over a number of years. Most existing models demonstrate only classificatory ability not real predictive ability.

The Taffler model is only available commercially so the ratio weightings and variable transformations remain confidential. The ratios used represent an optimum statistical selection and are consequently sometimes obscure. A similar approach has subsequently been adopted by Lincoln (1984) and Houghton and Smith (1991) in Australia.

The Taffler variables are:

X_1 = profit before tax/current liabilities $\left(\dfrac{PBT}{CL}\right)$ contributing 53% of the explanatory power of the model;

X_2 = current assets/total liabilities $\left(\dfrac{CA}{TL}\right)$ contributing 13%;

X_3 = current liabilities/total assets $\left(\dfrac{CL}{TA}\right)$ contributing 18%, and

X_4 = the no-credit interval (*NCI*) indicating the number of days the company can continue to trade when it can no longer generate revenues. It may be calculated as

$$\text{No Credit Interval} = \frac{\text{Defensive Assets} - \text{Actual Liabilities}}{\text{Projected Daily Expenditure}}$$

i.e., $NCI = \dfrac{\text{current assets} - \text{inventory} - \text{current liabilities}}{\text{sales} - PBT + \text{depreciation}} * 365$

and contributes 16% of the model's explanatory power

Rather than the relative obscurity of the four ratios employed being seen as a deficiency, Taffler views it as a distinct advantage in that the ratios are less prone to window dressing and creative accounting. He suggests that impending insolvency cannot be hidden in the accounts, however they are stated, if they are analysed in a holistic manner.

To date economic theory has played a negligible part in the development of failure prediction models. Given the absence of a substantial theoretical underpinning most research studies have been exploratory, trying to establish the model, method, variables and firms which give the best predictions. Research to date has demonstrated that the classification performance of predictive models is not highly sensitive to the mathematical relationship chosen or the statistical method employed. Linear additive models based on linear discriminant analysis are the simplest to construct and interpret, and their outcomes are not dissimilar to any comparable model.

A review of early warning models of impending failure highlights a number of common issues which require emphasis.

DEFINITION OF FAILURE

There are numerous definitions of business or corporate failure ranging from the strict legal sense of liquidation to an inability to repay monies when due. Differences in the definition of 'distress' are apparent in a number of studies and must be linked to the objectives of users of the model(s) concerned. Comparisons between the outcomes of different models are therefore difficult.

THE TIMING OF FAILURE

Most discriminant models will identify those companies exhibiting financial distress. Within this set they can highlight those most at risk: the worst companies, those most likely to fail within the following year. However, the precise timing of failure is determined by the bankers through their decision to appoint receivers or withdraw financial support. Financial profiles alone are unable to specify a precise timing. The shorter the time between the prediction and the likely event the easier the prediction task is, but the less useful in maximising economic gain. A timescale of one or two years between prediction point and decision outcome is the most common compromise adopted, which is sufficiently long to enable some positive actions to be taken but also sufficiently short to facilitate accurate predictions.

CHOICE OF SAMPLE COMPANIES

Linear discriminant analysis requires two distinct samples for classification procedures to function appropriately (i.e. a clearly failed set and a clearly healthy set of companies). Random sampling procedures, however desirable, would not systematically yield such a clear distinction. It is not appropriate to view continuing companies as distinctly different from their failed counterparts. Some companies still trading will have similar financial profiles to those of failures, and may themselves eventually fail. Discriminant analysis in this area requires the specification of clearly 'failed' and 'healthy' sets of companies. Many models have been fitted on highly artificial combinations of failed and non-failed companies. The use of a 50% failed proportion is not uncommon, even though the population percentage will be closer to 1%.

CHOICE OF VARIABLES

The lack of underpinning theory and consequent search activity has contributed significantly to variables found successful in early studies being used in subsequent studies. Only Taffler (1982), Lincoln (1984) and Houghton and Smith (1991) have conducted significant new searches.

This is disappointing because many of the variables employed in early studies have been those found useful for large US manufacturing companies. International evidence suggests that there are considerable differences between the discriminant models constructed in different countries, both in terms of the financial ratio variables included and the weighting accorded them.

Similarly, there are considerable differences between the models constructed for separate industry groupings with consequent dangers of over-aggregation from ignoring industry differentiation. Nevertheless, a long succession of authors has attempted to apply Altman's US model to companies elsewhere, a use for which it was not intended, and even more erroneously to apply manufacturing models to non-manufacturing companies or to unlisted companies. Differences between countries and industries mean that no single optimum combination of financial ratios will exist, although we might expect that particular ratios have widespread applicability.

PREDICTIVE ABILITY

Existing models are only predictive in the sense that they identify those companies currently trading who have financial profiles similar to previous failures. As with all similar models the 'distressed' set will over-predict failure, in that it will also contain some companies who effect recoveries and some who will be taken over before they are allowed to fail.

There is substantial difference in the error classification costs between a Type I error (predicting a failed company as non-failed) and a Type II error (predicting a non-failed company as failed). Pacey and Pham (1990) estimate the former to have financial consequences approximately 41.5 times greater than the latter. As a result, most new models reflect the relative costs of a Type I error and aim to ensure that no potentially failed case is missed at the predictive stage.

Case 24: British Motors provides a more extensive dataset, allowing the construction of a more complex model, together with the application of the model to a new set of companies. It highlights the benefits and limitations of the use of such models.

Rather than specifying a set of companies who will fail in the next two years, existing models identify a 'distressed' set from which the failures will come. Approximately 25% of all companies will be designated as 'distressed' at any one time, but only about a third of these will fail in the short term. This overprediction is a cause for concern in all failure prediction models.

Included in the 'distressed' set are those companies who might effect a financial recovery if they implement appropriate turnaround strategies. This provides a positive angle for early warning models in that it identifies some cases in need of remedial action. Slatter (1984, p. 105) identifies a number of generic recovery strategies that might be adopted, depending on the cause of the 'distressed' state. He specifies seven major causes of decline and potential failure:

- poor management
- inadequate financial control
- high cost structure
- lack of marketing effort
- competitive weaknesses
- financial policy
- ill-advised acquisitions and projects.

Each of these is associated with a particular set of generic recovery strategies:

- **Poor management** he associates with autocratic leadership, an ineffective board, the neglect of core businesses and lack of management depth. Appropriate remedial action would require new blood in the management team, organisational change and decentralisation.

- **Inadequate financial control** is associated with a poorly designed accounting system, misuse of information, the distortion of costs through misallocation of overheads and an organisational structure which hinders rather than facilitates control. This would be improved by new management and decentralisation if accompanied by tighter financial controls.

- **High cost structure** is associated with operational inefficiencies, competitor control of raw materials and proprietary knowledge, low scale economies and high labour costs. Cost reduction strategies and a revised product-market focus are appropriate for recovery. Cost reduction strategies would include those directed towards:

  - raw material costs — aimed at improved buying practices, better utilisation and the possible substitution of materials;
  - unit labour costs — aimed at increasing productivity and reducing head-count;
  - overhead costs — targeting manufacturing, marketing and distribution.

- **Lack of marketing effort** is associated with inadequate or inflexible response to changing patterns of demand and product obsolescence. Improved marketing pursues a revenue generating strategy embracing:

  - changed prices;
  - more selling effort;
  - rationalising of the product line;
  - focused promotion; and
  - a closer focus on customer needs

- **Competitive weakness** is reflected by lack of strength in both price and product competition and an absent product-market focus. A reliance on old products will be apparent, with inadequate differentiation and no new product ideas on the horizon. Cost, marketing and product weaknesses must be addressed, with growth via acquisition considered as a means of overcoming deficiencies in the product-market area.

- **Financial policy weakness** is characterised by high debt-equity ratios, expensive sources of funding and conservative financial policies. A new financial strategy will likely include debt restructuring and revenue-generating policies.

- **Failed acquisitions** are characterized by the purchase of losers at a price which is set too high. Poor post-acquisition management often results in a quick re-sale. Ill-advised big projects, which threaten the company's survival, are associated with start-up difficulties, the loss of major contracts and the under-estimation of capital requirements and market entry costs.

Asset reduction is the most appropriate recovery strategy in the circumstances, embracing:

- reducing fixed assets — through divesting operating units and specific assets, management buyouts and sale and leaseback arrangements;
- reducing working capital — through extending creditors and reducing both inventories and debtors. This would include cancelling orders, returning goods, the sale of surplus raw materials, tighter credit and possibly factoring arrangements for debtors.

The extent to which these strategies are appropriate will also be determined by the severity of the crisis and peculiar industry characteristics. Where short-term survival is threatened we might anticipate a recovery strategy comprising four strands:

- cash generation,

- asset reduction,

- debt restructuring, and

- very tight financial control, encompassing cash management, cost reduction, product refocus and improved marketing.

Case 25: Whittlesford Hardware provides an example of a company subject to financial distress and for which some of the above strategies may be appropriate.

REFERENCES

Altman E I, 'Financial Ratios, Discriminant Analysis and the Prediction of Corporate Bankruptcy', *Journal of Finance*, Vol 23, September 1968, pp 589–609

Ashton R H, 'The Robustness of Linear Models for Decision Making', *Omega*, Vol 4 No 5, 1976, pp 609–615

Beaver W H, 'Financial Ratios as Predictors of Failure', *Empirical Research in Accounting: Selected Studies: Supplement to Journal of Accounting Research*, 1966, pp 71–111

Box G E P and Jenkins G M, *Time Series Analysis: Forecasting and Control*, Holden-Day, San Francisco, 1976

Castagna A D and Matolcsy Z P, 'The Prediction of Corporate Failure: Testing the Australian Experience', *Australian Journal of Management*, Vol 6 No 1, 1981, pp 23–50

Houghton K A and Smith M, 'Loan Risk and the Anticipation of Corporate Distress: West Australian Evidence' in K Davis and I Harper (eds), *Risk Management in Financial Institutions*, Sydney, Allen & Unwin, 1991, pp 61–74

Izan H Y, 'Corporate Distress in Australia', *Journal of Banking and Finance*, Vol 8, 1984, pp 303–320

Kahnemann D and Tversky A, 'Subjective Probability: A Judgement of Representativeness', *Cognitive Psychology*, July 1972, pp 430–454

Lincoln M, 'An Empirical Study of the Usefulness of Accounting Ratios to Describe Levels of Insolvency Risk', *Journal of Banking and Finance*, Vol 8, 1984, pp 321–340

McDonald G C and Schwing R C, 'Instabilities of Regression Estimates Relating Air Pollution to Mortality', *Technometrics*, Vol 15 No 3, August 1973, pp 463–481

Nie N H (ed), *SPSS-X User's Guide*, McGraw-Hill, Chicago, 1983

Pacey J W and Pham T M, 'The Predictiveness of Bankruptcy Models: Methodological Problems and Evidence', *Australian Journal of Management*, Vol 15 No 2, December 1990, pp 315–338

Simnett R and Trotman K, 'Identification of Key Financial Ratios for Going Concern Decisions', *Charter*, April 1992, pp 39–41

Slatter S, *Corporate Recovery: A Guide to Turnaround Management*, Penguin Books, London, 1984.

Sorter G H and Benston G, 'Appraising the Defensive Position of a Firm: The Interval Measure', *Accounting Review*, October 1960, pp 633–640

Taffler R J, 'Forecasting Company Failure in the UK using Discriminant Analysis and Financial Ratio Data', *Journal of the Royal Statistical Society* (Series A), Vol 145 No 3, 1982, pp 342–358

Taffler R J, 'The Assessment of Company Solvency and Performance using a Statistical Model: A Comparative UK-based Study', *Accounting and Business Research*, Vol 15 No 52, 1983, pp 295–308

Taffler R J, 'Empirical Models for the Monitoring of UK Corporations', *Journal of Banking and Finance*, Vol 8, 1984, pp 199–227

Thorngate W, 'Efficient Decision Heuristics', *Behavioural Science*, May 1980, pp 219–225

CASE 22: THE REDFERN MUTUAL ASSURANCE COMPANY

This case provides the opportunity for the use of regression procedures in the development of a competitive market diversification. It raises awareness of the importance of non-quantitative factors, particularly political and legal aspects, in the implementation of a satisfactory policy.

The Redfern Mutual Assurance Company is based in Liverpool but contracts life assurance business worldwide in association with a number of overseas sister companies. The home market for new life policies is static and Redfern is looking further afield for growth in the short to medium term. It is particularly attracted by the opportunities in North America and Northern Europe where endowment assurance life policies are commonly used to secure the bank lending which provides home loan mortgages.

Cameron Pettigrew is the company's chief actuary, with the ultimate responsibility for setting the premium rates for all Redfern policies. His 'pricing' policy effectively determines the competitiveness of Redfern products worldwide. Premium rates are currently set with reference to a number of factors which have been shown through empirical studies to affect mortality rates. The lower the life expectancy of the assured, then the higher is the premium to be charged for the life cover provided. Pettigrew currently takes into account:

- age — the older the life assured the higher the premium. Redfern will normally decline new business from proposers in excess of 75 years of age;

- gender — females will pay a lower premium than males of the same age because of their greater life expectancy. In most developed countries this difference is of the order of six years. Redfern allows for the difference by treating females as males equivalent to four years younger for premium setting purposes;

- state of health — all new proposers make a statutory declaration of their current health. New proposers over the age of 45 are required to undergo a full medical, if over 65 the medical is at the proposer's expense. Any irregularities recognised result in a weighting being attached to the standard premium (e.g. evidence of rheumatic fever in early life may lead to heart problems later on. Redfern would react by either declining the business or charging a life premium two and a half times that of the normal rate).

- personal habits — all new proposers make a statutory declaration relating to smoking, drinking and drug dependence. Non-smokers are rewarded with a 10% discount off standard premium rates.

Cameron Pettigrew and his fellow actuaries are now reviewing alternative personal characteristics to determine whether they can make premium adjustments which increase the competitiveness of their products. They have decided to conduct a study of their US operations to determine additional contributory factors, as the first stage of evolving and implementing the launch of a new life assurance product which engineers a competitive edge over their rivals in the insurance industry. Sociology and environmental science have provided evidence to suggest that biographical data (e.g. level of education and race) and environmental factors (e.g. climate and pollution levels) may impact on levels of mortality, expressed as deaths per 100 000 population. They have collected data for a number of potentially useful explanatory variables across 60 US cities and intend to investigate any relationship with levels of mortality in those cities.

Case	Rate	Pre	Jan	July	Humid	Educ	Non	Coll	HC	NOX	SO2
1	921.870	36	27	71	59	11.4	8.8	42.6	21	15	59
2	997.875	35	23	72	57	11.0	3.5	50.7	8	10	39
3	962.354	44	29	74	54	9.8	0.8	39.4	6	6	33
4	982.291	47	45	79	56	11.1	27.1	50.2	18	8	24
5	1071.289	43	35	77	55	9.6	24.4	43.7	43	38	206
6	1030.380	53	45	80	54	10.2	38.5	43.1	30	32	72
7	934.700	43	30	74	56	12.1	3.5	49.2	21	32	62
8	899.529	45	30	73	56	10.6	5.3	40.4	6	4	4
9	1001.902	36	24	70	61	10.5	8.1	42.5	18	12	37
10	912.347	36	27	72	59	10.7	6.7	41.0	12	7	20
11	1017.613	52	42	79	56	9.6	22.2	41.3	18	8	27
12	1024.885	33	26	76	58	10.9	16.3	44.9	88	63	278
13	970.467	40	34	77	57	10.2	13.0	45.7	26	26	146
14	985.950	35	28	71	60	11.1	14.7	44.6	31	21	64
15	958.839	37	31	75	58	11.9	13.1	49.6	23	9	15
16	860.101	35	46	85	54	11.8	14.8	51.2	1	1	1
17	936.234	36	30	75	58	11.4	12.4	44.0	6	4	16
18	871.766	15	30	73	38	12.2	4.7	53.1	17	8	28
19	959.221	31	27	74	59	10.8	15.8	43.5	52	35	124
20	941.181	30	24	72	61	10.8	13.1	33.8	11	4	11
21	891.708	31	45	85	53	11.4	11.5	48.1	1	1	1
22	871.338	31	24	72	61	10.9	5.1	45.2	5	3	10
23	971.122	42	40	77	53	10.4	22.7	41.4	8	3	5
24	887.466	43	27	72	56	11.5	7.2	51.6	7	3	10
25	952.529	46	55	84	59	11.4	21.0	46.9	6	5	1
26	968.665	39	29	75	60	11.4	15.6	46.6	13	7	33

Case	Rate	Pre	Jan	July	Humid	Educ	Non	Coll	HC	NOX	SO2
27	919.729	35	31	81	55	12.0	12.6	48.6	7	4	4
28	844.053	43	32	74	54	9.5	2.9	43.7	11	7	32
29	861.833	11	53	68	47	12.1	7.8	48.9	648	319	130
30	989.265	30	35	71	57	9.9	13.1	42.6	38	37	193
31	1006.490	50	42	82	59	10.4	36.7	43.3	15	18	34
32	861.439	60	67	82	60	11.5	13.5	47.3	3	1	1
33	929.150	30	20	69	64	11.1	5.8	44.0	33	23	125
34	857.622	25	12	73	58	12.1	2.0	51.9	20	11	26
35	961.009	45	40	80	56	10.1	21.0	46.1	17	14	78
36	923.234	46	30	72	58	11.3	8.8	45.3	4	3	8
37	1113.156	54	54	81	62	9.7	31.4	45.5	20	17	1
38	994.648	42	33	77	58	10.7	11.3	48.7	41	26	108
39	1015.023	42	32	76	54	10.5	17.5	45.3	29	32	161
40	991.290	36	29	72	56	10.6	8.1	45.5	45	59	263
41	893.991	37	38	67	73	12.0	3.6	50.3	56	21	44
42	938.500	42	29	72	56	10.1	2.2	38.8	6	4	18
43	946.185	41	33	77	54	9.6	2.7	38.6	11	11	89
44	1025.502	44	39	78	53	11.0	28.6	49.5	12	9	48
45	874.281	32	25	72	60	11.1	5.0	46.4	7	4	18
46	953.560	34	32	79	57	9.7	17.2	45.1	31	15	68
47	839.709	10	55	70	61	12.1	5.9	51.0	144	66	20
48	911.701	18	48	63	71	12.2	13.7	51.2	311	171	86
49	790.733	13	49	68	71	12.2	3.0	51.9	105	32	3
50	899.264	35	40	64	72	12.2	5.7	54.3	20	7	20
51	904.155	45	28	74	56	11.1	3.4	41.9	5	4	20
52	950.672	38	24	72	61	11.4	3.8	50.5	8	5	25
53	972.464	31	26	73	59	10.7	9.5	43.9	11	7	25
54	912.202	40	23	71	60	10.3	2.5	47.4	5	2	11
55	967.803	41	37	78	52	12.3	25.9	59.7	65	28	102
56	823.764	28	32	81	54	12.1	7.5	51.6	4	2	1
57	1003.502	45	33	76	56	11.3	12.1	47.3	14	11	42
58	895.696	45	24	70	56	11.1	1.0	44.8	7	3	8
59	911.817	42	33	76	54	9.0	4.8	42.2	8	8	49
60	954.442	38	28	72	58	10.7	11.7	37.5	14	13	39

Figure C22.1: Dataset for Redfern Assurance Company

Management Science

The data collected for modelling is presented in Figure C22.1 and details the ten explanatory variables under investigation, grouped as follows:

Group		Variable	Symbol
Climate	1.	Precipitation Levels (Annual mean in inches)	Pre
	2.	January Temperature (Average minimum °F)	Jan
	3.	July Temperature (Average maximum °F)	July
	4.	Relative Humidity (% average at 1pm)	Humid
SocioEconomic	5.	Education Levels (Mean school years for >25s)	Educ
	6.	% Non-White	Non
	7.	% White Collar	Coll
Pollution	8.	Hydrocarbon levels	HC
	9.	Nitrous oxide levels	NOX
	10.	Sulphur dioxide levels	SO2

You are required to identify those variables with a significant impact on mortality rates and evaluate the possibility of incorporating these into life assurance premium calculations.

CASE 23: CHARITY SHOPS

This case allows the use of a regression model with cross-section data to provide evidence of the usefulness of a number of variables in improving sales performance. It provides the opportunity for a cost-benefit analysis for changes in circumstances.

Charity Shops operate nationwide from their Swindon base, remerchandising and retailing donations of clothing, books, ornaments, etc, brought directly to the shop or collected by group members.

They have engaged consultants to investigate the potential cost effectiveness of modifications to the current operation of the chain in the light of disappointing sales turnover levels. Four particular policies are under urgent consideration.

(a) The refurbishment of existing shops.

(b) The expansion of existing sites, when possible.

(c) The opening of additional outlets.

(d) The installation of professional shop managers.

Currently each shop is led either by an individual or a collective shop management committee, made up entirely of volunteers, responsible to a regional officer. A local supervisor oversees the operations of a small number of shops in his or her region.

Regional officers have authorised a sample survey of shops in order to determine what action might be taken to remedy the lack of sales growth. The data in Figure C23.1 provides the results of a survey conducted by consultants to examine the characteristics of a sample of 56 Charity Shops, and provides information on 12 separate features:

Variables for Which Data is Available

1. Gross turnover in year (£000).
2. Type of leadership: 0 = individual responsible to a regional officer.
                        1 = collective leadership of local volunteers.
3. Age of shop operation (years).
4. Gross rental value of shop (£ per quarter).
5. Sales area (sq m).
6. Decor of shop: rated 1 (very poor) to 5 (first class permanent fittings).
7. Population of area (000 people).
8. Site rating: Rated 1 (worst possible site) to 6 (prime site).
9. Number of helpers.
10. Supervisor visits per month.
11. Days open per week.
12. Hours open per week.

You are required to make recommendations of the strategies that you might adopt to improve the sales performance of Charity Shops. Your report should highlight the benefits and limitations of the use of regression models.

Shop	Turn-over	Leader	Shop Age	Rates	Area	Decor	Popu-lation	Site	Helper	Super-visors	Days	Hours
1	52.0	0	7	625	54	1	14	4	30	0	6	40
2	90.0	0	7	265	26	4	162	3	30	3	6	25
3	76.0	0	8	175	32	5	17	5	14	1	6	22
4	52.0	1	9	580	28	5	94	4	20	2	5	22
5	46.0	0	7	250	27	5	18	2	8	3	5	26
6	24.0	0	10	265	20	3	16	3	6	2	5	23
7	29.0	0	12	315	27	1	184	3	10	2	6	21
8	61.0	0	10	200	22	5	15	5	8	0	6	25
9	15.0	0	9	95	16	1	9	1	15	1	6	24
10	49.0	0	9	445	30	1	18	5	10	1	4	16
11	13.0	0	7	210	17	1	28	1	5	0	3	14
12	55.0	0	10	450	27	2	41	3	15	1	6	24
13	51.0	0	8	375	21	4	38	5	20	1	5	30
14	57.0	0	14	550	24	2	130	3	10	1	5	26
15	30.0	0	15	313	22	1	37	3	15	1	5	13
16	15.0	0	8	291	35	3	4	6	15	2	5	23
17	60.0	0	8	100	22	5	17	5	25	1	3	12
18	70.0	0	7	129	15	3	34	6	20	2	6	30
19	50.0	0	10	127	30	5	11	3	20	4	5	20
20	40.0	0	5	215	27	5	11	5	50	4	6	21
21	50.0	0	11	140	26	5	12	4	20	4	4	16
22	86.0	0	4	970	25	5	15	6	40	2	6	40
23	33.0	0	7	285	22	1	14	2	12	0	6	16
24	62.0	0	8	414	60	5	176	4	20	1	6	24
25	55.0	0	9	208	17	4	8	3	30	1	4	24
26	50.0	0	8	128	31	4	4	3	6	4	5	23
27	31.0	0	9	235	22	1	153	2	1	1	4	25
28	101.0	0	11	775	32	3	167	2	24	3	6	33

Shop	Turn-over	Leader	Shop Age	Rates	Area	Decor	Popu-lation	Site	Helper	Super-visors	Days	Hours
29	22.0	1	8	390	32	4	7	2	20	2	6	36
30	21.0	1	8	520	23	4	8	6	15	2	6	36
31	36.0	1	3	800	42	1	16	3	12	0	4	24
32	25.0	1	9	2850	32	1	48	5	12	0	4	20
33	75.0	1	8	545	32	5	41	5	16	3	6	28
34	62.0	1	7	135	32	2	222	2	13	4	4	20
35	14.0	1	2	191	22	3	19	3	8	1	3	10
36	32.0	1	8	303	29	2	26	1	25	1	4	16
37	69.0	1	13	534	30	3	46	4	20	1	5	15
38	47.0	1	13	534	21	3	49	4	25	1	4	16
39	27.0	1	7	188	21	2	38	3	12	1	5	16
40	48.0	1	15	500	25	2	63	2	15	1	5	20
41	40.0	1	9	525	26	4	153	1	15	2	5	24
42	92.0	1	1	830	52	5	180	3	30	3	6	36
43	19.0	1	8	400	33	1	11	5	10	0	4	16
44	35.0	1	8	720	23	1	41	4	12	0	4	22
45	47.0	1	7	480	23	5	20	3	15	0	6	33
46	60.0	1	9	925	46	4	112	4	18	0	6	42
47	57.0	1	9	900	33	2	101	4	24	0	5	30
48	26.0	1	12	315	27	1	93	2	20	0	6	38
49	101.0	1	10	355	32	4	18	6	30	2	6	30
50	36.0	1	10	370	22	1	74	2	22	2	6	23
51	39.0	1	12	275	37	1	34	2	10	2	5	20
52	108.0	1	10	138	15	5	18	2	45	1	6	25
53	77.0	1	9	142	30	5	23	5	16	4	3	17
54	85.0	1	8	1675	39	3	16	2	20	3	4	17
55	23.0	1	9	166	19	1	60	3	20	1	5	25
56	46.0	1	11	280	38	1	32	5	12	2	3	12

Figure C23.1: Charity Shops Data

CASE 24: COUNTRYWIDE STORES

This case provides the opportunity to use regression analysis to model sales turnover in terms of a number of explanatory variables. Interpretation of the resultant equation highlights both the potential for improvement and the limitations of the approach.

Countrywide Stores operates a chain of over 400 variety stores across the UK. Countrywide has engaged consultants at its London Head Office to evaluate the cost effectiveness of modifications in the operation of the stores nationwide. Four particular policies are under urgent consideration:

(a) A complete refurbishment of the whole chain in order to project a more up-market and modern image.

(b) A move away from small sites to larger ones located out of town, with the potential for both extensive car parking and further expansion.

(c) Insistence on the mobility of existing and potential store managers to promote movement between locations.

(d) Revision of the current policy relating to the product-mix and the number of lines currently stocked.

A sample of 40 stores has been surveyed to identify their individual characteristics and overall performance, in order to provide a benchmark for excellence within the group. 1993 Data is available in Figure C24.1 for each of the following 20 variables:

1. Sales (£000).
2. Gross profit (£000).
3. Sales floor area (sq m).
4. Display counter length (m).
5. Total store frontage (m).
6. Number of sales staff (full time equivalent).
7. Manager: 1 = manager in 1st year of appointment at store.
   0 = otherwise.
8. Years since last store refurbishment.
9. Number of car park spaces in shopping centre.
10. Catchment area population in thousands.
11. Percentage of catchment area population aged 65 and over.
12. Percentage of catchment area population in social class A (professional and managerial).
13. Sales/sales floor area (£/sq m).
14. Gross profit/sales floor area (£/sq m).
15. Gross profit/sales (%).
16. Sales/sales staff (£/person).

Strategic Management Accounting

17. Display counter length (m)/thousand m² sales floor area.
18. Sales staff/thousand sq m sales floor area.
19. Frontage (m)/thousand m² sales floor area.
20. Gross Rental Value/m² total store floor area (i.e. the current market rate, representing a measure of desirability of store position).

You are required to make recommendations of the strategies that might be employed by Countrywide to improve the performance of the group. Your report should embrace an interpretation of the outcomes of appropriate forecasting models constructed.

Store	Sales	Prof	Floor	Counter	Front	Staff	Manager	Refurb	Car Park	Popu-latn
1	3650	1150	940	93.2	15.2	25	0	10	1706	141.43
2	5350	1890	1420	162.7	5.7	41	1	10	1019	95.15
3	5870	1990	1780	110.8	6.0	51	0	0	2117	53.10
4	4430	1580	1290	163.7	6.8	34	0	0	530	59.84
5	6090	1880	1010	126.2	9.6	44	0	8	125	15.76
6	2920	940	680	89.4	4.5	22	0	1	1085	165.44
7	6350	2180	1400	126.2	7.7	46	1	12	575	26.58
8	6080	1900	980	101.6	4.2	35	1	10	600	64.28
9	5220	1800	840	97.0	10.3	37	0	11	730	90.32
10	5060	1600	1530	202.7	5.3	35	0	15	970	50.25
11	5440	1940	910	98.0	4.4	33	1	14	170	26.23
12	7160	2130	2120	160.2	15.0	69	0	0	1000	55.66
13	7160	2120	990	115.3	6.5	51	1	8	429	43.35
14	3560	1090	580	71.8	6.2	28	1	15	660	42.83
15	5560	1700	1120	125.8	6.0	38	0	2	1056	47.11
16	3710	1360	870	108.2	3.7	30	0	7	400	31.32
17	5150	1730	480	145.1	4.1	37	0	3	900	53.10
18	4720	1610	1300	132.9	8.3	27	0	5	845	55.69
19	4070	1500	970	136.7	10.9	30	0	1	210	31.46
20	6190	1920	1070	106.1	14.0	36	0	12	730	54.53
21	4240	1590	940	100.1	11.2	24	0	10	294	26.74
22	4690	1370	860	103.5	6.8	33	0	1	590	53.10
23	4340	1570	860	108.1	13.3	24	1	7	227	13.42
24	3490	1150	660	77.2	5.2	28	0	2	321	18.29

Store	Sales	Prof	Floor	Counter	Front	Staff	Manager	Refurb	Car Park	Popu-latn
25	4960	1450	1450	156.8	7.2	36	0	0	425	33.07
26	6000	1860	690	82.8	5.6	44	0	2	550	8.92
27	6040	1860	940	125.2	22.2	44	1	6	440	39.48
28	5700	1760	810	87.4	5.2	38	1	17	450	27.81
29	3830	1250	470	59.1	5.7	24	1	17	515	9.06
30	5150	1590	1300	164.5	3.5	36	0	7	50	20.40
31	6020	1750	1250	148.9	6.6	43	1	7	670	41.56
32	4250	1240	460	66.0	2.4	35	0	2	200	30.12
33	6820	2050	1160	131.7	5.6	54	0	12	320	24.58
34	4700	1490	1440	144.5	3.1	37	0	4	380	28.61
35	4360	1370	720	90.3	5.6	27	1	2	475	19.76
36	5960	1880	950	125.0	7.2	39	0	7	1301	107.80
37	4520	1460	940	106.6	5.4	35	0	8	150	48.96
38	4820	1590	860	108.3	5.2	34	1	5	395	16.97
39	4560	1480	800	95.2	2.2	29	1	4	330	16.34
40	4390	1380	830	100.8	10.1	33	0	3	120	14.01

Figure C24.1: Store Data for Countrywide

Store	Retired %	Class A	Sal2 Flor	Prof2 Fl	Prof2 Sal	Sal2 Stf	Coun 2Flor	Staf 2Fl	Fron 2Fl	Rent
1	10.8	9.3	388.10	1220	31.45	145908	99.15	26.6	16.17	0.86
2	11.1	13.3	376.70	1337	35.50	130462	114.58	28.9	4.01	0.71
3	10.2	11.6	330.10	1123	34.03	115211	62.25	28.7	3.37	1.51
4	13.1	14.6	343.10	1226	35.74	130188	126.90	26.4	5.27	0.65
5	12.3	17.2	603.10	1869	31.00	138435	124.95	43.6	9.50	0.62
6	9.3	12.5	429.60	1377	32.06	132778	131.47	32.4	6.62	1.16
7	9.3	20.0	453.50	1561	34.43	138034	90.14	32.9	5.50	0.64
8	16.7	23.8	620.10	1948	31.42	173630	103.67	35.7	4.29	1.11
9	13.8	13.4	622.10	2145	34.47	141238	115.48	44.0	12.26	1.10
10	11.0	8.8	331.00	1047	31.63	144688	132.48	22.9	3.46	0.67
11	12.3	11.9	598.30	2128	35.57	164985	107.69	36.3	4.84	0.83

Store	Retired %	Class A	Sal2 Flor	Prof2 Fl	Prof2 Sal	Sal2 Stf	Coun 2Flor	Staf 2Fl	Fron 2Fl	Rent
12	10.7	18.9	338.10	1006	29.74	103887	75.57	32.5	7.08	0.88
13	14.9	13.8	723.40	2146	29.67	140429	116.46	51.5	6.57	0.96
14	10.7	13.5	613.60	1887	30.75	127101	123.79	48.3	10.69	0.85
15	11.0	15.9	497.00	1518	30.54	146477	112.32	33.9	5.36	0.76
16	9.0	10.5	426.40	1570	36.82	123660	124.37	34.5	4.25	0.65
17	10.2	11.6	1072.8	3596	33.52	139178	302.29	77.1	8.54	0.97
18	14.1	13.2	363.00	1239	34.15	174774	102.23	20.8	6.38	1.00
19	9.5	10.4	420.10	1553	36.97	135822	140.93	30.9	11.24	0.76
20	11.4	16.1	579.10	1794	30.98	172133	99.16	33.6	13.08	1.15
21	23.9	22.6	451.20	1698	37.64	176701	106.49	25.5	11.91	0.69
22	10.2	11.6	545.10	1597	29.30	142055	120.35	38.4	7.91	0.48
23	20.0	19.4	504.20	1826	36.22	180663	125.70	27.9	15.47	0.47
24	13.8	11.9	529.80	1742	32.87	124888	116.97	42.4	7.88	0.53
25	10.0	12.5	342.20	1003	29.29	137843	108.14	24.8	4.97	0.94
26	10.6	15.3	870.00	2702	31.06	136425	120.00	63.8	8.12	0.58
27	10.8	9.9	642.90	1986	30.90	137337	133.19	46.8	23.62	0.78
28	12.4	12.2	703.70	2167	30.80	150010	107.90	46.9	6.42	0.74
29	16.7	13.7	815.50	2668	32.72	159706	125.74	51.1	12.13	0.49
30	13.5	21.1	396.20	1228	30.98	143066	126.54	27.7	2.69	0.77
31	10.5	15.8	481.50	1400	29.07	139981	119.12	34.4	5.28	0.94
32	9.0	10.5	923.70	2693	29.15	121398	143.48	76.1	5.22	0.97
33	12.7	11.0	587.90	1770	30.11	126297	113.53	46.6	4.83	0.58
34	10.6	8.5	327.00	1041	31.84	127268	100.35	25.7	2.15	0.45
35	14.9	22.1	604.90	1906	31.50	161316	125.42	37.5	7.78	0.90
36	8.3	32.7	627.20	1986	31.66	152774	131.58	41.1	7.58	1.43
37	12.7	11.4	480.70	1549	32.23	129111	113.40	37.2	5.74	0.65
38	9.1	11.3	561.00	1852	33.02	141893	125.93	39.5	6.05	0.79
39	12.1	14.7	569.80	1849	32.44	157190	119.00	36.2	2.75	0.53
40	10.4	12.0	530.00	1667	31.45	133301	121.45	39.8	12.17	0.82

Figure C24.1: Store Data for Countrywide (cont)

CASE 25: WHITTLESFORD HARDWARE GROUP

This case examines a turnaround situation and provides the framework for the estab-
lishment of a recovery policy based on an analysis of past errors and current
deficiencies.

Sam Kinnear established Aaron's Alloys in the early 1950s to capitalise on the growth
of the motor industry in Coventry and the ready market for the products of a light
alloy foundry. The company grew steadily, with the motor industry remaining the
major customer: in 1990 it still accounted for over 60 per cent of total group sales.

The casting process requires dies that are clamped into the machine and which
contain a cavity for the injection of hot metal. The die sinking process is a highly
skilled trade, which was originally part of Aaron's Alloys before being floated as a
separate enterprise, Bunyup Tool and Dies, in 1970. Over 50 per cent of the
customers of Bunyup are from within the Whittlesford group.

Sam acquired Donegal Castings at the end of 1983 to complement the existing
business by providing a facility for aluminium mouldings. The latter were increasingly being specified by customers because of their strength and lightness. Sam
made no attempt to integrate the commercial activities of the two enterprises since
their customer bases were almost entirely separate: Aaron in the motor trade and
Donegal in garden and DIY tools.

Further expansion took place with the purchase of Collingwood Hardware at the
beginning of 1985. This operation cast and plated its own line of fittings for the
hardware trade, notably furniture and domestic appliances. The purchase was
mainly seen as a diversification but also provided in-house plating facilities for
Aaron's output. Collingwood remains the only member of the group which designs,
makes and markets its own products, rather than complying to precise customer
specifications: it deals directly with wholesale and retail outlets and places a special
emphasis on new product development and sales expansion. Figure C25.1 details
the scope of the group in 1985.

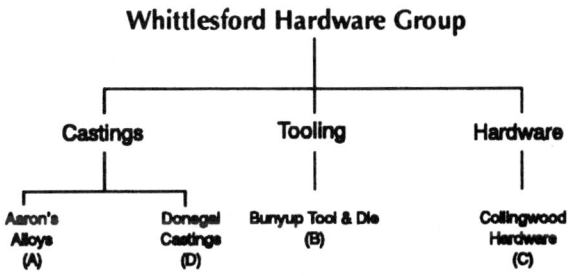

Figure C25.1: Group Structure (1985–89)

Whittlesford Hardware Group

(£000)	1983	1984	1985	1986	1987	1988	1989	1990	1991	1992
Profit and Loss Account										
Sales Revenue	4700	5200	5000	4100	4000	4300	4600	3500	3000	4000
Profit (before interest and tax)	105	190	250	20	(160)	60	(30)	130	90	270
Profit (before tax)	90	170	245	5	(200)	10	(70)	90	65	230
Taxation	15	30	95	(20)	–	–	–	–	–	20
Profit (after tax)	75	140	150	25	(200)	10	(70)	90	65	210
Extraordinary items	5	40	–	(60)	20	(90)	170	(700)	(55)	–
Dividends: Ordinary	25	35	55	49	–	–	–	–	–	44
Preference	5	5	5	6	6	6	6	6	6	6
Increase in Retained Earnings	50	140	90	(90)	(186)	(86)	94	(616)	4	160
Balance Sheet										
Net Current Assets	450	720	470	410	230	130	460	50	220	380
Non-Current Assets	1290	1430	1670	1530	1520	1480	1230	1060	1060	1060
Total Assets	1740	2150	2140	1940	1760	1650	1940	1280	1280	1440
Ordinary Share Capital	360	460	460	460	460	460	460	460	460	460
Reserves	1060	1550	1540	1340	1200	1090	1380	720	720	880
Preference Capital	100	100	100	100	100	100	100	100	100	100
Loans	220	40	40	40	–	–	–	–	–	–
Total Capital Employed	1740	2150	2140	1940	1760	1650	1940	1280	1280	1440

Figure C25.2: Summary Financial Data (1983–92)

Whittlesford Hardware Group

£000	1989 D	1989 Castings A	1989 Tools B	1989 Hardware C	1989 Total	1990 Castings A	1990 Tools B	1990 Hardware C	1990 Total	1991 Castings A	1991 Tools B	1991 Hardware C	1991 Total	1992 Castings A	1992 Tools B	1992 Hardware C	1992 Total
External Sales Revenue	1300	2300	350	650	4600	2600	400	500	3500	2060	420	520	3000	3000	500	500	4000
Cost of Goods Sold	760	1260	210	440	2670	1470	250	350	2070	1030	270	290	1590	1500	300	280	2080
COGS as % of Sales	58	55	60	68		57	62	70		50	64	56		50	60	56	
Gross Profit	540	1040	140	210	1930	1130	150	150	1430	1030	150	230	1410	1500	200	220	1920
Divisional Overheads	640	1030	100	180	1950	1050	125	125	1300	1000	120	180	1300	1290	180	170	1640
Group Contribution	(100)	10	40	30	(20)	80	25	25	130	30	30	50	110	210	20	50	280
Group Overheads					50				40				45				50
Pre Tax Profits					(70)				90				65				230
Total Assets	160	1250	190	340	1940	955	195	130	1280	1050	185	45	1280	1150	220	70	1440
Non-Current Assets	130	900	100	350	1480	950	100	180	1230	950	100	10	1060	920	120	20	1060
Net Current Assets	30	350	90	(10)	460	5	95	(50)	50	100	85	35	220	230	100	50	380
Current Assets																	
Inventory	300	400	70	160	930	550	80	150	780	500	70	165	735	700	90	150	940
Debtors	250	350	70	150	820	350	80	160	590	450	70	155	675	400	80	150	630
Cash	5	50	10	10	75	5	10	10	25	30	10	15	55	45	15	10	70
Current Liabilities																	
Creditors	315	300	20	230	865	550	35	250	835	500	35	200	735	515	45	180	740
Borrowings	210	150	40	100	500	350	40	120	510	380	30	100	510	400	40	80	520

Figure C25.3: Four Year Performance of Subsidiaries

Almost as soon as the group structure was complete, things started to go wrong. Donegal Castings was sold in 1989 in an attempt to stem increasing losses. This move was accompanied by retrenchments and a progressive slimming down of the other subsidiaries of the group. Figure C25.2 (see p. 230) provides summary financial data for the group over the period 1983–92 and Figure C25.3 (see p. 231) an analysis of the performance of the subsidiaries over the last four years.

Sam Kinnear believes that Whittlesford should have been aware of its troubles earlier and has brought in financial consultants, Taffler & Houston, to advise about future strategy. Their immediate diagnosis has been depressing. They have identified Whittlesford as a distressed company — one with a financial profile similar to previous failures — and advised that a recovery strategy be put into place. They have supplied the industry averages of Figure C25.4 to allow the analysis of specific aspects of group performance to take place.

	Metal Castings	Mechanical Tooling	Hardware Manufacturing
Sales Margin (%)	5	10	10
Capital Turnover (Sales/Net Total Assets)*	6	2	3
Inventory Turnover (Sales/Inventory)	6	4	4
Days Debtors	90	60	70

* Net Total Assets = Non Current Assets *plus* Net Current Assets

Figure C25.4: Industry Average Performance Measures

In addition to a financial analysis, the consultants have indicated that they will conduct a full evaluation of 'what is wrong with the group'. Their intention is initially to identify the principal errors made in the past under the headings Board/Management/Accounting/Marketing/Environment, to provide a basis for the detailed further analysis which needs to be undertaken within the business. They will use Figure C25.5 (see p. 233) as a framework for their discussion.

You are required to conduct an analysis of Whittlesford to determine its future viability and make outline recommendations for alternative strategies that might be adopted.

	Errors	Policy	Bankers	Profit Margin	Balance Sheet	Employees	Shareholders	Customers
STRATEGY								
BOARD ACTION								
MANAGEMENT								
ACCOUNTING								
MARKETING								
ENVIRONMENT								

Figure C25.5: Framework for Recovery Analysis

CASE 26: BRITISH MOTORS

British Motors (BM) seeks guidance as to opportunities that exist to improve its management information system by facilitating performance measurement and management reporting. The case provides the opportunity to develop and monitor the outcomes of a linear discriminant model designed to give early warning of potentially failed motor dealerships.

British Motors (BM) has 205 distribution dealerships across the country. Some of the dealerships are franchises but most are self-owned outlets. All rely on the strength of their BM connection for their wellbeing. The BM dealership within any suburb or locality is of treasured status and were the present holders to relinquish their ties, or be removed because of negligence or incompetence, then competition to replace them would be intense.

Each dealership is located by a five character identity tag (e.g. A2070). The dealerships are classified into 11 categories based on geographical considerations and distributed as in Figure C26.1. Each dealer reports to BM's Oxford Head Office on a weekly basis, and they prepare a monthly performance summary to give feedback to each dealership. Monthly HO comparisons form the basis of the monitoring of dealer progress.

Dealer Identity	Territory	No of Live Dealerships 1993	No of Failed Dealerships 1987–92
A	Anglia (Norwich)	21	2
C	Coventry and Midlands	14	1
D	Yorkshire	13	2
M	Manchester and North West	23	3
N	Newcastle and North East	18	4
P	Greater London	20	2
Q	South East	22	1
S	Swindon and the West	17	2
T	Northern Ireland	19	3
V	Scotland	20	4
W	Wales	18	3
		205	27

Figure C26.1: Distribution of British Motors Dealerships

BM has a number of concerns about its current provision of management accounting information which it wishes to address:

1. Current measures focus on short-term profit as the sole performance criterion. BM is concerned that such a restrictive view could be detrimental to the long-term strategies of the organisation and wishes to extend performance monitoring to a wider variety of financial and non-financial measures.

2. Monthly reports are too complex to be decision useful because of the content and presentation of the accounting information provided. Surveys show that reports receive, at best, a cursory review or, at worst, are completely disregarded. They do not satisfy the specific information needs of users nor do they allow dealers to appraise their own performance relative to others or to Head Office requirements.

3. There are insufficient means of identifying poor performers in advance of difficulties being experienced and Head Office backing being sought. No early warning model exists which discriminates between 'good' and 'bad' performance.

4. No 'benchmarks' are provided of good and unacceptable performance levels in particular aspects of business operations.

As a first step in addressing these issues, BM has employed a firm of local consultants to investigate the financial data relating to the dealerships. They have used financial information for 1992 relating to the 205 current dealerships and 27 other dealers who failed over the previous five years. This information has been used to provide a profile of dealers with the potential to fail in the future, and a model constructed to distinguish between good and poor performers.

The model includes seven items of financial information:

1. Profit before Tax (PBT)

2. Current Assets (CA)

3. Tangible Fixed Assets (FA)

4. Current Liabilities (CL)

5. Loan Capital, and Long Term Loans (LC)

6. Inventory (I)

7. Cash Flow (CF) = Retained Profit + Deferred Taxation

+ Extraordinary Expenditure + Depreciation

These data items have been used to generate an early-warning model based on four financial ratios:

$$Z = 2.546 + 3.494\ X_1 + 0.617\ X_2 - 6.075\ X_3 + 0.204\ X_4$$

where

$$X_1 = \frac{CF}{CL + LC} \text{ a cash-based profit measure } \left(\frac{CF}{TL}\right)$$

$$X_2 = \frac{CA}{CL + LC} \text{ a working capital measure } \left(\frac{CA}{TL}\right)$$

$$X_3 = \frac{CL}{CA + FA} \text{ a short-term financial risk measure } \left(\frac{CL}{TA}\right)$$

$$X_4 = \frac{CA - I}{CL} \text{ a liquidity measure, the quick assets ratio } \left(\frac{QA}{CL}\right)$$

These ratios and the resultant Z scores have been computed for both 1992 and 1993. Figure C26.2 shows the scores for the 27 (failed) dealerships: each of the failed cases is correctly classified in that it exhibits a negative Z-score. Figures C26.3 and C26.4 show both Z-scores and relative performance rankings for 1992 and 1993 respectively, for the 205 live dealerships, in order to aid the predictive purposes of the model.

You are required to investigate the management information requirements at BM and evaluate the degree to which its needs will be met by the new Z-score model. Your investigation should encompass improvements that might be made to the existing model and the likely predictive ability of non-financial factors.

Figure C26.2: Failed Dealerships (1987–1992)

Dealer	Profit	CA	FA	CL	LC	INV	CF	Z Score
A1125	−9778	215865	219523	209512	94994	288044	−6196	−0.081
A4039	1295	1376560	1221668	1581115	1518130	492007	17208	−0.743
C2013	−5486	47496	202455	214550	0	211462	3464	−2.631
D1065	90314	1549905	1246158	2557381	0	699303	95566	−2.438
D4113	49686	363838	87712	844753	0	228332	52717	−8.303
M1101	25233	104322	134875	149500	0	227960	28203	−0.330
M1158	−3614	59638	85443	178220	0	94510	−3614	−4.821
M4026	94020	883639	476148	925696	287947	807268	113215	−0.798
N1037	−5345	5372819	3209076	6742285	284798	3312743	45690	−1.561
N2090	63673	2713494	1337378	2672211	424499	1754578	118460	−0.714
N2098	139650	2810446	637327	2419062	166163	2087550	165848	−0.761
N4078	100776	1462712	144193	1593609	0	957466	131721	−2.559
P1021	2029	433546	1370292	982874	18000	902524	28235	−0.496
P1242	7048	1218144	237726	1134407	0	1472335	10723	−1.538
Q4118	30323	355408	25058	362661	5000	126580	31802	−2.217

Dealer	Profit	CA	FA	CL	LC	INV	CF	Z Score
S1038	109730	1651840	581273	1573341	27922	947631	147012	−0.686
S2174	−23115	64241	24904	102349	104410	134637	−20115	−4.717
T1022	86852	1156831	3973474	3590710	0	769559	101092	−1.387
T1187	24840	145038	161465	259399	0	410480	26942	−2.096
T3013	1603	56283	123111	136805	39032	151435	2337	−1.985
V1108	−22274	1495367	395454	1289299	207560	1184007	−770	−0.933
V1157	14636	168810	110361	194209	40000	155720	19427	−0.932
V1160	47523	1188420	129752	1228060	29167	997855	57453	−2.339
V4085	105335	341060	733364	900842	0	127308	118324	−1.807
W1055	66693	1241667	2334740	1048493	98035	819132	78950	−0.777
W1122	−52600	326821	147002	300305	0	308611	−25233	−0.914
W2097	−24270	10579	12987	38865	8971	26499	−24270	−9.193

Figure C26.3: Live Dealerships (1992)

Dealer	Profit	CA	FA	CL	LC	INV	CF	Z Score	Rank
A1039	18096	226726	122235	192722	14532	75972	18256	0.333	146
A1069	58256	301736	149506	134933	72392	225534	60096	2.755	50
A1080	42152	253664	49734	191510	1293	212909	45112	0.384	143
A1088	40173	406052	261423	472439	10045	265632	40173	−0.883	191
A1103	2000	430813	135024	151765	0	40742	3303	3.268	36
A1114	10205	870859	133805	673509	0	420583	29465	−0.440	174
A1144	55322	610032	288681	456916	109429	438292	82558	0.708	128
A1174	5285	148967	323248	112092	50000	114050	51908	2.853	46
A1208	47680	261284	39373	208952	0	216059	50246	−0.020	161
A2010	387118	2558438	297491	1321491	0	1506500	387118	2.115	70
A2029	−11537	670606	498673	547666	14894	364919	−2067	0.537	137
A2051	38048	294368	241493	235828	173522	172632	39663	0.760	124
A2070	22617	549361	339863	521566	38004	128734	22617	−0.106	163
A2078	31756	1212977	172667	606866	245000	358516	33856	1.190	113
A2089	13567	556569	64061	481943	0	420875	21719	−1.244	200
A2175	9465	239696	46707	141513	13119	104350	12457	0.977	118
A3049	−13713	170259	109775	216626	500	132303	−76190	−1.756	203
A4020	19069	163693	260309	189193	14802	139258	23184	0.754	125

Dealer	Profit	CA	FA	CL	LC	INV	CF	Z Score	Rank
A4031	−25764	77242	106634	134645	74733	127848	−14171	−1.988	204
A4106	18954	301099	25064	150198	4500	243599	30209	1.710	96
A5002	118299	1520401	143543	982304	0	1129865	144028	0.508	140
C1031	141045	3637147	391021	1038435	230299	3029411	405840	3.986	29
C1042	49464	510135	239093	432026	888	426642	55464	0.257	150
C1053	40513	630288	339706	305477	19274	467571	69432	2.686	52
C1072	168677	996640	500082	542794	604970	811745	176415	1.485	103
C1147	10933	446808	155828	402716	0	534550	23426	−0.670	184
C1177	138108	824518	237915	208835	104000	665196	155625	4.872	19
C2043	41335	1957480	566804	575139	99167	331235	143900	4.275	28
C2073	26564	1529936	938092	1117810	218829	1084643	57608	0.733	127
C2092	119736	733795	375773	386548	0	348194	148123	3.143	39
C2156	59843	222441	172772	94897	130220	140284	68967	2.944	42
C3063	49140	688844	95855	193766	0	402996	49140	4l426	25
C4023	−7272	552574	429358	660973	21703	372461	−5498	−1.016	194
C4053	69975	317081	29986	171518	0	402663	70940	2.028	77
C4083	225588	1729195	226029	374856	302287	1079622	232428	4.510	24
C4120	23830	476695	196948	355333	135281	226739	25210	0.264	149
D1076	249677	854501	223650	365003	0	379850-	257366	4.663	22
D1110	33408	200368	141416	58224	46675	232587	36241	2.851	47
D1132	31443	268781	4085	224394	0	112491	31443	−1.079	198
D1151	−23121	315205	211167	151444	0	523265	−8920	1.596	102
D2055	15865	371896	79927	132958	0	433022	18515	2.877	43
D2085	71204	571549	285490	354302	25000	255928	76104	1.847	86
D2096	100458	887490	1512145	1173908	0	1178820	144674	0.421	141
D3056	58161	1233717	1090224	1429492	132801	959104	67184	−0.514	177
D4027	19179	177950	69630	139509	0	100956	22905	0.596	132
D4046	95986	388348	418550	331737	210067	249450	109631	1.283	112
D4173	37180	549367	123738	426784	54970	355103	41697	−0.207	168
D5006	33426	521001	45292	300992	0	305644	33426	0.919	119
M1015	120688	586580	152683	62689	0	244207	126563	15.972	3
M1023	81177	547125	208012	329872	93828	371061	98460	1.610	101
M1064	28865	623550	200542	546868	43850	314297	62918	−0.347	173
M1075	98172	432242	157108	443518	0	315320	102349	−0.564	179
M1094	76881	1724487	85013	804347	200000	1044096	80161	1.356	109

Dealer	Profit	CA	FA	CL	LC	INV	CF	Z Score	Rank
M1109	286879	4616591	426298	3122100	1364641	1990287	380158	−0.113	164
M1120	129159	1691593	251407	1186460	1202	618544	135507	0.298	147
M1131	5787	333220	278550	258020	165450	145389	8987	0.692	130
M1139	−18937	642715	388614	696464	148145	447445	863	−1.026	195
M1161	32935	603318	354127	502822	150441	428395	33703	0.177	155
M1180	159404	423308	187266	196140	0	267884	168284	5.086	17
M1188	−20489	331152	150807	338708	0	355752	−15363	−1.293	201
M1191	19732	88594	23754	71868	0	35417	20100	0.549	136
M2035	61846	1099555	199963	776387	46348	393534	87053	0.296	148
M2054	14427	741091	8601	323265	0	493117	16359	1.674	98
M2076	41084	615612	54435	250963	0	534545	46499	2.497	61
M2140	152384	1148462	470204	522137	543750	593544	169551	2.024	79
M2170	−5079	688390	459309	661091	0	466393	23392	−0.119	165
M3036	84638	411999	49900	205064	24181	196908	84638	2.462	63
M3096	50030	315074	181547	219499	107397	197261	50030	1.100	115
M4015	40202	726535	187920	642835	0	570364	56202	−0.672	185
M4045	98051	672596	728625	847446	0	845999	111584	−0.220	169
M4075	196225	2714746	985073	990164	1705780	1412778	22332	2.099	72
N1026	32294	487322	243647	226894	91760	338312	57130	2.364	66
N1067	80684	1824762	641748	863487	0	958305	126431	2.439	64
N1086	9256	82640	94836	55981	720	162876	9985	1.852	85
N1112	223492	1231252	480919	620133	0	340178	232348	3.173	38
N1123	16028	504257	100902	209608	103216	2186098	47983	2.185	69
N1142	−57755	789595	391721	729040	119089	495904	−46755	−0.739	188
N1153	19048	449676	54623	139527	0	254277	22162	3.694	31
N2057	35616	593504	68911	271799	0	425446	42366	2.071	74
N2068	102114	1947576	168652	933143	0	819685	108230	1.807	90
N2087	369553	1886414	613426	1311715	0	930948	394392	1.445	105
N2102	57652	626566	407330	409682	5420	386004	101733	2.046	76
N2154	26906	401384	40548	194409	0	257375	30122	1.840	87
N3017	25018	378893	73668	62738	0	131267	27759	7.781	5
N3020	243536	773824	1132402	394635	450	1366108	243536	4.344	27
N4010	34339	294603	55633	192831	0	262831	38414	0.874	120
N4018	5217	498828	599102	333602	220152	414064	79695	1.811	89
N4123	25485	141641	449793	282173	0	471524	39604	0.209	152

Dealer	Profit	*CA*	*FA*	*CL*	*LC*	*INV*	*CF*	*Z* Score	Rank
N5000	95952	850791	567470	42603	0	529349	120516	26.108	1
P1018	146993	2252280	1061275	1506653	0	1513184	160102	1.177	114
P1040	58143	1162003	606126	1264820	170664	488382	97658	−0.954	193
P1051	67296	1299647	557014	1160171	64657	846670	93856	−0.248	170
P1070	103506	889818	246619	892295	0	374662	112491	−1.050	196
P1078	144365	1113673	207920	905674	212708	227454	150260	−0.334	172
P1081	30737	416624	76786	274169	0	166081	35716	0.750	126
P1104	58348	313454	53931	150114	0	90938	63635	3.136	40
P1145	70009	475950	181521	239864	0	529921	74219	2.589	56
P1156	141542	592230	226901	325581	257224	432129	186450	1.976	81
P1164	−12277	296738	211014	327630	0	148310	−11177	−0.842	190
P1186	55696	633800	335685	434028	237499	473202	63419	0.814	123
P2011	123316	1429507	371072	769241	0	1169474	125316	1.735	94
P2019	−19633	977804	84787	779322	20300	607336	1425	−1.052	197
P2030	30185	573129	378079	234423	0	421115	47835	3.403	35
P2116	85388	349785	57504	143196	779	153968	99904	4.613	23
P2176	42507	317514	14209	244728	44971	245495	47559	−0.626	181
P3039	23812	247616	33732	98826	3750	218739	26467	2.863	45
P4021	256992	912020	409189	541462	0	564347	27929	1.407	107
P4032	212185	1781982	458777	618225	178364	849285	505794	4.776	20
P4062	252084	1601159	427357	847765	0	677895	263682	2.481	62
Q1032	28098	519152	536633	580982	70600	496998	45046	−0.056	162
Q1043	35875	333113	122277	318966	9005	292428	35875	−0.674	186
Q1073	−18168	1190861	352802	1179375	0	288984	−14718	−1.360	202
Q1084	143912	871817	1377673	609508	0	652594	177247	2.872	44
Q1118	73735	602760	398941	470166	204000	532637	81771	0.700	129
Q1126	−49399	1802518	429047	1997013	0	652289	51456	−2.126	205
Q1137	20318	230475	169263	100897	89600	137981	25146	2.407	65
Q2014	62470	297406	471640	250462	122465	197484	76900	1.861	84
Q2033	92418	929149	78061	240204	67629	361795	108577	4.674	21
Q2074	71193	323550	558118	194829	52323	351143	168005	4.357	23
Q2093	248984	1903610	945628	811195	550000	1103377	277280	2.592	55
Q2179	10747	229469	387643	291085	0	95453	10947	0.392	142
Q3023	76617	590016	156430	155750	9500	438630	78552	5.341	14
Q3034	276471	2538371	195064	1084497	129167	476963	309150	2.704	51

Dealer	Profit	CA	FA	CL	LC	INV	CF	Z Score	Rank
Q3053	115874	162206	16039	54883	0	139042	115874	9.962	4
Q3064	45216	960482	13237	689226	0	429653	46756	−0.500	176
Q3094	272051	843052	229738	286578	0	668109	272051	6.180	10
Q3128	5040	119643	96365	79720	58280	90921	5040	1.040	117
Q4013	30181	336681	43519	152811	28496	220226	34241	2.065	75
Q4024	39127	319117	89695	171504	10000	173636	39127	2.008	80
Q4035	536433	3318212	1050439	1937970	687500	1479616	697183	1.752	92
Q4121	47654	792489	215276	581744	93404	549339	64659	0.183	154
S1016	339349	940117	1046962	461468	9600	463988	389067	5.463	12
S1027	82024	862338	343905	237969	19333	375272	177207	6.239	9
S1057	94036	428387	108602	237110	0	2146785	97842	2.576	57
S1068	75565	1530905	605590	683164	0	2175244	83241	2.219	68
S1154	121527	449555	228542	136416	10810	413538	125895	6.250	8
S1184	−19375	158287	57816	128943	0	106594	−16050	−0.675	187
S2017	25984	1108901	661978	1027650	41355	853015	157118	0.225	151
S2020	51842	653372	1581165	648166	559167	400778	304799	2.079	73
S3010	81428	581137	229005	254874	0	404148	92510	3.451	34
S3029	140807	2546750	286253	1856704	9158	1633058	159107	−0.195	167
S4011	131376	1209957	304565	755639	0	645832	153392	1.365	108
S4038	153640	925501	404687	274829	71644	415214	159599	4.927	18
S4041	82608	1145885	582117	690502	10498	832296	137028	1.903	82
S4049	43031	247652	93291	152542	63174	169540	48701	1.430	106
S4068	39039	298847	53848	135729	0	172401	42292	2.845	48
S4079	74643	1090086	392663	424267	1000000	778411	90841	1.653	100
S4135	46569	264082	30895	138601	1897	76713	46569	2.285	67
T1019	381392	3813822	1382988	986014	112688	689759	408469	5.480	11
T1030	34293	259407	158739	158379	58128	235382	41493	1.683	97
T1041	−32072	1504831	540556	1275652	500000	354179	−27432	−0.590	180
T1052	53106	439278	342956	244738	26628	203808	59106	2.601	54
T1071	63191	455470	166880	473361	0	284477	68928	−0.899	192
T1082	290247	1539874	1526084	930604	0	1202544	327228	3.026	41
T1146	72469	393933	456235	195793	210609	315494	783621	2.500	60
T1176	43134	254542	63091	129567	0	154162	45041	2.653	53
T2091	40338	976784	251821	831004	0	362994	56827	−0.448	175
T2106	40474	715386	51743	128860	0	581231	46066	6.412	7

Dealer	Profit	*CA*	*FA*	*CL*	*LC*	*INV*	*CF*	*Z* Score	Rank
T2136	80794	826995	497823	444426	172502	579683	102061	2.027	78
T2147	63864	526732	526989	698330	0	339441	79371	−0.563	178
T2166	489166	3087750	3227234	1230695	3500000	1440836	697372	2.553	59
T3032	36733	283924	90706	143614	0	275751	45558	2.557	58
T4052	226693	2110929	803301	606404	0	635080	242389	5.323	15
T4082	30271	384979	469310	438343	284700	153453	−30271	−0.281	171
T4108	32142	248205	55565	97728	0	161454	35393	3.605	32
T4116	15994	341130	200746	254066	74054	272790	16968	0.575	134
T4168	91458	417175	39553	33957	0	310707	99665	20.569	2
V1093	42434	907513	23738	429120	0	442945	46880	1.654	99
V1100	22755	196266	41520	171422	0	198067	23637	−0.647	182
V1127	126651	1035457	594260	305499	0	859186	145807	5.284	16
V1130	11625	524301	136234	441036	40000	415375	17431	−0.661	183
V1149	44084	415698	39361	230809	0	262232	50427	1.475	104
V1190	14785	44417	87505	27601	55000	103767	15385	1.819	88
V2034	−9110	40760	316332	136493	58500	106623	−6776	0.133	157
V2053	60545	591717	64900	227072	0	427496	67435	3.238	37
V2064	191181	1508635	54526	836550	228400	566001	205061	1.072	116
V2075	95540	356806	695534	140240	184174	267755	95540	3.574	33
V2120	86031	1852463	163292	895366	0	856862	94839	1.721	95
V2161	60332	966844	105477	654389	11961	678875	64099	0.1690	156
V2191	154113	2270887	1881880	2243435	606837	1740762	170808	0.013	160
V3024	48625	1045565	401531	859748	22046	795298	116041	0.187	153
V3035	12311	180055	202170	212085	16942	212687	13056	−0.172	166
V3054	12994	215854	70203	142828	24571	1492026	12994	−1.243	199
V3065	42238	1300438	27163	705955	200000	780155	45648	0.528	138
V3095	17984	480109	134486	320884	0	251636	19652	0.657	131
V4066	34944	380176	300194	346929	122703	231581	41019	0.340	145
V4171	81564	574914	192315	294773	0	547904	112640	2.769	49
W1066	18736	281659	283663	218543	117087	411836	24075	0.844	122
W1096	18422	45764	230678	78325	70238	107001	18422	1.289	111
W1111	111653	1558539	343030	820227	0	1090974	128179	1.760	91
W1141	9151	537031	241233	447206	10604	233784	20586	0.074	159
W1152	94974	658145	502904	330571	0	700943	159301	3.702	30
W1163	25346	295429	134228	208618	101112	203004	27826	0.589	133

Dealer	Profit	CA	FA	CL	LC	INV	CF	Z Score	Rank
W1171	−10379	166764	28991	129977	0	76279	−9723	−0.815	189
W1182	59351	329279	72628	107750	0	152277	70030	5.409	13
W2026	279287	1218314	122648	838690	0	1173704	289695	0.860	121
W2037	138593	1943436	329307	1108541	0	995176	159947	1.343	110
W2153	74404	766132	111082	531182	48236	446293	91870	0.360	144
W3016	320	41332	93548	33895	4182	65138	2080	1.737	95
W3057	22755	497097	189929	394957	0	395280	22755	0.084	158
W4050	72797	436397	261174	402966	25932	191384	96292	0.573	135
W4077	534346	463750	497966	441004	299495	361988	69234	0.520	139
W4080	44666	247091	156001	164159	0	148759	45882	2.099	71
W4114	64561	452956	46098	90897	0	155938	66777	7.748	6
W4133	34116	320346	89891	178981	0	166318	36478	1.888	83

Figure C26.4: Live Dealerships (1993)

Dealer	Profit	CA	FA	CL	LC	INV	CF	Z Score	Rank
A1039	21297	155927	122835	119302	14532	68823	21477	1.375	117
A1069	55017	194408	148603	30382	71783	200720	57025	5.090	24
A1080	42256	207706	50529	145905	1293	182186	45512	1.100	122
A1088	41299	335922	262860	400161	10884	225457	41299	−0.602	189
A1103	1683	464685	1335024	183777	0	56313	3148	2.758	57
A1114	12089	839720	134472	639583	0	406246	32105	−0.319	181
A1144	67352	480247	288681	314541	109429	371213	97157	1.631	107
A1174	7493	129963	322885	89941	50000	101225	55375	3.360	42
A1208	47816	236879	39373	183688	0	211198	51022	0.301	156
A2010	303527	2363225	303387	1023929	0	1227033	303527	2.899	54
A2029	−4880	491973	504093	444531	14280	357254	8017	0.619	147
A2051	34284	246560	241492	191448	173858	176612	36243	1.001	126
A2070	36041	571558	342362	537385	36490	150887	36041	−0.032	164
A2078	35180	1264712	183431	664412	245000	350723	38330	1.045	124
A2089	17002	503339	61665	422871	0	435966	26270	−1.017	200
A2175	13588	189899	46760	87061	12916	117393	16930	2.245	80
A3049	−7554	241324	113984	289597	0	182995	−90	−1.851	204
A4020	20075	123984	255801	149374	14585	105835	24704	1.174	120

Dealer	Profit	*CA*	*FA*	*CL*	*LC*	*INV*	*CF*	*Z* Score	Rank
A4031	−27545	36077	110948	94194	74658	105445	−14089	−1.6456	203
A4106	25262	29647	27193	144430	4125	202042	38666	2.153	86
A5002	137199	1480078	143578	922845	0	861462	164558	0.842	134
C1031	185915	4125162	395592	1481434	230299	2856045	454604	3.145	48
C1042	78548	574142	239331	467187	0	401744	85148	0.527	152
C1053	42197	718548	339706	389791	18876	441209	73601	2.168	85
C1072	192179	1186989	504808	731423	604970	703896	201940	1.130	121
C1147	14363	520474	157595	473627	0	506154	26557	−0.817	196
C1177	149271	787042	237915	160196	104000	676201	166788	5.781	15
C2043	49890	2062829	572202	679379	93333	363988	155225	3.839	35
C2073	39224	1614272	931686	1193388	211641	1020111	74567	0.694	141
C2092	131146	689961	375773	429009	0	274576	162148	3.012	52
C2156	69364	235395	173325	98970	128820	151082	79801	3.110	49
C3063	69981	720024	95855	205354	0	479281	69981	4.610	29
C4023	−6933	539647	429775	648163	20984	381698	−4729	−0.993	198
C4053	77178	281808	31034	131566	0	525646	78250	3.013	51
C4083	266037	1716267	229153	324130	301519	1124851	273855	5.128	22
C4120	27892	500834	196948	379071	131812	246593	29678	0.190	159
D1076	261701	837467	231565	342469	0	322258	270205	5.172	21
D1110	32797	206918	141416	93203	45857	230079	35630	2.683	63
D1132	43183	267532	5271	212591	0	106647	43183	−0.548	188
D1151	−6442	332964	210048	150980	0	515017	10177	2.207	83
D2055	22381	449303	79327	203249	0	479497	25738	1.986	93
D2085	90785	616130	288785	381927	25671	234941	95685	1.938	94
D2096	647	170932	1517702	457695	0	1087614	16280	0.846	133
D3056	49950	1135765	1097126	1222435	257024	994341	58973	−0.143	173
D4027	25251	203932	69626	157952	0	107146	29601	0.615	150
D4046	97717	368185	417311	311703	206193	259888	112137	1.401	115
D4173	40145	556501	124316	430991	55172	354375	45000	−0.174	174
D5006	31287	524064	45292	306194	0	283835	31287	0.852	132
M1015	138891	597815	152683	55021	0	213068	145466	19.469	1
M1023	88388	489661	206668	266340	91280	307838	108327	2.265	77
M1064	30666	447583	209301	409527	42395	308060	34846	−0.291	180
M1075	108167	457213	157604	458317	0	246246	112772	−0.413	183
M1094	80405	1616851	85013	692597	200000	947454	84275	1.718	103

Dealer	Profit	CA	FA	CL	LC	INV	CF	Z Score	Rank
M1109	303056	3236083	431864	1392158	1702289	1991657	406725	1.527	111
M1120	134259	1232960	257595	722877	1002	603828	142588	1.516	112
M1131	8613	321204	289974	255452	164200	187606	12213	0.687	143
M1139	26259	486077	403451	494078	139121	554728	46674	−0.125	168
M1161	39423	638433	354127	533421	148961	470367	40959	0.132	160
M1180	16345	481956	188965	239694	0	270411	17056	2.045	88
M1188	−5592	358475	150849	378380	0	402769	−4992	−1.453	202
M1191	27246	108430	23754	84091	0	36959	27706	0.801	138
M2035	96334	1072340	193235	704437	46348	447651	124721	0.807	137
M2054	22535	798112	8601	372178	0	488303	24467	1.466	114
M2076	47446	653382	53352	281288	0	523877	53944	2.325	76
M2140	−4584	1023994	479022	411414	540834	553142	1524	1.786	99
M2170	−12168	523496	471727	482982	0	499456	4983	0.313	155
M3036	97319	418583	49900	202845	23753	197519	97319	2.778	56
M3096	55863	221777	181547	120828	106938	201848	55863	2.217	81
M4015	31366	625297	186177	547314	0	600496	48741	−0.526	187
M4045	120516	535861	750278	691512	0	801635	136938	0.372	154
M4075	219552	2262912	992358	737156	1485780	1506639	249897	2.400	72
N1026	42111	461436	253006	201822	89396	342349	67939	2.743	58
N1067	104443	1838252	643778	920448	0	1022726	142988	2.249	79
N1086	13608	86597	95386	52354	695	140623	14520	2.551	69
N1112	263923	1114118	480919	586296	0	301375	273550	3.398	41
N1123	16467	527006	100212	231937	102507	291865	51012	2.012	91
N1142	12756	757089	387086	658524	97089	486705	24756	−0.134	172
N1153	12013	452962	53960	149185	0	236039	15736	3.297	43
N2057	37232	577446	68751	253965	0	375254	45332	2.347	75
N2068	124514	2072396	169380	1035649	0	829517	131747	1.663	106
N2087	454574	1668767	613647	1012494	0	892521	482469	2.689	62
N2102	79346	661211	434767	435669	5076	374806	126473	2.193	84
N2154	29971	402115	41198	133057	0	245535	33589	3.709	38
N3017	32154	378130	73737	56781	0	123388	35570	8.996	5
N3020	267407	625187	1165483	258267	400	1192262	267407	6.325	11
N4010	35983	308285	55633	205817	0	322687	37775	0.661	145
N4018	1840	479999	605032	321938	217308	400454	78762	1.853	98
N4123	30259	68693	448520	203178	0	471672	45651	0.749	139

Strategic Management Accounting

Dealer	Profit	CA	FA	CL	LC	INV	CF	Z Score	Rank
N5000	96921	888208	566403	77134	0	507639	121935	15.859	3
P1018	161342	2540417	1062429	1804913	0	1740249	227948	0.903	128
P1040	56555	745612	595416	837764	168877	516136	101689	−0.383	182
P1051	68398	1359180	555408	1211126	66255	875456	98474	−0.290	179
P1070	115572	850134	245467	828140	0	334716	125707	−0.755	193
P1078	145111	1096354	207920	886659	212708	185936	151771	−0.277	178
P1081	44865	431399	77977	276588	0	184148	49960	1.023	125
P1104	62085	285900	49961	114853	0	90342	69470	4.465	30
P1145	71231	429498	186197	195673	0	538512	76073	3.214	46
P1156	143593	787058	215513	349136	412861	480274	189698	2.117	87
P1164	−9555	262469	211014	290419	0	130325	−8235	−0.629	190
P1186	55856	639073	335463	437928	237499	444704	64570	0.824	135
P2011	153772	1269377	371072	709255	0	853363	15572	1.911	97
P2019	−7347	1030336	85537	819791	19600	612563	14588	−0.995	199
P2030	33616	663976	371749	313982	0	479469	53031	2.719	60
P2116	87844	339505	57504	130047	587	160726	102963	5.194	20
P2176	40721	253009	13718	182684	43805	178480	46452	−0.126	170
P3039	31020	258387	137743	108141	2250	234333	33497	3.437	40
P4021	283448	752505	418880	358040	0	540545	308058	5.113	23
P4032	252158	1914501	460877	709056	178364	532204	550427	4.629	28
P4062	287076	1799860	442428	1287065	0	836147	300123	0.889	129
Q1032	31552	539028	536633	601992	66428	460397	50731	−0.064	165
Q1043	43342	373857	123568	354597	8316	277117	43342	−0.676	191
Q1073	−19254	1199829	352802	1189020	0	280051	−15471	−1.371	201
Q1084	182395	903588	1379598	600598	0	668026	220486	3.239	45
Q1118	80828	727501	398813	534074	256045	609036	89931	0.676	144
Q1126	−69619	1346904	429898	1562470	0	662620	37390	−2.091	205
Q1137	22143	235457	169263	103289	89600	139570	28144	2.448	71
Q2014	57827	279653	471640	238363	119618	176948	74113	1.912	96
Q2033	108599	801750	78061	106665	65408	390814	125318	8.015	7
Q2074	79923	308987	582312	196730	51323	397639	178904	4.402	31
Q2093	305843	1940658	945103	889130	450000	1037634	337436	2.656	65
Q2179	16136	225199	388268	286851	0	76897	16536	0.497	153
Q3023	90845	609321	156430	161979	9000	420632	93635	5.611	17
Q3034	331915	2360003	194903	866848	126584	426408	365715	3.692	39

Dealer	Profit	CA	FA	CL	LC	INV	CF	Z Score	Rank
Q3053	115723	155579	16039	48407	0	138259	115723	11.241	4
Q3064	54285	980432	13137	700007	0	404166	55965	−0.423	184
Q3094	322038	926867	229738	330536	0	664139	322038	6.106	14
Q3128	6910	136527	96366	94936	58080	96202	6910	0.865	131
Q4013	30996	328303	43519	143618	28496	206044	35056	2.262	78
Q4024	42835	393399	89695	250881	10000	200957	42835	1.052	123
Q4035	458605	2931554	1063505	1806259	487500	1782677	625867	1.671	105
Q4121	31647	823329	219587	630734	91740	657123	50780	−0.126	169
S1016	362458	870362	1059813	396098	9600	429173	415397	6.428	10
S1027	95926	887721	344106	253234	18667	365818	195777	6.248	12
S1057	108959	355746	109186	148746	0	216660	113111	4.926	25
S1068	102700	1403239	605590	527939	0	2139438	111907	3.046	50
S1154	146054	370126	230969	36074	10727	353771	150968	18.424	2
S1184	−21120	178504	57816	150405	0	91806	−17570	−0.879	197
S2017	47972	1211633	662650	1108801	40996	806859	180607	0.226	158
S2020	78727	756712	1586420	704484	459167	427940	333259	2.217	82
S3010	100406	588107	231405	244611	0	456247	112143	3.928	33
S3029	146109	2569166	292025	1858713	21665	2141358	166909	−0.200	175
S4011	134224	1069985	305585	611662	0	519907	158065	2.010	92
S4038	182023	1003018	403160	320752	72452	410034	188858	4.790	26
S4041	88193	1246660	585617	789402	10036	877551	145467	1.622	108
S4049	48884	208205	93291	106112	62727	170149	55298	2.386	74
S4068	45176	263664	53848	124262	0	163344	48546	3.007	53
S4079	76864	986553	392663	315558	1000000	733522	95033	2.035	90
S4135	58109	272646	33617	138397	1847	131899	58109	2.655	66
T1019	442468	3999420	1382988	1105623	112688	950266	472930	5.242	19
T1030	45339	281785	164043	177590	54753	220230	53439	1.749	102
T1041	−46725	1145607	539396	929671	500000	449876	−40925	−0.259	176
T1052	67255	435642	342206	212054	26628	259638	74005	3.269	44
T1071	65146	424309	166880	439001	0	276394	70937	−0.735	192
T1082	321448	1785603	1528205	1142433	0	1329580	363065	2.608	67
T1146	82232	414097	455800	206423	210062	292457	88952	2.584	68
T1176	55919	236028	63091	98268	0	108922	57826	4.352	32
T2091	42564	909652	251821	759445	0	381100	61299	−0.263	177
T2106	47916	694665	50811	97202	0	525969	56895	8.563	6

Dealer	Profit	*CA*	*FA*	*CL*	*LC*	*INV*	*CF*	*Z* Score	Rank
T2136	91815	730261	503823	335566	178443	532488	113736	2.664	64
T2147	79128	528153	701848	704610	153639	358631	95730	−0.116	167
T2166	529396	2636469	3332459	1027491	3186340	1666315	746995	2.698	61
T3032	44555	284749	90706	136332	0	223706	56115	3.158	47
T4052	283351	2083273	803301	5518191	0	530252	301806	6.582	8
T4082	−19654	126608	469583	161284	293744	111163	−19654	0.943	127
T4108	35598	304898	55565	150639	0	139865	39175	2.388	73
T4116	20999	332891	200746	246780	67898	261768	22171	0.694	142
T4168	107245	385117	38731	291290	0	290484	116274	0.648	146
V1093	65998	1009742	23738	507478	0	481418	70751	1.490	113
V1100	28570	206956	41520	176099	0	191468	29630	−0.429	185
V1127	137248	1027665	593972	286077	0	858746	157164	5.731	16
V1130	9035	547279	135444	465814	40000	420946	15631	−0.768	194
V1149	55148	408640	34240	208766	0	297305	62008	2.037	89
V1190	17968	76977	87505	56828	55000	99426	18718	1.376	116
V2034	−25584	50874	316632	163601	58250	102267	−23941	−0.444	186
V2053	65176	480118	69030	114972	0	454707	73444	6.128	13
V2064	206085	1337621	53346	648244	228400	593371	221700	1.774	100
V2075	107737	394471	693854	144899	186519	237151	107737	3.829	36
V2120	92847	1795397	143482	447489	0	1008042	102949	4.782	27
V2161	70960	821573	105477	499491	8332	593044	75650	0.885	130
V2191	153851	2105172	1958512	2161022	602816	1796830	170346	0.030	162
V3024	50437	1087591	451394	945224	22424	773363	118833	0.005	163
V3035	13296	144292	216812	169129	37642	254922	14190	0.238	157
V3054	18658	222217	70203	156372	11396	134519	18658	0.618	148
V3065	44536	1238060	28897	643013	200000	736030	48256	0.728	140
V3095	30922	470668	134771	331534	0	216847	34485	0.615	149
V4066	35999	209102	302065	175407	12392	228492	42749	1.921	95
V4171	91402	627185	192334	337234	0	606722	125763	2.509	70
W1066	24237	245707	283870	178205	115310	369357	30445	1.239	119
W1096	24022	43342	230678	71783	68758	87500	24022	1.617	109
W1111	147914	1412701	343030	635695	0	1145995	166873	2.720	59
W1141	18433	502035	242321	449638	10604	230248	30618	−0.095	166
W1152	114149	757520	446177	356824	0	665245	182889	3.899	34
W1163	28790	277453	134826	188085	100513	216830	31580	0.816	136

Dealer	Profit	CA	FA	CL	LC	INV	CF	Z Score	Rank
W1171	−8500	180000	28991	141145	0	76849	−7680	−0.811	195
W1182	72314	356572	73609	115080	0	227856	77082	5.401	18
W2026	314617	1216238	128540	805644	0	1175051	326326	1.264	118
W2037	160868	1856147	329307	991349	0	1061294	187369	1.769	101
W2153	31784	658126	112522	466236	48236	432872	49950	0.098	161
W3016	1486	52028	93548	43166	4182	65905	3486	1.614	110
W3057	30662	578090	193030	471144	0	457954	30662	−0.129	171
W4050	90908	259194	255668	193772	29434	172593	115041	2.868	55
W4077	65605	446164	509343	433192	288106	442708	82264	0.574	151
W4080	59880	212334	156001	112410	0	228612	61098	3.727	37
W4114	76060	495505	46098	121731	0	202174	78492	6.437	9
W4133	46343	313327	89891	192145	0	148479	48705	1.718	104

CASE 27: BALMAIN BREWERIES

This case provides weekly time series data over a period of seven years, sufficient to allow the development of a forecasting model embracing both trend and seasonal components. It provides the opportunity of developing models of varying levels of sophistication and evaluating their success relative to the control limits in place.

Balmain Breweries is based in Central London and has successfully penetrated the home market for lager distribution. Cartons of Lager (each containing fifty 375 ml cans) are produced and packaged at their site close to London's Barbican Centre and distributed nationwide.

Conflict between production and sales is inevitable at Balmain, so much so that the production team is frequently in a no-win situation:

- Produce too much—so that inventory holdings are high in order to capture all possible sales. The levels of inventory necessary to ensure that lager is available at all retail points of sale are expensive and the quality of the product deteriorates rapidly.

- Produce too little—so that inventory holdings are pushed down to their minimum level. If all potential sales are still to be met, this requires a rapid response from production and the ready availability of stocks of all constituent ingredients. It may also mean expensive small batches and highly variable manpower requirements.

The data of Table C27.1 shows the number of cartons that were held in inventory at the distribution depot at the end of each week in the period 1986–92. The level of inventories reflects the likely levels of demand for canned beer, taking into account UK climatic and seasonal conditions, as well as the production capacity of the company. The data highlights the Christmas and New Year peaks and the strike of production workers in September 1988.

The policy of the brewery is to dispose of 'stale' beer, defined as that remaining undistributed in the depot for a period of six weeks because of overstocking. The company wishes to match production with demand in order to maintain a stock control policy which would allow them always to meet the demand of their distribution outlets (i.e. never run dry) while minimising the quantities of beer that are disposed of. The brewers recognise that thus far they have not been entirely successful and want tighter procedures in place to forecast outcomes for 1993 and 1994.

You are required to recommend to Balmain the inventory holding policy they should adopt in order to satisfy their objectives. Your report should consider the development of alternative models (both graphical and algebraic) which will assist Balmain in forecasting its immediate requirements.

Figure C27.1: Weekly Depot Data of Balmain Cartons

Week	1986	1987	1988	1989	1990	1991	1992
1	32	53	2	0	114	110	191
2	47	43	417	442	100	90	130
3	23	53	63	308	100	81	104
4	28	58	58	177	80	77	122
5	28	31	387	220	64	75	120
6	28	184	168	124	44	79	167
7	41	32	118	179	66	80	188
8	26	228	48	92	34	83	191
9	26	37	75	188	194	91	172
10	31	52	107	102	54	112	200
11	47	67	132	96	90	133	161
12	34	303	93	105	54	225	180
13	216	89	78	175	166	304	300
14	166	73	145	147	50	300	174
15	18	87	278	222	70	165	128
16	50	65	336	390	34	111	150
17	27	72	206	416	250	131	191
18	99	102	407	298	76	162	222
19	155	206	199	338	106	193	232
20	43	146	242	292	78	159	196
21	131	35	399	316	196	138	156
22	79	87	205	1030	178	180	224
23	166	244	669	868	184	200	271
24	48	118	886	710	292	181	243
25	28	62	3	644	240	95	130
26	83	127	55	429	378	139	124
27	77	208	617	420	268	231	302
28	397	411	725	245	294	402	362
29	145	259	243	266	482	369	470
30	346	383	540	154	638	398	448
31	441	347	536	306	320	508	476
32	191	228	593	500	412	540	441
33	508	337	518	222	74	549	362

Strategic Management Accounting

Week	1986	1987	1988	1989	1990	1991	1992
34	233	282	765	278	208	341	370
35	112	189	0	324	100	250	323
36	205	301	0	300	146	235	333
37	47	260	0	158	110	174	250
38	94	191	1	106	88	142	227
39	88	139	108	136	120	118	141
40	61	111	0	96	120	132	103
41	79	126	142	62	116	111	143
42	46	117	478	84	150	105	131
43	65	108	300	70	156	172	191
44	53	222	157	134	92	115	190
45	58	211	12	94	190	103	152
46	316	180	225	334	210	167	211
47	222	416	20	176	170	206	273
48	382	147	171	94	314	303	306
49	374	841	303	276	438	334	584
50	274	597	710	156	134	420	420
51	594	726	326	334	72	441	307
52	91	257	198	88	74	140	208

Index

Absenteeism 115
Absorption costing 48, 108, 115, 128
Accounting 64
  creative 167
  ethics 21
    CIMA guidelines 26
  information 39
  manipulation 32
  procedures 123
  rate of return 140
  responsibility 103
  standards 26, 36
  systems 83, 98
Acid test ratio 210
Acquisitions strategy 214, 215
Activity
  dictionary 112
  drivers 112
  on arrow 149
  on node 149
Activity based costing (ABC) 50,
  108, 109, 111, 113, 117, 138
Activity based management (ABM)
  45, 113, 117
Actuarial analysis 45, 218
Ad hoc reporting 100, 173
Added value 48
Additive models 186, 189, 190
Anchoring and adjustment 181
Assets 36
  reduction strategy 216
  stripping 37
Auditing standards 26
Autocorrelation 200, 203, 204
Availability, equipment 153, 154, 181

Backlog 40, 49, 117
Balance of payments 81
Batch production 146
Benchmarking 68, 82, 97, 170, 171,
  174, 175, 235
Best practice 82, 97, 167, 168, 170
Boston Consulting Group (BCG)
  matrix 46, 72, 74, 123, 136
  cash cows 76
  dogs 76
  questions marks 76
  stars 76
  strategies 76
Bottlenecks 63, 64, 71, 72, 92, 108,
  112, 114, 117, 118, 150, 151
Box–Jenkins method 180, 193
Brainstorming 83, 168, 174
Brand loyalty 71, 74
Breakdown maintenance 49, 89, 115
Break-even analysis 12, 14
Budgeting, participatory 39, 42, 43,
  46, 98, 104
Buffer stocks 115, 118
Business
  cycle 185, 186, 190
  ethics 21
  impact analysis 98

Cs, six of TQM 166
Capacity planning 64, 71, 72, 92,
  117, 121, 155
Capital v expense 104
Case study method 3
Cash flows 76, 128, 144, 210
Causal relationships 180, 194
Centred moving average 189
Classification, accuracy 213
Codes of Professional Conduct 24,
  43
Coefficient of determination 196, 205
Commodity prices 80
Competitive advantage 121
Competitive position 75
Competitive pricing 74
Competitiveness 67, 69, 71, 218
Computers
  hardware/software compatibility 83,
    98, 100, 101
  manufacturing aided by 79
  models 181
  security 104
  support 98
Constraints, binding 108, 117, 119
Conditional probability 143, 144
Confidentiality 26
Conflict of interest 24, 30
Constraints
  binding 108, 117, 119
  non-negativity 119
  production 108
  systemic 24, 28
Consumer demand 79
Control procedures 40, 42
Corner points 108, 119
Corporate cowboys 34, 87, 105
Corporate failure 21, 71, 207
Corporate maintenance 49
Corporate mission 45, 67
Corporate recovery 214, 215, 229
Corporate strategy 67, 71, 83, 85,
  102
Correlation coefficients 195, 198,
  200, 205
Cost
  appraisal 115
  capital, of, 141
  control, 110
  drivers 40, 41, 108, 110, 113, 117,
    123
  leadership 45, 46, 71
  measurement 42
  minimisation 107, 110, 121, 130
  pools 109
  quality, of, 115 166
  reduction 121
Cost benefit analysis 112, 146, 206,
  222
Costing 39, 89, 91
  absorption 48, 108, 115, 128
  activity based 50, 108; 109, 111,
    113, 117, 138

  jobs 89, 91
  undercosting 113
Costs
  direct 112
  discretionary 12, 80, 100
  fixed 12
  historic 111
  indirect 112
  misclassification 214
  prevention 49, 115
  relevant 12
  selling 112
  set-up 49, 71, 108, 109, 112, 113,
    117
  standard 43, 48, 63, 64
  sunk 12, 16
  variable 12, 87
Crashing 150, 151
Creative accounting 167
Creative thinking 83, 114, 169, 170
Creditors turnover 70
Critical path analysis 146, 148
Cross section data 179, 222
Cue weights 181
Cultural environment 23, 45
Current best practice 167, 168
Current ratio 70, 210
Customer
  analysis 122, 123, 136
  focus 50, 83, 115, 166, 167
  profitability 45, 75, 78, 107
  service 167, 178
Cycle time 71
Cyclical component 190

Data collection 40, 111
Data manipulation 111
Database systems 83
Debt
  burden 70, 81
  equity ratio 210
  rescheduling 81
Decision support system 67, 122, 179
Decision trees 143, 144, 164
Decomposition analysis 185
Defensive interval 211
Defensive strategies 72
Deflationary policy 80
Delegation 51
Delivery 71, 108, 116, 117, 123,
  147
Delphi technique 180
Demand
  consumer 74
  matching 71
Demographic factors 79
Deontological evaluation 23, 26
Design
  plant 105, 115
  product 115
Discounted cash flow (DCF) 90, 141,
  153, 159
  hurdle rate 141, 146

Index

Discriminant analysis 81, 180, 206, 210, 213, 234
Distress, financial 71, 81, 207, 214, 230
Distribution channels 72, 74
Diversification 87, 92, 105
  concentric 72
  conglomerate 72
Divestment strategy 76
Downtime 154
Dummy variables 179, 206, 210
Durbin–Watson d-statistic 200, 204
Duty of care 21, 26

Es, three of evaluation 46, 84
Early warning models 211, 235
Earnings per share 36
Economic
  growth 80
  impact 169, 175
  risk 46, 79, 80, 81, 85
Economic order quantity (EOQ) 128
Economies of scale 71, 76, 215
Effectiveness 46, 85
Efficiency 46, 48, 85
Employees
  empowerment 30, 103, 167, 168
  involvement 44, 166
    total employee involvement (TEI) 44, 114, 121, 167, 168, 178
Employment law 80
Environmental analysis 69, 78, 81
Equation misspecification 198
Equipment
  availability 153, 154
  failure 116
  productivity 48, 85
  utilisation 46
Error terms 198
Ethics
  decision making 21, 32, 45
  guidelines, CIMA 24, 26, 43
  integrity 24
  insider trading 36
Evaluation 84
Excess capacity 109, 119
Exchange rates 80
Executive information systems (EIS) 83, 104
Explanatory power 205
Explanatory variables 194, 205
Exponential smoothing 180, 192, 193
Export markets 80
External reporting 42

F-test 197, 210
Failure 71, 207
  corporate 21, 71, 207
  equipment 116
  external 115
  relevance-type 48
  types 48
  use-type 48
Feasibility study 112
Feasible region 107
Financial
  distress 71, 207, 210, 214, 230
  performance 69
  ratios 71
Financial accounting 41
Fishbone diagrams 168

Force fields 168
Forecasting 46, 98, 206
  methods 179, 193
  models 250
Foreign debt 81
Foreign exchange shortage 80
Franchising 87
Fuzzy logic 144

Gantt charts 146, 147
Gearing 70, 208
Geographical factors 79
Goals
  corporate 40, 42, 68, 85, 92, 111, 121, 174
  congruence 12, 37, 40, 42, 48, 67, 68, 85, 92, 121, 125, 174
  short term 12, 20, 37
  strategic 42, 68, 125
Government
  intervention 105
  policy 80
Grievance procedures 26
Gross domestic product 81
Group dynamics 168
Growth
  economic 80
  market 75

Heteroscedasticity 200, 203
Heuristics 146, 148, 180, 181
  decision making 180
Historic costs 111
Horizontal integration 72
Human information processing (HIP) 180
Human relations movement 44
Hurdle rate 141, 146

Idle time 117, 121, 147
Import controls 80
Indirect costs 112
Industry
  environment 23
  leadership 45, 46, 71
  means 69
  relatives 68
  yardsticks 82
Injury rate, industry 115
Inflation 80, 81
Informal systems 40
Information overload 180, 181
Information systems 43, 105
Innovation 113, 121
Insider trading 36
Insolvency 69
Integration 72, 101, 181
  horizontal 72
  vertical 72
Integrity 24
Interdependence of systems 120, 121, 150, 151
Interest rates 80
Internal control 42
Internal organisation 67
Internal rate of return (IRR) 141, 161
Internal reporting 39, 40, 83
Interval measures 211
Inventory
  control 39, 40, 51, 56, 87, 128, 193

holdings 123, 240
turnover 70
valuation 42
Investment appraisal 142, 145
Iterative procedures 193

Job costing 89, 91
Job crashing 150
Job satisfaction 44
Job scheduling 71, 120, 146, 147, 180
  Gantt charts 146, 147
Justice 23, 28
Just-in-Time (JIT) systems 45, 50, 114, 116, 118, 166

Key result areas 41, 98

Labour productivity 8, 48
Large scale production 71, 76
Lateral thinking 83, 168, 174
Lead times 48, 114, 116, 122, 128
Leadership 71
Leading indicators 180
Linear correlation coefficient 195, 198
Linear discriminant analysis (LDA) 206, 234
Linear models 70, 180, 189, 213
Linear programming 108, 117, 118, 120, 130, 131
Linear relationships 194, 205
Liquidity 70, 208, 236

Machine utilisation rates 48
Maintenance
  corrective 49
  expenditure 40, 49, 115, 155
Makespan time 146
Management
  activity based (ABM) 113, 117
  value added 114, 166, 178
Management accounting
  function 97
  Japanese 42, 68
Management accounting information systems (MAIS) 29, 39, 40, 67, 115, 122, 180, 235
Management information systems (MIS) 53, 114, 116
Managerial control 61
Manual systems 83, 175
Manufacturing overhead 201
Market
  diversification 72
  growth 75
  impact 69
  leadership 71, 76, 78
  penetration 105
  power 71
  share 75, 78, 121
Marketing costs 61, 79, 110
Mass production 126
Mission statements 67
Monetary policy 81
Monitoring systems 39
Monte Carlo methods 181
Motivation 43, 170
Moving averages 180, 186, 189
Moving sum 187
Multicollinearity 200–3, 205
Multivariate methods 180

Index

multiple cost drivers 112
multiplicative model 186, 189, 191
Multivoting 174

Needs analysis 176
Net present value (NPV) 141, 161
Network analysis 146, 149, 151
No credit interval 211, 212
Non financial indicators (NFIs)
  39–42, 100, 106, 111, 112, 113,
  114, 117, 121, 122, 133, 134,
  153, 175
Non-negativity constraints 119
Non value adding activities 110, 111,
  115

Objective function 108
Objectives 67, 68
Obsolescence 121, 215
Offensive strategies 72
Operational strategies 67, 71
Ordinary least squares regression
  (OLS) 195, 198, 199, 200, 206
Organisations
  culture 168
  environment 23
  performance 46
Outliers 205
Overhead, allocation of 64, 108, 113,
  138, 201, 220

Ps, four of quality improvement 169
Payback period 140, 161
Performance evaluation 46
  benchmarking 68, 82, 97
  effectiveness 46, 85
  efficiency 46, 48, 85
  measurement 46, 67, 71, 85, 106
  relative performance 69, 236
  reporting 98
  yardsticks 69
Performance indicators 41, 67, 169,
  172
Planning 39, 42, 51, 92, 98
Politics
  political factors 79
  political risk analysis 81
  unrest 81
Portfolio, balanced 76, 78
Post audit methods 101, 145, 146,
  159, 161
PRAISE system 168–70, 176
Prediction models 179
Predictive ability 179, 214
Present value 141
Pressure groups 81
Price 71, 74, 88, 107, 117, 133, 138,
  218
  inflation 80, 81
  variances 48
Pricing, competitive 74
Probabilities 143, 144, 164, 181, 182
  distribution 142
  prior 181
Product life cycle (PLC) 72, 73
Product mix 20, 107, 113, 117, 119,
  130, 131, 225
Production
  batch 146

scheduling 63, 127
  set-up 71
Productivity 46, 85
  equipment 48, 85
Professionalism 23, 26
Profit maximisation 107, 110
Profitability 69, 107, 122, 208, 236
Program evaluation review technique
  (PERT) 149
Purchasing patterns 109, 123

Qualitative analysis, Delphi technique
  180
Quality
  assurance 168
  control 49
  drivers 105, 113, 115
  improvement process 168–70, 173
Quantitative analysis 178
  Box–Jenkins method 180, 193
Queuing 48, 118, 120, 147

Random sampling 182, 184, 213
Recovery strategies 78, 214, 215, 229
Regression analysis 180, 186, 189,
  194, 197, 199, 206, 218, 222,
  225
Reorganisation 54
Resource use 46, 85
Responsibility accounting 103
Reporting
  external 42
  internal 39, 40, 83
Reward systems 44, 46, 170
Risk
  economic 46, 79, 80, 81, 85
  political 81
Risk management 140, 142, 146,
  164

Safety stocks 115
Sample estimates 197
Scatter diagrams 194, 205
Scheduling 64, 109, 146, 147
Scientific management 43, 44
Sensitivity analysis 3, 12, 15, 107,
  108, 144, 157, 161, 165, 193
Set-up
  costs 49, 71, 108, 109, 112, 113,
    117
  external factors 117
Short termism 12, 20, 37, 44
Shrinkage 111, 165
Simulation methods 147, 181, 183
  Monte Carlo methods 181
Situation audit 68
Smoothing constants 192, 203
SPAMSOAP 42
Spreadsheets 107, 144, 164, 187, 196
SPSS-X 193, 205
Standard operating procedures
  (SOPs)
  process control 115, 213
  processes 170, 172
  significance 196, 204
  tests of 196, 200, 204
  statistical methods 54, 180
Stock
  control 56, 128

turnover 70
Stock market crash 21
Stock-outs 49, 51
Strategies
  offensive 72
  operational 67, 71
STRIPED reports 6
Supply chain 45
SWOT analysis 3, 6, 9, 68, 78, 83,
  174
Synectics 168
Systems
  balanced 120
  manual 83, 175
  on-line 42, 101
  stable 117

T-test, student's 197
Takeover targets 36, 69, 71
Tariff barriers 80
Taylorism 43, 44
Teamworking 44
Technology
  change 71, 72, 74, 79, 98
  leading edge 71, 122
Throughput 49, 116–19, 147
Time
  horizons 85, 116
  trends 185
  timeliness 40, 67, 111
Time series analysis 179, 180, 185,
  192, 200, 250
Total quality control (TQC) 114
Total quality management (TQM)
  44, 83, 100, 115, 166, 170, 173,
  178
Total quality service (TQS) 168
Trade cycles 185, 186, 190
Training 112, 167, 170
Transfer pricing 92
Transportation 108
Turnover
  creditors 70
  debtors 70
Type 1 errors 213, 214

Undercosting 113
Utilitarians 23, 28

Value adding activities 40, 41, 48,
  100, 110, 111
Value chain 45
Variables
  dummy 179, 206, 209
  explanatory 194, 205
Variance analysis 42, 43, 104, 175
  unfavourable variances 48
Vertical integration 72

Waiting time 147
Warranty claims 115, 166
Waste 48, 63
Work in process/progress 40, 46, 48,
  114, 118
Working capital 39, 70, 236
Work study 43

Z score 207, 211–13, 236
Zero defects 49, 114, 115, 167

Strategic Management Accounting
text and cases

Dr Malcolm Smith

Datadisk Contents

No	Case	Filename
10	Willingham Furniture Ltd	Willing.wk3
13	Fibro Ltd	Fibro.wk3
15	Pitcairn Electronics	Pitcairn.wk3
18	Westralian Alumina	West.wk3
22	Redfern Mutual Assurance	Redfern.wk3
23	Charity Shops	Charity.wk3
24	Austwide Stores	Austwide.wk3
25	Whittlesgord Hardware Group	Whittle.wk3
26	Turbaust Motors	Turbaust.wk3
27	Balmain Breweries	Balmain.wk3
E	Exploration Holdings	Explore.wk3
F	Ferrous Castings	Ferrous.wk3
G	Gresham State Bank	Gresham.wk3

Lotus 1-2-3, readable by Excel